Musical Voyages
4th edition

Dr. William E. Doyle
El Camino College
Torrance, CA

www.ArtMusicHistory.com
Pacific Coast Publishing
Los Angeles, CA

Pacific Coast Publishing

Musical Voyages
4th edition
William E. Doyle

This book is dedicated to the memory of my parents.

Publisher:	Pacific Coast Publishing
Book layout and cover art:	Steve Richter, Wendy Stockstill
Art work:	Ashkan Tirgari, Tamara Tanabe
	Wendy Stockstill
Cover photos:	William E. Doyle
Original music:	*Kronos Fanfare, Voyage*
Special thanks:	James Hurd, Anthony Moreno
	Kenner Bailey, Cindy Tseng
	Allan Tudzin, Michelle Levert
	Michael Lloyd, LA SuperNova

Pacific Coast Publishing

©2015
Pacific Coast Publishing
Los Angeles, California
U.S.A.
www.ArtMusicHistory.com

Printed in the United States of America
10 9 8 7 6 5 4 3 2 1

ISBN 978-1-935920-48-9

Table of Contents

Movement II. ~ Music for Instruments

Movement III. ~ Mostly Vocal Music

Preface

This 4th edition is now enlarged after recent studies in India and Nepal. It is amplified to meet the growing awareness of the merits of both older and more recent music as well as the emerging field of 'non-Western' music. However, it also retains the aim of earlier versions – to provide information that will make for intelligent listening to the musical masterpieces that have met the test of time and are now a part of our musical world.

Musical Voyages is neither a history of music nor a technical manual on the performance of music. It is, however, a Music Appreciation textbook that is organized into various musical 'movements' that will in succession, take you deeper into the realm of both Western and selected non-Western musical cultures. The 'narrative' of how to use this textbook is described below.

Textbook Organization

The structure of this textbook is akin to that of a musical work and is organized into 'movements' that flow one into the other. Music is an art whose material consists of sounds organized in time. Through the many types of patterns in which these sounds can be arranged, music can serve as a medium for the expression of ideas and emotions – some literal, others ambiguous. In order to be able to discuss these ideas and emotions, a musical vocabulary is necessary. Movement 1 focuses on this 'language' of music that will allow you to talk intelligently with other musicians and music-lovers.

After mastering the language in Movement 1, you are ready to begin looking at various 'genres' or types of pieces. Movement 2 takes you into the major instrumental genres including the sonata, concerto, and symphony. Sacred and secular vocal music are the source materials for Movement 3 – starting with ancient Greek and Roman fragments and moving forward in history to the mass, madrigal, oratorio and opera, and other important vocal genres.

Movement 4, the last five chapters of this textbook, contains a wide array of Western musical styles and works including newer forms such as jazz, minimalism and musicals, piano and guitar music, ballet and chamber music. In addition, many –ism's such as impressionism, expressionism, primitivism, and serialism, are discussed and this section ends with an introduction to seventeen various world music locations – from Japan and Bali, to Nepal and the Aboriginal music of Australia, Papua New Guinea and many more. *Composer Profiles*, a full *Glossary*, *Index*, and an *Index of Composer's Works* can be found in Appendices A – D.

In the textbook, you will notice that after a piece of music has been discussed (i.e., Chapter 4, *Courante* by Michael Praetorius), there is a *Check Box*. This indicates that there is a listening or video example associated with the discussion of that piece. After you read the chapter, consult with your instructor for the location of the music examples (CD, mp3, YouTube, video, website, etc.) and then listen to these musical selections.

Use the *Worksheets* in Appendix E of your textbook to help keep you focused on the musical elements in these pieces. They are perforated and can be used during in-class assignments and at concert events. The *Guided Listening Worksheets* and *Concert Reviews* are new and reflect the teaching of this course as a listening-based, Music Appreciation course.

RUDOLFINUM
Sukova Síň

13. 7.

2010

19:00

HAYDN
MOZART
BEETHOVEN

VIENNA HONOR ORCHESTRA USA

DOYLE WILLIAM
Dirigent/Conductor

PROGRAM/PROGRAMME:
S. BARBER, E. LALO, J. HAYDN
W. A. MOZART, C. SAINT-SAËNS
L. VAN BEETHOVEN, W. DOYLE

CONCEPTIO

X

"This is the moment of embarking. All auspicious signs are in place."
Deng Ming-Dao, author

"Children should be trained in music so as actually to take part in its performance."
Aristotle, an ancient Greek philosopher

"You are teachers? You mean there are people who know less than you do about music?"
Composer Arnold Schoenberg, to kindergarten teachers in Los Angeles

Leopold   "What are you doing?"
Wolfgang   "Writing a concerto for the clavier."
Leopold   "Let me see it."
Wolfgang   "It is not finished yet."
Leopold   "Never mind, let me see it. It must be something very fine."
Conversation between the 4-year-old Mozart and his father

How We Listen to Music

To appreciate music you must listen to it. Talking and reading about music is not a substitute for listening to it. You must be able to recognize a melody when you hear it—and then remember it so that you can tell what has come before it and after it. Music exists in time. It is abstract and therefore more difficult to understand and remember.

Most rock or popular music starts with an introduction. We seldom listen to this but instead focus our attention on the words and the main melody that follows. In "Classical" music, however, the composer often puts his best and most important musical ideas first in the music. This is when your mind is fresh and you are the most attentive. You must develop a new habit of paying attention to the first five to ten seconds of music, and then remember it. The music that will follow is related in some way to what you just heard. One suggestion is to try to sing along with the melody when it is repeated.

All music is expressive. All music has meaning. Can that meaning be put into words? No, not really. As we will see, the meaning of a piece of music often defies description. Perhaps a mood is created, or just a general feeling or impression.

Active listening (as opposed to passive listening) is a combination of the expressive and musical levels—to be inside and outside of the music. It is the ability to shift your focus to feel the expressive elements of the music and then to understand how, on the musical level, the composer has made you feel these things. Active listening is the goal of this music appreciation course. So, to quote the jazz musician and composer Quincy Jones, "Listen Up!"

Musical Perspectives

We can observe music from three different perspectives. First, there is the composer. The composer represents the beginning of the creative process of musical composition. Next there are the performers. These are the musicians that will interpret the musical notation and bring the composer's ideas to life. After all, music on a piece of paper is lifeless! Without an actual performance, a piece of music is just a series of lines and dots. Finally, there is the listener who will experience the composer's ideas as interpreted by the performers and communicated to the audience. Each one of these viewpoints is unique and will have a relationship and connection to the others. We will examine each one, starting with the composer.

The Composer - and the creative process in music

There are essentially two types of music (program and absolute) and two broad categories of music (vocal and instrumental) that are used by composers. Program music makes use of extra-musical references that are often taken from the field of literature. One example is the tone poem *Don Juan* by Richard Strauss. Although Strauss composed the piece for a symphony orchestra, the music attempts to describe to the listener the story of Don Juan and his many escapades.

Absolute music, on the other hand, does not have an extra-musical meaning or significance. It is music for the sake of music. A good example would be the symphonies of Mozart. These entertainment works for the Viennese aristocrats and courts do not contain any musical characters or references. Their meaning is solely a musical one.

A composer's style consists of essentially two elements—his or her personality and the age during which they lived. Many composers, as they matured, found their own musical personalities changing as much as the time periods changed. Beethoven, for example, lived at the end of the Classical era and the beginning of the Romantic era. His personality, which was rather coarse and rugged, also underwent tremendous changes.

The changes were due to his health problems. So, at different times during the life of Beethoven, we will see how his music was influenced by events in his life and by the changes in society's style and taste.

Aaron Copland, the famous American composer discussed in Chapter 13, identified four different types of compositional styles:

1. Spontaneous - Franz Schubert.
2. Constructive - Ludwig von Beethoven.
3. Traditional - Johann Sebastian Bach.
4. Explorer or Pioneer - Claude Debussy.

We will examine many different works and composers throughout the semester. You will see how each of the composers mentioned above affected music and musical styles during their time and throughout history.

The Performer - the interpreter of the music

As a music listener, you need to be aware that the music you are hearing is not the composer's music, but rather the interpretation of the composer's music by the performer. To put it another way, it is not really the composer that one hears, but rather the interpreter's conception of the composer. Music, like theater, is an art form that exists only when interpreted. Music, on a piece of paper, is not really music—a performance medium is needed to bring it to life.

Once a composition is completed, the composer must turn it over to the interpreter. Musicians, like composers, are affected by changes in style, taste, and personal experiences.

Every musical composition has an essential element(s)—something that makes it special and unique. The interpreter tries to be aware of these elements and attempts to bring about a performance of this music that is as true to the composer's original intent as possible. A piece of music is a living entity—one that is often redefined according to the practices of the era and the interpretation of the musicians. That is why a piece of music is capable of being viewed from different perspectives and from different points of emphasis.

 Interpretative differences.

So, you the listener must become aware of the interpreter's role in the performance of a musical composition. To accomplish this, you should try to:

1. Understand the composer's original intent (as much possible).
2. Recognize to what degree the performer has reproduced that intent.
3. Listen to music in the active mode.

The combined efforts of the performer and interpreter will only have meaning if the listener is an aware listener—this is the role of the listener in music. This is, according to Copland, the purely musical level of listening. As he suggested, "Listen intently, listen consciously, and listen with one's whole intelligence." We will discuss this in more detail after we examine the interpreter's physical tools—the various families of instruments (Chapter 2).

The Listener - this is where you come in!

What does the music mean? What is the composer trying to say? Music is sound. A musical composition has many notes put together in such a way that we get pleasure out of hearing them. Music is not about anything. Music is just music.

Music is put together (form) with different rhythms and melodies, using different instruments and voices in such a way that what finally comes out is exciting, interesting, or moving. Since it is a musical form, it has a **musical** meaning. Although it may suggest various images and feelings, it really is not about those images or feelings. Of course, if there is a story connected with a piece of music, it gives it an extra-musical meaning to the music. The music, however, is not the story even if there is a plot connected to it.

An example of this is the famous old-time radio show *The Lone Ranger*. This radio show used a very well-known piece of music for its theme music. Many people still associate this music with the Wild West and with the two main characters from the show, Tonto and the Lone Ranger.

 Theme from *The Lone Ranger*.

The composer of this piece, Gioacchino Rossini, was an Italian opera composer. He did not even know what the Wild West was! What is this piece about? The name of the opera it comes from is *William Tell*, and the libretto (story) is about a legendary 14th century Swiss patriot of the same name. Although the rhythm and excitement of the music may suggest the Wild West, they could also suggest other things.

What does music mean then? It is the way it makes you feel when you hear it. The meaning is all in the way music moves, since music is movement. It is always going somewhere, shifting, changing, and flowing from one note to another. The meaning of music can be found in the music itself. You will find the meaning in its melodies, its harmonies, its rhythms, its tone colors, and especially in the way it **develops** itself (form).

Development in Music

All music, to some degree, depends on development. The more it develops, the more "symphonic" it is. The basis of all development is repetition. The less exact the repetition is, the more symphonic it becomes.

How do composers use repetition in a non-exact way to develop their themes (melodies) into symphonic pieces? Here are five devices that composers most commonly use to develop their themes in a composition:

1. Variation - change a musical component (rhythm, dynamics, etc.).
2. Sequence - repeat a melody in a higher or lower register.
3. Imitation - literal repetition.
4. Diminution - break a theme down into smaller parts.
5. Augmentation - extend a theme into longer sections.

In most symphonic music the composer will take a melody and orchestrate it. What is orchestration? Well, orchestration is how a composer arranges his music for performance by an orchestra, a jazz band, a chorus, etc. A good orchestration is orchestration that is exactly right for that music. It lets the music be heard in the clearest, most effective way. One example is the ballet piece *Boléro* by the French composer Maurice Ravel. *Boléro* is considered a fine example of orchestration. In fact, that is all it really is! We will examine this work in Chapter 2.

Music, as you can see, has its own meanings that are right there inside the music. You do not need any stories or pictures to tell you what it means. The meaning of music is **inside** it and nowhere else.

What Makes Music Classical?

People use the word "Classical" to describe a particular type of music. It is actually easier to describe music that is not Classical. For example, jazz, pop, folk, or rock music is not Classical music. Some of the words that are used to describe it are not very accurate either—good, serious, art, and symphonic to name a few.

"Classical music is an exact music," according to the late American composer and conductor Leonard Bernstein. In this exact music, the composer has written the notes, the speed, and the instruments that are required. And, within limits, there is a certain manner in which it is to be performed. How do we know what that way is? Well, the composer has told us through the musical notation and description.

Popular, folk, jazz, and rock are all open to the performer's interpretation and improvisation. Seldom is the piece performed exactly the way the composer or song writer wrote it. In some cases, it may not have been notated or written down at all!

Classical is a term that has many meanings. Classical refers to the music of the period from 1750-1820. It indicates the music of the so-called "First Viennese School" of composers. The composers of this school were Haydn, Mozart, and Beethoven in his early years. These composers were interested in the perfection of form and shape, in proportion, elegance, balance, and symmetry. Their music is composed of many simple and graceful melodies that are easy to sing, remember, and dance to.

The term Classical also refers to something that is timeless. Even though these composers were searching for perfection and ideal form, they had something to say with their music. That is why their music can still make people feel a wide range of emotions. This is how a piece of music will endure. Mozart, for example, had a particular gift for melody and for beauty. When we listen to a piece by him, we feel something. Many of his melodies are moving and full of expression. These special feelings are the true marks of his genius.

Beethoven, on the other hand, was the last composer of the Classical era and the first one in the Romantic era. He was a Classical composer who went too far and began composing music that was full of expression and feeling. He had so much to say that he could not keep himself confined to all of those rules and regulations of the Classical era. In this way, Beethoven became the bridge to the Romantic era.

So what does the word Classical mean? To use the term specifically, it refers to the music of the Classical era (1750-1820). However, we usually use it to generalize and to represent the music of the great European composers from the Middle Ages through the 20th century. Since this music has endured, it has the quality of being classic or timeless.

How to Listen to Classical Music

First, acquaint yourself with the music ahead of time. The more you know about the composer, his style, and the motivation behind the piece, the more you can begin to understand what the piece is all about.

Listen to the instruments, melodies, and rhythms of the piece. In many Classical works you will not find any words (lyrics), so concentrate on the elements of music and how they are combined. The first five to ten seconds are important. In Classical music the composer puts the best and most important music first. This is what will be repeated, imitated, or developed later.

Development and contrast are two of the keys to Classical music—and these take time. So get comfortable and be patient with the music. Active listening is the key to understanding and appreciating music.

Do not expect to hear everything on the first listening. The best way to learn and understand the music is by "repeated listening." So put your tape recorders and the *Review Tapes* in the Music Library (MU 126) to good use.

Most Classical pieces require more concentration than popular or rock pieces. Building your concentration and your ability to really "listen" to the music will take some time and practice. You may be used to listening to popular music that only lasts from three to four minutes. A Classical piece of music usually lasts quite a bit longer. Again, repeated listening and practice with the *Worksheets* (Appendix E) will help develop and extend your concentration level.

If you find yourself daydreaming, simply bring your attention back to the music. A piece of music will conjure up many types of feelings and emotions for you. It is only natural to go "channel surfing" to the music.

Classical music uses a somewhat confusing "naming" system. There are basically two types of music and two broad categories of music. The two types of music are absolute and program music, and the categories are vocal and instrumental music. We will examine these distinctions and the naming system in later chapters.

Where to Find Classical Music

You can start by examining the Calendar Section your local Newspaper. On Sundays, most newspapers offer a large Calendar Section with a complete listing of what is happening in film, art, drama, theater, and music.

You can also begin to experiment with listening to the Classical music stations on the local FM airwaves. If you really get hooked, you should know that there are several Classical music magazines and a variety of music clubs. With the developments in current technology, you will also find an array of Classical music on CD-ROM.

If you are a television fanatic, you can always tune into the many PBS specials throughout the year. There are usually several great shows every month. You can also go to your local video rental store and check out their selection. Or you can wait for the movie *Amadeus* to make its annual return to network television!

Record stores are also great places to learn about Classical music. Many stores now have a large Classical department, and sometimes they even have a separate store for Classical music! The people who work in these stores are generally quite knowledgeable about this music and are happy to recommend specific works and recordings to you. Just ask!

How to Attend a Concert

If you are going to attend a concert, first check the papers for a program that interests you. Then buy a good seat so that you will be able to see and hear the music. Prepare before you go—read up and listen up before you go to the concert. Since a concert generally lasts between one and one and one-half hours, try not to go tired to a concert. That is no way to enjoy and experience this wonderful art form. Here are ten other items of "Concert Etiquette" to consider:

1. Know how others dress at these occasions.
2. Get there early - Classical concerts start on time.
3. Applaud at the end of a piece, not between movements!
4. Do not unwrap candy - cellophane wrappers are annoying.
5. Buy a program and read it before the concert begins.
6. Enjoy the sound, the atmosphere, and the history of the experience.
7. Stay until the end since there may be an encore.
8. Take a few notes between pieces and at the intermission.
9. Write your concert review right away.
10. Attach a ticket stub and/or program.

Now we are ready to take a journey *Inside Music.*

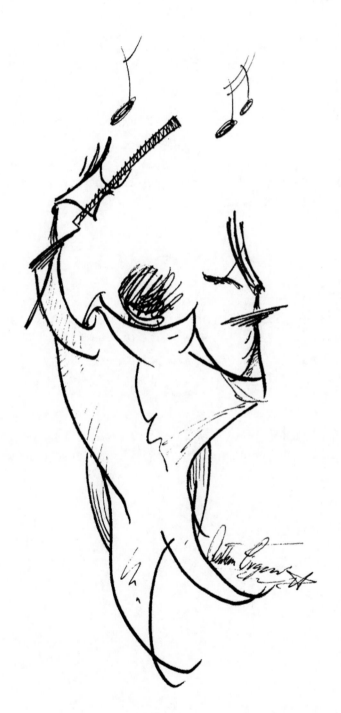

"If melody was all of the music, what could we prize in the various forces that make up the immense work of Beethoven, in which melody is assuredly the least?"

Igor Stravinsky, a 20th century composer

"When admiring a painting, do not examine the paint. When meeting an artist, do not look at the brush."

Ancient Taoist phrase

Emperor Joseph II once said, "My dear Mozart, that is too fine for my ears, there are too many notes." Mozart replied, "There are just as many notes as there should be."

The work in question was Mozart's opera *The Abduction from the Seraglio*

At the premier of <u>Boléro</u>, a woman next to me stood up and yelled out, "He's mad!" Ravel replied, smiling, that she had understood the piece.

Description of the premier of Ravel's ballet *Boléro*

The Musical Palette, part one

The various musical components (elements) are the composer's raw materials. The combined effect is what is most important. Although one element may dominate a piece of music, seldom do you hear only one element by itself. As the painter Claude Monet said, the goal of an artist is "to fix sensation," or capture feeling on a canvas.

A composer chooses certain instruments, rhythms, and melodies in much the same way that an artist chooses and mixes colors. In order to be able to listen inside the music, we will first examine how we perceive music. Then we will take apart the music and look at the various components of music individually.

Musical Perception

Musical perception lies at the heart of our musical experience. According to Dr. Robert Cutietta, coordinator of music education at Kent State University (Ohio), "The actual processing of music is largely holistic, intuitive, and nonverbal." What does this mean?

Well, even after a semester of a music appreciation course many students are still unsure of the elements of music. But these elements are the common **starting point** for a music appreciation course! This means that students were struggling and guessing all semester when it came to the listening portion of their exams. Let's see if we can do something to minimize or eliminate this problem. We will begin with musical perception and then move onto the musician's vocabulary—the building blocks of music.

It has been my experience that students do not usually hear what is notated or written in a piece of music. Music notation allows a composer to measure and quantify sound. For the performer, it gives a written blueprint for musical sound. To the listener that is not familiar with music notation, they hear the music according to preconceived categories and then interpret everything they hear based on these categories. This means that the perception of a piece of music will vary from individual to individual.

The most fundamental process in perception is categorization. When listening to a piece of music, people will immediately try to categorize it into country, rock and roll, jazz, Classical, etc. In making this categorization, the mind has processed some very complex information (rather quickly, I might add), in a holistic manner. This means that you hear the music first in an overall and general manner (outside) rather than in an elemental (inside) manner. Dr. Cutietta has identified five perceptual elements that are the basis for our first look at music from the outside. The five perceptual elements are:

1. Motion
2. Energy
3. Flow
4. Fabric
5. Color

The first three elements relate to the movement of the music. They deal with the speed, strength, and manner of how the music is moving. As you can imagine, the three are related to each other.

Motion can be described in terms of the amount of forward movement that the listener perceives. Most New Age music (anti-stress) seems to have little forward motion and is static or still. In contrast, the opening of a fast-paced action movie is probably an example of music with considerable forward motion. All music moves with some degree of strength. This is its energy. Regardless of how much motion is present, there is energy. The freedom with which the music is moving is the music's flow. The music can move freely or in a restricted manner.

If you were to put together a tape for dancing, chances are the various musical selections would be energetic and have an unrestricted (free) flow. If you wanted to make a tape of all relaxing music, then the various selections would all have a static (still) motion with a weak energy.

The fourth perceptual element is fabric. Fabric, as in clothing, refers to how the musical parts are combined and interwoven. Often it results in a perception of the overall thickness or thinness of the music. The perception of musical fabric can be affected by the density of rhythm and the amount of instruments or voices.

Color, the fifth perceptual element, is perhaps the most important and (of course) the most difficult to put into words. When a composer assigns a particular instrument to play a certain melody, it is usually done based on the color (timbre) of its sound. Although in our section on instruments we will classify both an oboe and a clarinet as "woodwinds," they do not have the same color from a perceptual standpoint.

Sound, by itself, is still only one part of the overall element of color. Sounds combine to produce an overall hue in the same way that a painter will mix colors to come up with a compound color. To borrow an analogy from painting, pieces of music can be categorized as dark, bright, green, blue, etc. Certain rock bands are recognizable by their characteristic sound. Even if you are not familiar with a piece of music that they are playing, you can recognize what band it is by the sound (hue) of the piece. This is an example of your brain interpreting color. While the traditional elements of music are at work behind the scenes to contribute to these categories, we perceive music first in terms of these five perceptual components.

☐ Perceptual elements.

Rhythm

Most music historians agree that if music started anywhere it probably started with the beating of a rhythm. Perhaps our hearts were the first real percussion instruments. We are, in a sense, rhythmic beings. Everything we do is based on rhythm—the way we breathe, move, walk, and talk. Many thousands of years passed before man learned how to write down the rhythms that he played or sang. Today our system of notation is highly developed, but it is still not perfect.

During the time of the Greeks, music was probably used to accompany prose or poetry. The music followed the rhythm of poetry and prose. Later, around 1150, rhythm was grouped into measured units. This helped to supply music with a rhythmic structure all it's own so that it would not have to rely upon poetry or prose. This allowed music to move from an **oral** tradition to a written one, as measured music could be passed on from generation to generation. It also gave composers the ability to notate music, allowing for several voices or instruments to perform at the same time (polyphony, homophony).

Rhythm is the beat or the pulse in music. The speed at which the beat moves is the tempo. Music can move at slow, moderate, or fast speeds (tempi), or some combination of these three.

The grouping of beats into patterns creates a meter. If the music is heard in a pattern of strong and weak beats, then it is a duple meter. If it is grouped into a pattern of strong-weak-weak, then it is a triple meter. Duple meter and triple meter are the two basic meters of music. Music is also composed in combinations of duple and triple meters. This creates a mixed meter.

☐ Examples of duple and triple meters.

In the late 1800's Western music began experimenting with the use of polyrhythm. Polyrhythm is the simultaneous combination of duple and triple meters. This could be found in the music of African drummers and Balinese percussionists, as it was not a new idea. Polyrhythm has been around for a long time.

Jazz is an outgrowth of these African polyrhythms. For example, swing, hot jazz, and bebop have all experimented with the use of polyrhythm. Music that uses polyrhythm has a freer feel to the music. Removed from this music are the monotonous repetitions of ONE - two, ONE - two, **or** ONE - two - three, ONE - two - three. In the hands of many 20th century composers, this effect was used to create a primitive feel (Igor Stravinsky, Chapter 13).

Remember, even the most complex rhythms are meant for your ears. After repeated listening, the greater complexities of modern rhythms will make more and more sense to you, adding to your greater enjoyment of contemporary music.

☐   Examples of polyrhythm.

Melody

While rhythm is associated with physical motion, melody is connected to our mental emotions. What makes a good melody? A good melody is satisfying in its proportions, and gives us a sense of completeness and inevitability. It will generally be long and flowing, with high and low points of interest, and a climactic moment usually near the end. It will have a variety of notes and avoid unnecessary repetitions. A sensitivity to the rhythmic flow is also important when creating a melody. Most of all, the melody will have an expressive quality that will create an emotional response in the listener.

From a technical standpoint, a melody is constructed from a set of raw materials known as a scale. A scale is merely an arrangement of notes that have been passed down to us by great musical theorists. There have been four main systems of scale building: Oriental (pentatonic), Greek, Ecclesiastical (church modes), and Western (major and minor).

We will deal mainly with the Western system in this course. This is a system that has been with us from the beginnings of the Baroque era (c.1600).

☐   Major and minor examples.

A melody can be many different things. It can be a tune, a theme, a motive, a long melodic line, a bass line, or an inner voice. To most people a melody is a tune, something you go out whistling or singing that sticks in your head.

In symphonic music we are interested in development, so a tune is not really what is needed. Tunes do not need development since they are already complete. A theme however, is usually incomplete (on purpose). Many people will, at first, describe these themes as unmelodic. One example is the beginning of *Symphony No. 5* by Beethoven—"Ta-ta-ta-tum!" This is a theme and it is not a melody in the sense of a Mozart melody. And it works very well. Why? This theme is perfect for further development. In other words, since it is incomplete, it leaves Beethoven plenty of room to expand, contract, sequence, imitate, or vary the theme—to develop the theme in a myriad of ways.

Counterpoint (polyphonic texture) sometimes causes problems for people. Counterpoint is not the absence of melody, but rather an abundance of melody. Many works from the Baroque era are often described as too melodic because the composer has combined several melodies simultaneously creating a polyphonic texture. If you listen to each one separately, you will hear a melody that is easily recognizable and complete all by itself.

So, what is a melody? A melody, in the broadest sense of the word, is really any series of notes. What about the melodies that sound unmelodic? This leads us to the question of taste and experience. What kind of music do we usually listen to? Do we get what we expect from a piece of music? Does the melody move in such a way that I can predict it and feel comfortable with its movement?

The more you listen to music in an active mode, the more you will be able to accept melodies that at first may not seem to be very melodic. This is especially the case with a melody that does not repeat, or a long, complicated, polyphonic melody.

A melody is a continuous thread. It is supposed to lead you from the beginning to the end of the piece. While it may disappear at times, you can be sure that it will return at some point and that it disappeared for a reason. Most melodies are accompanied by secondary, or background, material. A good composer is able to keep you focused on the melody no matter how much background music is going on behind it. It is your job to try to follow the melody and its various appearances from the start to the finish of the piece.

▢   Examples of various melodies from different eras.

Timbre

Timbre, or tone color, in music is comparable to the use of color in a painting. It is the particular (distinctive) sound produced by an instrument or voice. There are certain sounds that the listener will recognize and enjoy. This section of the course will allow you to become familiar with all the various timbres that voices and instruments have to offer.

As you listen to a piece of music, try to sharpen your awareness of vocal and instrumental tone colors. Then figure out why a composer chose that voice or instrument. Often a composer will choose a particular instrument for the expressive qualities of the instrument. An instrument is usually chosen because of how it can express the meaning behind the musical idea.

Before the Baroque era (1600-1750), it is unlikely that composers wrote music with a particular instrument in mind. Many times the music does not even list which instruments the composers were writing for. Composers would be just as happy with a string ensemble as with a group of woodwinds and brass. Today composers not only specify which instrument is to play which part, but often the music is composed with particular instruments in mind. This is because of range, technique, volume, and other acoustical properties of the instruments or voices. There is a typical or characteristic way of writing for each instrument or voice.

Instruments

The orchestra is divided into four sections—strings, woodwinds, brass, and percussion. Each of these sections is a family of instruments. The string section, which is the most frequently used section, is made up of the violins (first and second, or high and low), the viola, the cello, and the string bass, or just the bass.

The woodwind section is composed of the flute, clarinet, oboe, and bassoon. Related, and more modern, instruments include the piccolo, the bass clarinet, the double bassoon, and the English horn. More recently, the saxophone has been added to this complement of woodwind instruments.

The brass family is made up of the trumpet, French horn (or horn), trombone, and tuba. There are usually two to four trumpets, four horns, three trombones, and one tuba in the orchestra from the time of the Classical era (1750-1820) onwards.

The fourth section of the orchestra is the percussion section. Percussion instruments come in two types—pitched and non-pitched. Pitched percussion instruments include the timpani, xylophone, bells, and related instruments. Non-pitched percussion instruments include the snare drum, bass drum, triangle, castanets, wood blocks, cymbals, gongs, etc.

As for voices, the highest and generally lightest voice is the soprano. Next is the darker, more heavy female voice known as the alto. The highest of the male voices is the tenor. The lowest and deepest male voice is the bass.

Electronic instruments are the newest family of instruments. Today, the synthesizer and the computer are combined to develop new and fascinating musical resources—from sampled sounds, to exotic world music sounds, and instrumental or vocal sounds that are not possible from acoustic instruments.

Vocal Characteristics

Soprano	Coloratura - virtuosic, extended high range.
	Lyric - lighter.
	Dramatic - lower range, more powerful.
Alto	Lower range than soprano.
Tenor	Heroic, lyric.
Baritone	In between tenor and bass.
Bass	Baritone, lyric, profondo.

Timbre Classifications

Chordophones	Any instrument that has a string that is plucked, bowed, or struck.
Aerophones	Woodwind and brass families (from the flutes to the tubas).
Membranophones	Percussion instruments with a "head" or membrane that is struck. Pitched and non-pitched:
	pitched - timpani
	non-pitched - snare, toms, bass, tambourine.
Idiophones	Percussion instruments without a membrane head.
	pitched - xylophone, marimba, celesta, chimes, bells, piano
	non-pitched - claves, triangle, temple block, cymbal, gong, castanets, etc.
Keyboard	Often considered a separate family; piano, organ, harpsichord, etc.
Electrophones	Synthesizers, MIDI controlled instruments, drum machines.

Boléro by Maurice Ravel

We will examine the orchestra and the families of instruments of the orchestra. The musical example, which became a "musical hit" after the movie *10*, is *Boléro* by the French composer Maurice Ravel. This piece is an experiment in tone color (timbre).

Boléro
  completed in 1928

First performed at the Paris Opera
Choreography by Bronislava Nijinska
22 November 1928

Originally entitled *Fandango*, Ravel later changed the name of this ballet to *Boléro*. The music has little to do, however, with the Spanish folk dance known as the boléro. It was written as a ballet score and became a smash hit at its premier. Today, it is often performed in concert halls as an orchestral work without the ballet.

The setting of the ballet is an Andalucian inn. Several male dancers (gypsies) are lying about on chairs and on the floor. The lead female dancer dances into this room. She dances slowly at first, then more intensely. As the music increases in intensity, she dances on a table with greater and greater abandon. The men, intoxicated by the rhythm and aroused by her dancing, eventually join her in the boléro dance. The ballet ends with an explosion of musical color and wild abandon.

Musically, the two themes are "impersonal folk tunes of the usual Spanish-Arabian kind," according to Ravel. He saw the piece as an "experiment in a very special and limited direction . . . " He also believed that the music would not be successful without the ballet. He was, of course, quite wrong. It was enormously successful at its orchestral premier and remains one of Ravel's most popular orchestral works.

The music begins with an ostinato (a repeated rhythmic pattern) in the snare drum accompanied by a string pizzicato (plucked strings). The ostinato then accompanies two themes, each being eight bars long, which alternate with one another. For example, theme one is played by the flute, then repeated by the clarinet. Theme one is then followed by theme two in the bassoon's high register. This is immediately repeated by the small E-flat clarinet. Sectional repetition is the basic form (organization) of the piece.

There are seventeen repeats of this process with no development; just repetition of the two themes with various changes in the instrumental timbre. The only thing that will change is the orchestral accompaniment. As the instrumentation changes, the music gradually crescendos until there is a sudden change of key (modulation). Then an amazing cascade of sounds is heard from the entire orchestra (tutti) as the ballet ends.

A study in orchestral timbre, Ravel experimented with adding instruments together to create a new color. One of the most unusual orchestral colors he creates results from the combination of two piccolos, a horn, and a celesta. Since the piece is highly repetitive, hypnotic, and concentrates on gradual changes, it is similar to the 20th century musical style known as Minimalism (Chapter 16).

☐   *Boléro* by Maurice Ravel

The following three compositions will help sharpen your awareness of instruments and musical timbres. All three of these works, along with Ravel's *Boléro*, can be found in the Music Library (Mu 126). They are also readily available on c.d. and cassette.

Camille Saint-Saëns (1835 – 1921) had an extraordinarily long and productive musical career. He was active as a composer for 83 years beginning at age three, and he continued to compose almost non-stop until the day he died. His career as a pianist was equally distinguished and he remained an active performer until his final days. His *Carnival of the Animals* (1886), which he refused to publish during his lifetime, is most commonly heard today in an arrangement for full orchestra. Many of the 'animals' are scored for specific instruments and one movement includes some 'finger-strengthening exercises' for pianists. The piece was first performed in its entirety in 1922, the year after his death.

Sergei Prokofiev (1891 – 1953) composed his orchestral 'fairy tale' *Peter and the Wolf* in 1936 and it premiered later the same year in a Moscow Philharmonic children's concert. Each character in the story is represented by an instrument in the orchestra; the bird by a flute, the duck by an oboe, the cat by a clarinet, the grandfather by a bassoon, the hunters by the timpani and bass drum, and the wolf by three menacing French horns. Peter, represented by the strings, is the boy who outsmarts and captures the wolf.

Benjamin Britten (1913 – 1976) wrote the *Young Person's Guide to the Orchestra* as both an instructional piece for young adults and as a tribute to Henry Purcell. Britten borrowed a theme from Henry Purcell's *Abeldazer* and created a set of variations and a fugue on it. First performed in 1946, Eric Crozier's text for the *Young Person's Guide to the Orchestra* is optional. All three of these works are often performed in a purely instrumental setting without narration.

"J.S. Bach was so fond of harmony that, besides a constant and active use of the pedals, he is said to have put down such keys by a stick in his mouth, as neither hands nor feet could reach."

Charles Burney, a music historian (c.1789)

"Oppressed by the excessive heat, he had divested himself of everything but his shirt, and was busily employed writing notes on the wall with a lead pencil, beating time, and striking a few chords on his string-less piano."

The Austrian poet Alois Jeitteles, after watching Beethoven at work on a new composition

"Thus without music no discipline can be perfect, for there is nothing without it. For the very universe, it is said, is held together by a certain harmony of sounds."

Isidore of Seville, c.600, Medieval author on music

The Musical Palette, part two

While many music cultures of the world use rhythm and melody almost exclusively, European concert music invented and developed harmony. Melody and harmony, "ebony and ivory" according to Stevie Wonder and Paul McCartney, are intimately related to each another. We will examine harmony, its relationship to melody, and how musical texture results from the use of melody and harmony together.

Harmony

By comparison to rhythm and melody, harmony is more complex. While rhythm and melody came naturally to composers, harmony had to be invented. Harmony was invented in the ninth century. Until that time most European music was a single melodic line. Today, this is still true among many other musical traditions. The anonymous European composers (church musicians, monks) who began experimenting with harmony created a revolution in musical thinking.

The earliest form of harmony is called organum. Organum is a primitive sound that is the result of a parallel melody being added above or below the original melody. Several hundred years later descant harmony was invented by some ingenious French composers. In descant harmony, two melodies move independently and usually in opposite directions from each other.

The last form is called faux-bourdon, or false bass. In this style of harmonization, certain intervals that were once not used became acceptable. This allowed the music to continue to evolve, as it is still doing today.

Harmonic theory is based on chords, tonality, modulation, consonance, and dissonance. Chords are a simultaneous sounding of notes (tones). Certain chord patterns have been established over the years and are still in use today. Tonality refers to the home-base, or most important note that the piece centers around. We refer to harmony as either major or minor harmony or tonality.

The overall psychological effect of the harmony is often the best way to determine which is which. Major harmony tends to be the brighter, happier sound. The minor tonality ranges from dark and somber, to melancholy and even angry. Modulation, for reasons of relief and variety, is the movement away from the home-base. This is usually accompanied by a return to the home-base or key center.

Consonance and dissonance refer to two opposite poles in music. Consonance is the release, while dissonance is the tension in music. Depending on how much music you listen to will determine what is consonant and dissonant to you. Often, how the composer has scored the music (in other words, what instruments play it) and the required volume level will affect your determination.

One other important invention was the combination of two different harmonies simultaneously. This is called polytonality, and it had its roots in the years before World War 1. Stravinsky and Bartók, to name only two, both became fascinated by this new musical resource and by the new dissonances that were derived from the simultaneous combinations of two keys.

Despite the advances in harmonic language, today most music still centers on the major and minor tonal systems. The music is not, however, the same musical language from the time of Handel and Bach. Today it is often richer, more complex, and contains more tension (dissonance) in it.

☐ Harmony - major and minor, consonant and dissonant, polytonality.

Musical Texture

Musical texture is related to the idea of texture in the art world. If you could touch an oil painting, a watercolor, and a photograph, you would feel a difference in their texture. In music, unfortunately, we cannot feel the texture. Instead, composers put music together in such a way that they use three basic sound textures.

The first texture is the simplest to understand because it is just one melody. This is monophonic texture. It is comparable to a photograph that has only one object in it. In music, Gregorian chants are the perfect example of monophonic texture.

Homophonic texture is perhaps the most common musical texture. It consists of one melody with some sort of background or accompaniment. This was the invention of the early Italian opera composers who wanted to find a way to have their melodies and the text stand out from the music.

The third type of texture is polyphony, or polyphonic texture. Musically, polyphony makes the greatest demands on the listener. It is composed of two or more melodies that are simultaneously layered on top of each other. These separate and independent strands of melody require you to listen to this texture in a different way. Do not expect that on the first listening you will grasp all the melodic material. Since the texture is more dense (thick), you will need to listen to the piece several times, each time focusing on a different melodic strand. This is called linear or horizontal listening.

In Western musical history, almost all the music written between 1400 and 1750 is polyphonic (contrapuntal) in texture. You will need to listen with different ears to the polyphonic music of Bach as opposed to the homophonic music of Mozart.

Today, many composers have returned to the polyphonic style of musical composition. They have done so, however, in a more modern sense. This music allows for more dissonance (tension), and a freedom from the strict rules of music composition before the year 1750.

There are also many musical examples that do not fall into just one category. Many pieces will use all three textures, although one type of texture may dominate the entire work.

☐ Monophonic, polyphonic, and homophonic textures.

Expressive Elements - Dynamics and Tempo

While telling a story to a friend, our speech will encompass a broad dynamic spectrum, ranging from softly whispered words to a full-throated scream. Not only will our vocal dynamics change, but also the rate of speed at which we speak. As we become more excited, our tempo will speed up. When we are almost finished with the story, our tempo will slow down. This is the verbal clue to our listener that the story is ending. In music, the two expressive elements that are directly related to the story above are dynamics and tempo.

Dynamics and dynamic contrast provide an entire musical range of color, emotion, and intensity. They will help to delineate the sections (form) of a piece of music. Dynamics are the volume levels in music—the loudness or softness of the musical sound. The changes between these can be either abrupt (terraced) or gradual (crescendo, decrescendo). The musical systems for notating dynamics and dynamic changes are listed below.

Dynamics

ppp	—	extremely soft
pp	pianissimo	very soft
p	piano	soft
mp	mezzo piano	moderately soft
mf	mezzo forte	moderately loud
f	forte	loud (strong)
ff	fortissimo	very loud
fff	—	extremely loud

Dynamic Changes

Crescendo	To gradually get louder.
Decrescendo	To gradually get softer (also, diminuendo).
Terrace	Abrupt changes; alternating forte to piano.

Tempo

The tempo of a piece of music is defined as the speed at which the beat or pulse of the music is moving. How fast or slow the pulse of the piece is moving can be broken down into various "inexact" tempo markings. I say inexact because these tempo markings are very subjective and open to different interpretations. Each tempo has a mood or characteristic associated with it. Many times the differences are very subtle.

Composers also use various descriptors and tempo changes in a musical composition. Listed below are some of the most common terms for tempo markings.

Tempo Markings

Grave	extremely slow, solemn
Largo	very slow, broadly
Lento	slow
Adagio	slow, easily
Andante	moderately slow, walking
Moderato	moderate
Allegretto	moderately fast
Allegro	fast
Vivace	very fast, animated
Presto	very fast

Descriptors

Agitato	agitated
Assai	very
Cantabile	in a singing style
Con brio	with spirit
Con fuoco	with fire
Con moto	with motion
Grazioso	gracefully
Ma non	but not
Maestoso	majestically
Meno	less
Molto	very
Non troppo	not too much
Piu	more
Poco	little

Tempo Changes

Accelerando	To speed up.
Ritardando	Slow down.
Rallentando	To gradually slow down.
Rubato	Borrowed time, a flexible tempo indication.

Test Piece: Try out your new musical vocabulary on the following piece by the conservative Romantic composer Johannes Brahms. This piece was composed in the year 1877.

A   Moderate triple meter with some rubato, crescendo and decrescendo.
B   Tempo change, fast duple, steady (no rubato), dynamic changes and terrace effects.
A   Moderate triple with some rubato, crescendo and decrescendo, then a ritardando.
C   Tempo change, fast duple, steady (no rubato), good terrace effects.
A   Moderate triple with some rubato, crescendo and decrescendo, then a rallentando.

☐   Johannes Brahms, Allegretto grazioso. In an **A B A C A** form.

Ensembles and Concert Venues

As discussed in Chapter 1, follow the basic rules of concert etiquette; prepare before going to a concert, arrive early, read the program, and stay until the end of the concert! The term concert refers to a musical performance requiring the cooperation of several musicians. This is a very open-ended definition. In general, you will find instrumental, vocal, or combined concerts. The difference between a concert and a recital is the size of the performing ensemble. Recitals usually feature a small (or even just one) group of musicians. Originally, a recital meant a concert given by one musician or a concert of music by one composer. Today the term is nearly synonymous with a concert. To further complicate matters, sometimes a recital program is called chamber music.

In large concert halls you will generally find symphonies, concerti, program music, bands, musicals, ballet, modern dance, chorus with orchestra, and operettas. Chamber ensembles or recitals include art songs, sonatas, character pieces, mixed instrumental chamber ensembles, a cappella or chamber choir, church choir, and madrigal groups.

In this course you will experience a wide variety of types (genres) of music: both choral and instrumental, with large and small forms including opera, ballet, program music, sonata, concerto, concerto grosso, symphony, oratorio, choral music, entertainment pieces (serenades, suites), film music, musicals, and some of the more contemporary musical styles of the late 20th century.

Magnum Opus

"Magnum opus" refers to the system of numbering the various musical works of a composer. As discussed in Chapter 1, there are two types of music (absolute and program music) and two broad categories of music (vocal and instrumental). To understand how composers number their works, let's take a look at some of the more common catalogue systems.

Opus (Op.)

The word opus is Latin for "work." It is usually the composer's way of cataloging and listing his works chronologically. Unfortunately, it is seldom accurate. Some pieces are lost, some are forgotten, and often minor works are left out. Many times the music publishers made mistakes in the printing and numbering of the pieces. In the 1950's, for example, the publisher of Antonin Dvorák's music had to completely renumber his symphonies because of mistakes and omissions that they had made over the years!

When did it begin?

Handel was one of the first composers whose musical works had opus numbers attached to them. It was probably Beethoven who made them universally accepted.

How many works are in an Opus?

During the Baroque and Classical eras there were groups of similar works published under the same opus number. At this time, no standard system had been established. For example, there are six string quartets in the Opus 18 of Beethoven.

Other Systems

WoO vs. Op. for Beethoven

WoO means, if you can understand German, Werk ohne Opuszahl. In English it translates to "work without opus number." The highest opus number for Beethoven is Op. 138. There were, however, more than 200 pieces of his that were not on his main opus list during his lifetime. These were added to the Beethoven opus list and published in 1955 by Georg Kinsky. It was Kinsky who came up with the WoO designation.

Schubert gets a D.

The D in the Schubert catalogue marking stands for Otto E. Deutsch, the great Schubert expert. His catalogue of the music of Franz Schubert was published in 1951.

Haydn - Hob. (H.) or Op.

The Dutch bibliographer Anthony van Hoboken spent 30 years compiling a thematic F.J. Haydn catalogue which tends to be rather confusing. Still, you may run into it today. More common, however, are the old Opus numbers.

BWV for J.S. Bach

BWV is an abbreviation for Bach-Werke-Verzeichnis, or Bach Works Catalogue.

K. for Mozart

Ludwig von Köchel was a botanist and very good at classification. He began cataloguing Wolfgang Amadeus Mozart's music in the 1850's—drawing on the composer's and his father's (Leopold) partial catalogues. His numbers are labeled as KV for Köchel-Verzeichnis (Köchel catalogue) and KE when referring to the revisions made by Alfred Einstein in 1937.

HWV for Handel

This is the catalogue designation for G.F. Handel's works as compiled by B. Baselt and edited by the G.F. Handel Society in 1979. HWV stands for Handel-Werke-Verzeichnis, or Handel Works Catalogue.

C.P.E. Bach and Gluck

These composers often have a W or Wq number after the Belgian bibliographer Alfred Wotquenne.

R. or P. for Vivaldi

The designation of R or P comes from the musicologist Peter Ryom. Ryom did his catalogue work on the music of the Baroque composer Antonio Vivaldi.

Musical Form

Form is organization. Music is not a series of random notes and sounds. In most pieces of music the composer is adhering to a preset form or idea. If the music is based on polyphonic techniques, then the form is **imitative**. Music in **sectional** form is composed of large musical blocks with cadences. One of the distinguishing features of sectional form is the repetition of the musical material.

A piece of music that is associated with a piece of literature will use **dramatic** form. In other words, the music is composed to follow the story line or to convey the drama in the story. Music of the 20th century is often characterized by **free** or **open** forms, where the composer is often drawing on elements of randomness and improvisation. These are the four basic types of musical forms.

Whether you know it or not, you are probably already familiar with musical form. Most pieces of popular or rock music start with an introduction. Usually the introduction is instrumental—without words or lyrics. Then, when the vocalist enters, the first verse begins (A). At the end of the first verse the singer stops singing. This is a **cadence**—a moment of rest or repose. When the singer reenters, the second verse begins. The second verse uses different lyrics but the same music (A). After the second verse ends, a cadence again occurs just before the chorus section begins. The chorus, also known as the hook, is composed of different lyrics and music (B). This is then followed by verse three (A). This is known as song form or, in musical shorthand, **A A B A**.

☐   Song form with introduction.

Film Music – Dramatic Form

Another type of musical form that you are probably familiar with is dramatic form, especially as it is used in a movie or on television. In the history of Western music, however, this is a rather recent development. Usually the film is shot first and the music is added later. In this way, the music can be written to follow the dramatic action of the movie. What happens then is the music becomes secondary to the film. Many times you may not even notice the film music. Here are five important ways in which music will serve the action on the screen.

1. Create a convincing atmosphere of the time period, the place, and the setting.
2. Underline the psychological nature of a scene, the unspoken thoughts of a character, and the unseen implications of a situation.
3. Create a neutral background.
4. Build a sense of continuity and keep the action moving forward.
5. Underline the theatrical build-up of a scene and bring the dramatic action to its conclusion.

When we discuss program music, ballet, and opera, you will see many parallels between them and film music. Opera was, in many ways, the film equivalent in the 19th century. It was the biggest spectacle and visual form of entertainment for the aristocrats and the common people.

Stomp Out Loud

Using ordinary objects to make sounds, the ensemble Stomp is a unique combination of percussion, movement and visual comedy. Featuring choreographed performances from the stage show along with stage and street work, *Stomp Out Loud* (1997) makes new and unusual rhythms out of everyday sounds. From dangling precariously from a massive billboard, to utilizing the sounds of 'waterphonics,' brooms, poles, and buckets, this ensemble creates an explosive mixture of music and dance as they 'shake, rattle, and roll' anything that makes a sound! Stomp, which originated off-Broadway, is a unique exploration of rhythm, percussion and musical timbre. Listen for the use of dramatic form in these excerpts.

☐   *Stomp Out Loud* (excerpts)

Blast!

Produced in 2001 by Cook Group Inc. and Star of Indiana, *Blast!* brings together 68 brass, percussion and visual performers in a unique explosion of music and theater. *Blast!* is a novel art form that evolved from competitive drum and bugle corps. This show is both a musical spectacle and 'music in motion.' Using diverse musical materials (classical, blues, jazz, rock, and techno-pop), *Blast!* explores the 'music and motion' genre with creativity and artistry. With the inclusion of harmonic elements, this show from London's West End is the perfect way to enjoy both watching and listening to the seven elements of music.

☐   *Blast!* (excerpts)

"The principal function of form is to advance our understanding."

Arnold Schoenberg, a 20th century composer

"You can see the form of a painting, or a church, more or less all at once because their forms exist in space. But with a piece of music, you actually hear form. And it takes <u>time</u> to hear the form."

Leonard Bernstein, American conductor, composer, and author

While saying Mass, a theme for a fugue suddenly struck him. He quitted the altar to the surprise of the congregation, hastened into the sacristy to write it down, and then returned to finish his office.

Description of Antonio Vivaldi in Venice

". . . and I offer myself in the most dutiful obedience, whenever your Royal Majesty may graciously require me, to show my unwearying zeal in the composition of music either for church or orchestra . . ."

J.S. Bach, in a letter to the King of Poland in 1733

Form in Music

Form in music is the organization of a piece that helps the listener to keep the main musical ideas in mind as it develops, changes, and comes to a conclusion. Essentially there are four types of forms—dramatic, sectional, imitative, and those that are open or free in form. Musical composition is a process of creating sound by putting the components of music together piece by piece.

We will now examine some of the most important musical forms that are sectional and imitative. A summary of the most important forms can be found in Appendix B.

Musical Structure

In Chapter 3 we took a look at song form and the labeling of the major sections of a piece of music. We also saw what dramatic form was and how film music revolves around the dramatic action of the film (plot and dialogue).

We will continue to examine musical forms in this chapter concentrating on the important sectional and imitative forms that are common to Western music. Keep in mind that sectional forms are usually homophonic in texture while imitative forms tend to be mostly polyphonic.

Sectional Forms
Michael Praetorius - Dance Music

Although musical virtuosi existed from the beginning of time, it was during the Renaissance that their accomplishments began to achieve real importance. During this era their abilities became regarded as truly artistic ones. This was because there were more compositions that featured instruments and instrumental accompaniments. In Renaissance cathedrals, for example, instrumentalists often accompanied the chorus in performance.

Musicians were employed not only by the courts and churches but also by the towns. Many towns created and maintained bands of musicians (wind, brass, percussion) to perform at various civic functions. These musicians, however, were not paid as well as their counterparts in the wealthy courts of Europe.

One musician, Michael Praetorius (1571-1621), published a collection of music in 1612 that is really the first European orchestral music collection. This furnished the music for the French kings at all of their various social events. The collection is the *Terpsichore musarum,* and includes a rather new social dance of the time known as a Courante. This refined French dance will also find its way into the dance music of the Baroque era (1600-1750) and into a genre of music known as the suite (Chapter 15).

This dance composition features various Renaissance wind instruments including cornettos, sackbuts, recorders, shawms, plucked string instruments, and bells. The musical form has two parts and is known as binary form. It is arranged in an **A A B B** format.

☐   "Courante" by Praetorius.

Giovanni Gabrieli - Sacred Music

Gabrieli's *In ecclesiis* is a vocal and instrumental composition that is organized around the principle of alternating verse and chorus (refrain). Called a motet, it is a polyphonic sacred composition for voices that was popular in the Renaissance and Baroque eras.

Giovanni Gabrieli was born c.1556. He was the music director at St. Mark's Cathedral in Venice. Acting on the order of the Council of Trent to make church services more interesting, he surveyed the huge interior of

St. Mark's, where he was the organist and composer. Then he experimented with placing groups of singers in one alcove of the nave, brass players in another, a boy's choir in a third, and string players in the fourth. This resulted in music that is concerted, or stereophonic. Gabrieli was attempting to bring contrasting mediums of sound together.

The words concert and concerto are derived from this "concertato" principle. As Gabrieli alternated choirs and instruments from the left and right, front and rear, the music enveloped the audience in a new way. He also brought two other innovations to the music world; he specified which instruments were to be used, and added expression (dynamic) marks to his music. The overall form of the piece is a binary form with an alternating verse and chorus. Here are the sections and the translations from Latin to English.

Introduction	Triple meter, major tonality, organ only, ends in a clear cadence.
Verse 1	"In ecclesiis benedicte Domino" - Praise the Lord in the congregation; moderate tempo, duple meter, for sopranos (I) and organ.
Alleluia	Triple meter, faster, sopranos (I), chorus II, organ.
Verse 2	"In omnia loco" - In every place of worship praise him; duple meter, moderate tempo, tenors (I), chorus II, organ.
Alleluia	Triple meter, faster, tenors (I), chorus II, organ.
Sinfonia	Instrumental interlude - duple meter, brass and organ.
Verse 3	"In Deo, salutari meo" - In God who is my salvation and glory; dance-like character, alternating altos (I), tenors (I), and brass.
Alleluia	Triple meter, forte, alternating choirs and brass
Verse 4	"Deus meus, te vocamus" - My God, we call thee; duple meter, dynamic level of piano, alternating sopranos (I), tenors (I) and organ.
Alleluia	Triple meter, alternating choirs - Chorus I & II, organ.
Verse 5	"Deus, adjutor noster aeternam" - God, our eternal judge; duple meter, alternating soft and loud, choirs and brass, with organ.
Alleluia	Triple meter, alternating choirs and brass, with organ. Final Cadence - long full chord, forte.

☐   *In ecclesiis* by Gabrieli.

G.F. Handel - Dance Forms

The *Music for the Royal Fireworks* is one of the few instrumental works from Handel's later years. The story behind the piece involves the signing of the Peace of Aix-la-Chapelle in 1748. When it was completed, King George wanted to celebrate. A public display of fireworks was planned for Green Park in April of 1749, and Handel was commissioned to write a piece for the ceremony. At a rehearsal for the ceremony supposedly more than 12,000 people turned out to hear the music. This caused an enormous traffic jam that blocked the London Bridge for most of the afternoon!

The piece is actually a Baroque suite (Chapter 15). At that time a suite was a collection of popular dances. In this suite, Handel composed a Bourrée, a Réjouissance (Rejoicing), and a Menuet. The Bourrée is an elegant court dance that Handel scored for two upper parts and a bass line. The Rejoicing adds snare drums to the ensemble. It is played three times; trumpets, woodwinds, and strings, then horns and woodwinds, and finally tutti (all). The final Menuet begins as a canon (imitation) and has a middle section in the minor key. It is similar in instrumentation to the Rejoicing. You will notice in all three of these movements the use of sectional form, with changes in instrumentation occurring in the repeated sections of the Rejoicing and Menuet.

Music for the Royal Fireworks, HWV 351
  composed in 1749

I.   Overture
II.   Bourrée
III. La Paix
IV.   La Réjouissance
V.   Menuet I
VI.   Menuet II

[ ]   *Music for the Royal Fireworks* by Handel. (II, IV, and VI.)

W.A. Mozart ~ Rondo Form

A sonata, as we will see in Chapter 5, is a piece for a solo instrument. Typically, it follows a three movement plan (form) of Allegro, Andante, and Allegro.

The third movement of Mozart's *Sonata in C major*, KV. 545, is in a rondo form. A rondo is characterized by the returning of the original theme (A). Typically, it follows an A B A C A pattern. In a rondo form, the most important feature is the alternation of new material with the main A section. See how many times the A section returns in this piece. You will notice, as with many pieces by Mozart, that the melody is easy to remember; short, simple, and singable.

Sonata in C major, KV. 545
  composed in 1788

I.   Allegro
II.   Andante
III. Rondo

[ ]   *Sonata in C* major by Mozart. (III. Rondo)

W.A. Mozart ~ Menuetto and Trio

The *Symphony No. 35*, "Haffner," by Mozart was originally intended as a serenade (outdoor entertainment music) for his childhood friend, Siegmund Haffner. The music was written to be performed at a ceremony honoring Haffner, who was being elevated to the rank of nobility.

This symphony is similar to a serenade in form and style. At this time, symphonies were not profoundly challenging orchestral pieces. They were meant to be light, entertainment pieces. Rehearsals for orchestral concerts were rather unusual at this time. The music was usually performed on sight (sight-read) and therefore not very difficult to play.

The *Symphony No. 35* comes at the end of a long series of light, multi-movement works that were composed for specific occasions. Mozart was, after all, a practical man who had a family and debts to pay—especially living in Vienna. It is not until we get to *Symphony No. 38*, "Prague," with its heightened drama, strong contrasting themes, frequent interplay and juxtapositions of winds and strings, that we begin to see Mozart changing the symphony into a major genre (form). From this time on, the symphony began to dominate the music of the Western world well into the 20th century.

The Menuetto and Trio form, or just Menuetto, is usually found in the third movement of a symphony. The basic form is **A B A**, or ternary form. The A section is the minuet with a contrasting or lighter trio section (B). Originally, the trio section was written to be performed by only three instruments.

Symphony No. 35 in D major, K. 385
    composed in 1782

I.   Allegro con spirito
II.   Andante
III.   Menuetto, Trio, Menuetto
IV.   Presto

☐   *Symphony No. 35* by Mozart. (III. Menuetto and Trio)

W.A. Mozart - Theme and Variations

In 1784, Mozart wrote his *Piano Concerto No. 17 in G major*, K. 453, for one of his students, Ms. Babette Ployer. She was the daughter of the agent to the Archbishop of Salzburg. Ms. Ployer gave the world premier of the concerto in Döbling, Austria in June of 1784.

As the story goes, a few weeks after this concert Mozart heard a starling bird singing a tune quite like the main theme of the third movement of his *Piano Concerto No. 17*. He was so surprised at this coincidence that he decided to buy the bird and keep it for a pet. When the bird died, Mozart buried it and wrote a short poem for its gravestone.

The third movement (finale) is a set of variations on the starling theme. This theme sounds similar to Papageno's music from the opera *The Magic Flute* (1791). The theme has two parts, and each section is repeated before the variations begin. The orchestra begins with the main theme, and the piano enters on the first variation. Here is the overall outline of the third movement:

Theme	Orchestra only, A A B B (binary).
V. 1	Piano enters.
V. 2	Winds, accompanied by the strings and the piano.
V. 3	Piano alternates the melody with the winds.
V. 4	In the minor key (G minor), the strings and piano alternate.
V. 5	Alternations of orchestra and piano, forceful, return to major key. The piano holds onto the theme; sequence and cadential extension.
Presto	The tempo changes, it is now faster.
Coda	This is the closing section, new melodies combine with the main theme. This is not another variation, just a closing section. It ends with the piano and orchestra alternating musical phrases.

Piano Concerto No. 17 in G major, K. 453
   composed in 1784

I.   Allegro
II. Andante
III. Allegretto, Presto

☐   *Piano Concerto No. 17* by Mozart. (III. Allegretto, Presto)

W.A. Mozart - Sonata-Allegro Form

It takes time to hear form. You have to develop a good memory for the notes, themes, and melodies you've just heard. The problem is that you have to do this while listening to new material. In the Classical era, sonata-allegro form was usually found in the first movement of a symphony. Since this form is a little more challenging, composers probably put it at the beginning of the symphony when your powers of concentration are most acute.

What made this form so popular? First, it makes sense. This form is constructed in the same manner that a paper is written. It begins with an introduction (exposition), in which the composer exposes you to the two musical themes. Usually this is played twice so that you can really concentrate on what the themes sound like. Once you know what the themes are you will be able to understand and enjoy the development section. This is where the composer shows us his compositional skills.

The second section is the body (development). This is the part of your paper where you develop the ideas you presented in the introduction. The composer in this section develops his two musical themes—see Chapter 1 in case you need to review what the process of development is all about.

The movement concludes with a recapitulation. It functions to recap the main ideas from the first part (exposition). It is almost a repeat of the introduction with a longer closing section called a coda. The function of the coda is to bring the music to a close.

As you can see, the musical form is balanced and utilizes the element of contrast. The balance and logic of its form (introduction, body, conclusion) and the contrasts of musical elements are what make this form so popular with many composers. Balance and contrast are the two secrets of sonata-allegro form. Overall, the form is **A B A**. Here is the outline of Sonata-allegro form:

A   Exposition (usually played twice)
         Theme 1 - rhythmic in character.
         Theme 2 - melodic in character (contrast).
         Codetta - cadence section.
B   Development
         Theme(s) - in various keys with the use of imitation, sequence, diminution, augmentation, and/or
         variation. (the process of development, Chapter 1).
A   Recapitulation (almost the same as the exposition)
         Theme 1 - rhythmic.
         Theme 2 - melodic.
         Coda - closing section.

The first movement of the *Serenade for Strings in G major* follows this format. The melodies are easy to remember and the distinctions between sections are quite obvious. We will examine the first movement, Allegro, of this light, outdoor entertainment piece by Mozart written in 1787.

Serenade for Strings in G major, K. 525
   composed in 1787

I.   Allegro
II.   Romanza
III.   Allegretto
IV.   Allegro

☐   *Serenade for Strings* by Mozart. (I. Allegro)

Imitative Forms
J.S. Bach - Two-Part Inventions

Originally composed for the harpsichord in 1723, these pieces were not only intended as studies for amateur keyboard players, but also as models in the two-part contrapuntal style. These inventions were meant to demonstrate how to play and compose for two voices (parts). Today, they are performed on everything from a piano to a synthesizer.

   J.S. Bach was the master of transcription. He pursued a lifelong exploitation of all the forms and developments in the music of his time (except for the opera). He was fascinated with the music of Vivaldi and transcribed (adapted) four of his concerti for the organ. Not only did Bach "borrow" music from Vivaldi, a form of flattery and quite legal during his time, but he also borrowed music from other colleagues, his pupils, and even from himself! He often reworked and adapted many of his works to different settings and instruments.

   In the spirit of Bach, we will listen to contemporary recordings of his *Two-Part Inventions*. The reason for this is that the synthesizer is capable of a variety of timbres whereas the harpsichord is not. On a synthesizer you will hear how Bach combines two melodies in a polyphonic setting very clearly.

☐   *Two-Part Invention No. 1* in C major and *Two-Part Invention No. 8* in F major by Bach.

☐   *Two-Part Invention No. 4* in D minor by Bach.

J.S. Bach - The Fugue

The *Toccata and Fugue in D minor*, BWV 565, is assembled in three parts; a toccata, a fugue, and a closing section with a series of sound medleys. The dynamic contrasts and changes in tempi make the closing section another toccata. Overall, the form is ternary—**A** (toccata), **B** (fugue), and **A** (toccata). The toccata, the first section of this piece, is a show-off piece for the organist. The word toccata comes from the Italian verb "to touch." It is imitative, ornamented, and has a complex melody that uses the full range of the organ.

   A fugue, including the one in this piece, is an imitative form that is one of the high points of the Baroque era. It begins with a subject (theme) in a monophonic setting. This allows you to focus on the theme all by itself. The reason for this is that it will be imitated four times in succession before coming to a cadence. After the fugue subject is heard four times, a series of episodes (imitation) will occur until Bach returns to the main theme at the end of the fugue. In this piece, Bach ends with a toccata that is a series of sound blocks.

   Bach composed this c.1708 while he was working at the court in Weimar for Duke Wilhelm Ernst. Duke Ernst was a devout Lutheran and an enthusiastic patron of Bach's music.

☐   *Toccata and Fugue in D minor* by Bach.

Movement II. – Music for Instruments

5 Le concert c'est moi

"Then we stopped at an old music shop near the harbor. I began browsing through a bundle of musical scores. Suddenly I came upon a sheaf of pages, crumbled and discolored with age. They were unaccompanied suites by Johann Sebastian Bach . . . Those suites opened up a whole new world. They are the very essence of Bach, and Bach is the essence of music."

Pablo Casals, a cellist

"I have seen compositions declared to be his which are assuredly not bad and in which I perceived no sign of a twelve-year-old boy; and I cannot well doubt that they are his own, for when I tested him at the harpsichord in various ways, he played me such things as are prodigious at that age and would be admirable even in a grown man."

Description of W.A. Mozart by Johann Adolf Hasse, an opera composer

"I want to seize fate by the throat."

Beethoven as a young composer

The Sonata

The sonata is defined differently in each historical period. Even within an era, there are certain exceptions to the genre. For our purposes, we will define it in its most general terms. A sonata is a piece for solo or small ensemble, usually instrumental, and typically in three movements. The first movement is commonly in a sonata-allegro form.

The history of the term sonata goes back to the 13th century where it was used to denote any instrumental piece. Toward the end of the 16th century it was used in reference to the Italian lute repertory and was also applied to any instrumental works that were being composed. Usually it was used to designate an instrumental work. The consistent traits of the sonata throughout the centuries include:

1. Instrumental music without voices.
2. Absolute music without a program.
3. Concert music without a specific social function.
4. Solo or chamber music for one to four players, without orchestral parts.
5. Cyclic music in two to four movements.
6. Use of extended forms of absolute music (sonata-allegro, rondo, etc.).

In the Baroque, Classical, Romantic, and 20th century eras, the sonata had identifiable traits that were unique to each era. Although it was the Romantic composer Franz Liszt who said "Le concert c'est moi" (The concert, it is me), we will begin in the era in which the sonata originated—the Baroque Era (1600-1750).

Baroque Sonata

The word sonata comes from the Italian verb "sonare," which means "to sound." The other Italian word, considered its opposite, was "cantare" which means "to sing." Unfortunately, for about seventy-five years, the terms sonata (sonare) and canzona (cantare) were often used interchangeably. It was only in the late Baroque, also known as the high Baroque, that the term sonata was used exclusively to denote instrumental works.

A sonata was composed for both church and court, but only very rarely in the theater. It could be found in concerts of all types, and was extensively used in amateur and home music-making. While the term sonata was used for instrumental works, often the instrument itself was not specified.

Musically a sonata features a polyphonic texture, fast harmonic rhythm, and melodic lines unfolding through repetitions, sequences, or various types of imitation. Composers increased their ability to extend the musical forms during this period, so that the pieces became longer.

During this era, the number of movements was usually three or four. The music itself included explicit and expressive tempo indications. One of the most popular plans for the sonata was an alternation of fast and slow movements of different character and key (tonality). Contrast in both tempo and key was a major determination in the ordering of the movements. A binary form with repeated halves was the favorite movement plan both for sonatas and dance forms. Quite often the opening and closing measures were very similar to each other (closure).

Historically, the sonata's development began in northern Italy during the early 17th century. It was carried abroad by visitors and natives who traveled and worked elsewhere.

J.S. Bach

Johann Sebastian Bach's solo works for violin, cello, viola da gamba, flute, and lute are usually classified either as sonatas or as suites, although sometimes as partitas. Some are for a single instrument without an accompaniment: the six sonatas and partitas for violin (BWV 1001-06), the six suites for cello (BWV 1007-12), a partita for flute (BWV 1013), and seven works for lute (BWV 995-1000 and 1006a). These works are very idiomatic for the particular instrument, and skillfully create harmonic and contrapuntal effects despite the absence of an accompaniment. Bach also wrote sonatas for a solo instrument with continuo, while there are still others that feature a solo instrument with a written-out harpsichord part.

The works of Bach that we will examine include the *Sonata No. 1*, *Sonata No. 2*, and the *Partita for Solo Violin No. 3* from the *Six Sonatas and Partitas for Violin*, BWV 1001-06. These were written during his main instrumental phase from 1717 to 1723. It was during this time that Bach was at the court of Cöthen as Kapellmeister to Prince Leopold. The Brandenburg Concerti, his orchestral suites, and some of his best-known keyboard works are also from this period.

Sonata No. 1 in G minor, BWV 1001
I.   Adagio
II. Fuga (allegro)
III. Siciliana
IV. Presto

Sonata No. 2 in A minor, BWV 1003
I.   Grave
II. Fuga
III. Andante
IV. Allegro

Partita No. 3 in E major, BWV 1006
I.   Preludio
II. Loure
III. Gavotte (en Rondo)
IV. Menuet I, Menuet II
V.   Bourrée
VI. Gigue

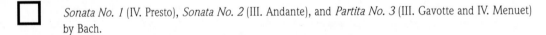

Sonata No. 1 (IV. Presto), *Sonata No. 2* (III. Andante), and *Partita No. 3* (III. Gavotte and IV. Menuet) by Bach.

Classical Sonata

Some of the Classical era definitions and attitudes overlap with both the Baroque and Romantic eras. The Classical sonata begins with the keyboard sonatas of Scarlatti, Alberti, and the son of J.S. Bach, C.P.E. Bach. During this era, there will be a change in keyboard instruments from the harpsichord and clavichord to the pianoforte. The most important sonata composers were those of the First Viennese School—Haydn, Mozart and Beethoven. There is less confusion as to the use of the word in this era, though one still sees it as meaning any instrumental genre.

Sonatas continued to be used at the courts but declined in use in the church. They were almost never found in the theater. The new social functions of the sonata include:

1. A diversion for the amateur or dilettante.
2. A launching vehicle for a professional performer or composer.
3. A training piece for a student composer.
4. An occasional piece in private and public concerts.
5. A convenient musical work for use in church.

The sonata, as you can see, was not the main stay of concert life. This distinction fell to the operas, arias, songs, choral ensembles, concerti, and other large instrumental ensembles during the Classical era. Historically, the keyboard sonata is tied to the Classical sonata. In the Baroque era there were very few keyboard sonatas; perhaps only about thirty in the years just before the death of J.S. Bach. Clavichord sonatas were composed by the sons of Bach and their followers in North Germany. The first piano appeared in 1709 (by Cristofori), and while some piano sonatas were published in 1732 (by Giustini), the real circulation began in the 1760's.

Violin and other string instruments contributed to the quality of sonata composition. However, these instruments did not undergo the development in their construction that the piano did at the time. Additionally, there was a large body of sonatas composed for a solo guitar by Sor, Molitor, and Giustini. There were even a few sonatas for solo winds, including the flute, clarinet, and horn. It was the solo keyboard setting, however, that ranked the highest throughout the Classical era. Musically, the Classical sonatas demonstrate:

1. A homophonic texture.
2. A slow harmonic rhythm.
3. The use of repeating phrases and sectional form.
4. The use of many contrasting themes (polythematic).
5. An increase in chromaticism, changes in key, and a bolder use of dissonance.

This musical development of the sonata was a flexible process and continually evolved. There is almost no point in looking for any consistent trend in the number and order of the movements during this period. The first movement is, however, usually in a textbook sonata-allegro form. The second movement may also be in sonata form, but with a less complex development section and often in binary or ternary form. The third and fourth movements were often in a variety of forms, including minuet, scherzo, rondo, variation, or other dance forms.

W.A. Mozart

Wolfgang Amadeus Mozart did not begin writing piano sonatas until 1774. By then, he was already a famous composer in Vienna with a tremendous output of music. While his early sonatas show the tremendous influence of the composer Haydn, his later sonatas display a maturing of his style. This mature style of Mozart would later influence Beethoven.

The *Sonata No. 14 in C minor*, K. 457, was completed in October of 1784 while he was in the middle of composing some of his greatest piano concerti. It is the only one of Mozart's solo works that fully exploit the dynamic range and expressive possibilities of the piano. The dramatic statements, the short lyrical phrases found in the outer movements, the interruptions in the melodic flow in the finale, all separated by the tranquil middle movement (Adagio), influenced the piano music of Beethoven.

In the third movement you will also find the use of silence, a moody quality to the melody (minor), and use of the full range of the keyboard. These elements, combined with a harmonic ingenuity and melodic richness, are characteristic of the mature musical style of Mozart.

Sonata No. 14 in C minor, K. 457, for piano
   composed in 1784

I.   Molto allegro
II.   Adagio
III. Allegro assai

Sonata No. 14 by Mozart. (III. Allegro assai)

Ludwig von Beethoven

After making his permanent home in Vienna in 1792, Ludwig von Beethoven made his initial musical reputation by his piano playing. He was a brilliant performer and improviser, as well as the finest piano player in his time. In his thirty-two sonatas that were published with opus numbers, Beethoven displays his virtuosity as a performer, his experimentation as a composer (sonorities, harmonies), and a unique musical style heightened by his oncoming deafness. Many of the slow movements of his works seem to be a private world of contemplation and meditation—the meanings of which we can only imagine.

The late Classical style of the sonata shows an intensification of the traits from early in the period. This includes:

1. Extended and more complex main themes.
2. More lyrical themes, often taken from folk melodies.
3. Accompaniment patterns that feature driving rhythms.
4. Richer musical textures.
5. Freer treatment of dissonance.
6. Greater rhythmic variety.
7. Expanded harmonic language.

The *Piano Sonata No. 8 in C minor*, Op. 13, "Pathétique," is one of the two sonatas that Beethoven himself subtitled. The other one is "Les Adieux," Op. 81a. The rest were subtitled by his publishers. Beethoven dedicated this piece to his friend and patron in Vienna, Prince Carl von Lichnowsky, in whose house he had lived for a short while.

The "Pathétique" sonata, meaning "strong emotion", is one of the most performed of all the thirty-two piano sonatas composed by Beethoven. It is also the most important of the early Beethoven piano sonatas and was written during his "C minor" period. At this time, the key of "C minor" was practically the only minor key he used in important compositions. The sonata shows Beethoven's growing dissatisfaction with the restrictions of classical forms.

This sonata consists of three movements: a dramatic allegro movement in a sonata-allegro form that begins with a slow introduction, a lyrical middle movement in a rondo form, and a third and final movement in a fast tempo also in a rondo form. The desperateness of the opening movement indicates a growing awareness of his hearing loss. The melancholy of the second movement creates a feeling of deep expression and emotion.

The overall rondo form of the third movement is A B A C A B A, with a coda at the end of the movement. In it, the tonality alternates between minor and major. The symmetry of the sections creates an overall balance and clarity of design that is common to the Classical spirit that influenced this piece. The beginning of the third movement rondo theme comes from the first four notes of the first movement, and musically unifies the piece.

This process of musical unification is called "cyclic" treatment.

Beethoven composed piano sonatas during every style period throughout his life. He used them as a vehicle for experimenting with form and in advancing piano technique. This also led to the further development of the piano as an instrument. The sonata was a genre that he was very comfortable and familiar with. Few composers since then have used it as he did—as a portrait of the composer's most intimate musical ideas.

Piano Sonata No. 8 in C minor, Op. 13, "Pathétique"
   composed in 1798-99

I.   Grave - Allegro di molto e con brio
II.   Adagio cantabile
III. Rondo (Allegro)

☐   *Piano Sonata No. 8* by Beethoven. (I. Grave and III. Rondo)

Romantic Sonata

The sonata continued as a genre for social diversions in the Romantic era (1820-1900). It continued to be used at private concerts as well as a teaching device for students and aspiring musicians. Wagner suggested to a music school in Munich that the sonata, especially Beethoven's, "should be the starting point of a fine musical education."

By the 1830's, the sonata flourished as a genre in public concerts. The sonatas of Beethoven became the most frequently performed. The Romantic sonatas were generally not at the same level as those of Beethoven.

Most sonatas from the Romantic era are for piano, or for an instrument with piano accompaniment. Only rarely is it used for a large instrumental group, such as Richard Strauss's *Sonatina for Sixteen Winds*. The piano is now essential to the sonata concept and to Romantic music in general.

The Romantic sonata is considered an expansion or exaggeration of the Classical ideals, and not a complete break with it. The newer characteristics of the Romantic sonata include:

1.   More lyrical and balanced themes (as compared to Beethoven).
2.   New types of piano accompaniments.
3.   March and waltz patterns as accompaniments.
4.   Richer sound, but still with basically homophonic textures.

The late Romantic sonata is an international pooling of styles. There were also attempts at infusing some sonatas with nationalistic traits (i.e., the Russians, Sibelius). Unfortunately, many were not composed at the same level of musical creativity as their earlier counterparts.

Richard Strauss

In 1888, Strauss wrote his *Sonata for Violin and Piano* in E-flat major, Op. 18. This work demonstrates many of the aspects of the late Romantic sonata. In the first movement, for example, there are three themes in a typical late romantic pattern; a heroic, triplet melody, followed by a nostalgic second theme, concluding with an unrestrained third theme. This is then followed by a long development section and a recapitulation that counterbalances the three themes of the exposition. The second movement was completed in 1888, a year after the rest of the score. It is in an **A B A** form but with a twist — a new theme appears halfway through the movement.

The finale is composed of surging, expansive themes that provide many opportunities for ornamentation by the soloist. This movement is full of typically lush Romantic melodies and rich musical textures.

Sonata for Violin and Piano in E-flat major, Op. 18
  composed in 1888

I.   Allegro, ma non troppo
II. Improvisation: Andante cantabile
III. Finale: Andante; Allegro

☐   *Sonata for Violin and Piano* by Strauss. (III. Finale)

20th Century Sonata

The continuity of the sonata has been lost in the 20th century. The title no longer implies a work for piano, or for an instrument with piano accompaniment.

Debussy's three late sonatas (1915-17) show a refinement of his own unique style. His *Sonata for Flute, Viola, and Harp* opened the way for other unusual instrumental combinations, such as the *Trio for Brass* (1922) by Francis Poulenc.

Claude Debussy

Claude Debussy, a French Impressionistic composer, described his *Sonata for Flute, Viola and Harp* as ". . . the music of a Debussy I no longer know. It is terribly melancholy and I do not know whether one should laugh or cry—perhaps both?"

It was written during World War I at a time when Debussy was very ill. As a composer, Debussy wrote melodies that were really just short melodic fragments. These melodic fragments in his works fit together like pieces of stained glass—one color leading to another color.

Debussy's *Sonata for Flute, Viola and Harp* features three unusual instruments and instrumental colors (timbres). It is sensuous music with a variety of tempi and moods. The flute themes recur intermittently in the minuet-like Interlude and in the frantic Finale, as all three movements are thematically linked. The flute writing is similar to his landmark composition from 1894, the *Prelude to the Afternoon of a Faun*. The sonata ends in a final burst of color from all three of the instruments.

Sonata for Flute, Viola, and Harp
  composed in 1915

I.   Pastorale
II. Interlude
III. Finale

☐   *Sonata for Flute, Viola, and Harp* by Debussy. (III. Finale)

"... not to judge their imperfection by the strictness of that fine and delicate taste which all the world knows You have for musical works; but rather to take into consideration the profound respect and the most humble obedience to which they are meant to bear witness."

J.S. Bach, to the Margrave of Brandenburg

"To tremble in the icy snow, to be buffeted by the village wind, to stamp one's frozen feet, to feel the excessive cold make one's teeth chatter."

Antonio Vivaldi, excerpt from his sonnet on winter

"Oblivion and neglect are the worst fate that can befall a composition, especially a new one. It does not so much signify what the critic writes; that he should write something is the important matter."

P.I. Tchaikovsky

The Concerto and Concerto Grosso

A concerto is an instrumental work that maintains contrast between an orchestra and either a smaller group or a solo instrument. The word concerto means "things happening together." It features the use of three different textures—the small group (or a soloist), the big group, and the two groups together. To many composers, the contrasting mediums of sound were like a musical battle as the performers stepped "Once more unto the breach" (Shakespeare, *Henry V*, Act 3).

Generally a concerto has three movements in the order of Allegro, Andante, and Allegro. Before the year 1700, the term concerto could apply to a great variety of forms. During the time of the three great Baroque masters, Vivaldi, Handel, and Bach, there were two common forms—the concerto and the concerto grosso.

The word concerto comes from the Italian "concertare," which means to arrange or to get together. The first musical application of this term was in describing a vocal ensemble, or "the bringing together of voices." In 1618, Michael Praetorius (Chapter 4) wrote that the common usage of this term included nearly all sacred compositions of instruments and voices.

The earliest publication of a concerto was the *Concerti di Andrea et di Giovanni Gabrieli* from Venice in 1587. Here the term implied a performance by combinations of voices and instruments. In the first half of the 17th century, the concerto became a common term for Italian vocal music accompanied by instruments. Some were large scale antiphonal works, as in the case of Gabrieli, but most were small compositions. Two consistent elements found in the concerto were the use of a continuo and the substitution of voices for instruments.

Antonio Vivaldi

The Baroque composer Antonio Vivaldi was born in Venice. He was the son of a violinist at St. Mark's Chapel, and was educated as both a clergyman and a musician. He was ordained but, because of his poor health (asthma), he chose music as a career. Known as the priest with flaming red hair, he spent the years 1704-40 at the Ospedale della Pietà as a conductor, composer, and teacher. La Pietà was a music conservatory and a home for orphans and illegitimate children. Music was an important part of the curriculum, and the children were expected to excel at it. They were given instruction in singing and on playing the violin, flute, organ, viola, bassoon, and the cello. The conservatory in Venice had an "orchestra" of approximately forty girls. Audiences flocked to the regular Sunday and festival concerts to see Vivaldi's orchestra expertly playing and singing.

In his role as a composer, Vivaldi wrote more than 450 concerti (plural of concerto), 23 sinfonias (predecessor to the symphony), 75 solo or trio sonatas, 49 operas, and countless cantatas, motets, and oratorios that he was expected to furnish for various festivals and religious feast days in Venice. Today, Vivaldi is remembered primarily for his instrumental music, particularly for his concerti.

Essentially, a concerto (solo concerto) is a work for a small orchestra and a soloist. Since Vivaldi was a virtuoso violinist, many of his concerti feature the violin. A concerto grosso (big or grand concerto) generally featured two to four soloists with a small orchestra for accompaniment. Frequently, two violins and a basso continuo are featured in contrast to the larger orchestra.

The basso continuo was a Baroque musical characteristic. Composed of the harpsichord, cello, and bassoon (if available), it functions as the rhythm section does in a band today. It provides a steady beat, fills in any missing parts, and adds to a thin or empty sounding musical texture. Notice how in this concerto the harpsichord, cello, and bassoon act as a backdrop for the solo recorder (flute), oboe, and violin.

▢   *Concerto No. 1 in F major*, RV 98 by Vivaldi. (I. Allegro)

The orchestra during the Baroque era was not standardized. Today, a composer can count on writing for a standard group of instruments that are organized in a certain way on the stage. This was not the case in the Baroque era. Often, depending on what the servants or musicians played, the composer would have to revise or rewrite a piece of music from court to court, or church to church.

Usually, however, the orchestra had a string ensemble that consisted of first and second violins, one or two violas and celli, and maybe even a string bass. Depending on the orchestra and the musicians, the composer might even have a few woodwind or brass players to write for. For really festive occasions, the timpani (kettle-drums) might be brought out and used to perform a fanfare with the trumpet players.

Vivaldi helped to standardize the three movement, symmetrical form of the concerto. The first movement is Allegro (fast) in tempo. The second movement is an Andante or Adagio (slow). The third movement balances the form by returning to an Allegro (fast) tempo. He also wrote brilliant solo parts for the violin that he would play in concert. Vivaldi is also known for writing memorable melodies and using dramatic and exciting rhythms.

The Four Seasons, (*Le Quattro Stagioni*), Op. 8, is Vivaldi's most famous work. It was enormously successful in his time and is again popular in the 20th century. It is a set of four concerti that he composed in 1725. They are based on four Italian sonnets that Vivaldi probably wrote himself. The entire work is full of fresh melodies, zesty rhythms, inventive instrumental color and sound, and has a great clarity of form.

The compositional style of *The Four Seasons* was unlike anything that had been heard before. You will hear chirping birds, chattering teeth, the gentle murmur of a spring breeze, and feel the oppressive heat of summer in Venice. The second movement of "Spring" (La Primavera) for example, features three different musical descriptions—a shepherd (the solo violin), the barking of a dog (viola), and the rustling of the leaves (the string orchestra). Other examples include a storm in the last movement of "Summer" (L'Estate) and drunken peasant workers in the second movement of "Autumn" (L'Autumno).

Vivaldi was one of the most prolific and likable of the Baroque composers. He was also responsible for some of the most important musical contributions to the following generation of composers. *The Four Seasons* shows off Vivaldi's personality in a very humorous, whimsical, and engaging style.

All the seasons are constructed in the three movement patterns of Allegro, Andante, Allegro. Here is how the program for the "Spring" season appeared in a printed concert program from 1725.

La Primavera
   composed in 1725

I.   Allegro
II.   Andante
III. Allegro

☐   Excerpts from *La Primavera* by Vivaldi.

Vivaldi was especially influential on the German composers who were to produce the Classical concerto. After 1730 or so, the Italian public seemed to tire of Vivaldi. The church fathers chastised him for ignoring his priestly duties and for having an affair with a well-known Venetian soprano. In 1738, after working for La Pietà for thirty-five years, the directors fired him. Two years later Vivaldi traveled to Vienna looking for employment from Emperor Charles VI. Charles, however, had recently died. After several terrible months in Vienna, Vivaldi died in July of 1741. He was buried in a pauper's grave.

J.S. Bach

Bach adopted the Italian design of Vivaldi. His *Brandenburg Concerti* are considered the supreme achievement of the Baroque concerto. They are similar to Vivaldi's in design, but grander in scale and have a deeper range of emotion and expression. The six *Brandenburg Concerti* were dedicated to Margrave Christian Ludwig of the Brandenburg Court. He was the youngest son of the "Great Elector" Frederick William who employed a small orchestra at the court in Berlin. These courtly entertainment pieces of the highest order were assembled by Bach from the various orchestral works he had composed during 1718-20.

The *Concerto No. 3*, BWV 1048 in G major, probably originated in the ensemble music at the court of Cöthen. The musical texture features three groups of strings: three violins, three violas, and three celli that are independent of the continuo (harpsichord) part. The absence of a soloist, or solo group, sets this work apart from the typical concerto grosso tradition. The division of the strings into three groups of three instruments gave Bach a rich contrapuntal texture to use two ways: within each string section, and between the three string groups. The first and third movements, both at an Allegro tempo, use a rondo form and are very much indebted to the style and formal design of Vivaldi.

For the middle movement, Bach only wrote out two chords. Music historians believe that Bach probably improvised at the harpsichord as the strings held out the two chords. The adagio, as brief as it is, adds a moment of repose and reflection.

Brandenburg Concerto No. 3, BWV 1048 in G major
  composed c.1720

I.   Allegro
II. Adagio
III. Allegro

☐   *Brandenburg Concerto No. 3* by Bach. (III. Allegro)

W.A. Mozart and the Classical Concerto

In the Classical era, polyphony gave way to a homophonic idiom, the fugue to the sonata-allegro form, and the sober church spirit to the gallantries of the aristocratic salon. Stylistically the change was neither sudden nor complete, but it was unmistakable. Sonata-allegro form became the standard for the first movement. Within sonata-allegro form the orchestra generally plays the first theme by itself, without the soloist. Then the solo instrument enters either with the principal subject or with a brilliant introductory passage, followed by the principal theme. A repetition, with considerable modification, of the first tutti usually follows, now divided (alternating) between the principal instrument and the orchestra. The second movement is in an andante or adagio tempo, and is sometimes in a theme and variations form. The third movement (finale) is usually in a rondo or sonata-allegro form as well.

The cadenza is the part of the concerto where the orchestra stops playing and the performer (as a virtuoso) displays their technical brilliance. With such composer-performers as Mozart and Beethoven, the cadenza reached its height as a medium for spontaneous improvisation. Cadenzas which Mozart wrote out were intended for his friends and pupils. There are no written cadenzas for the majority of his mature piano concerti.

The most important Classical era concerti are those by Mozart and Beethoven. Mozart's first attempts were adaptations of other works, with his earliest independent concerto being the *Concerto for Bassoon*, K. 191.

In 1775 Mozart composed five concerti for violin that were influenced by the pre-Classical violin concerto and the Austrian serenade. He also wrote wind instrument concerti for either various music patrons or for outstanding performers. His concerti reveal a composer whose interest was in beauty and melody, and not technical display. This will differ from Beethoven. Beethoven's early concerti were very conservative and lyrical, while his later works imposed great technical demands on the performer.

In his brief thirty-five years, Mozart wrote 23 piano concerti that can be organized into four groups: Salzburg, early Vienna, the 1784 and the post-1785 group. This organization is based on where and when he was living at the time they were composed.

In 1782 Mozart made his final break with the Archbishop of Salzburg. The unbroken series of piano concerti that Mozart composed in Vienna between 1782 and 1786 suggests that this was one of the essential means by which he sought to win the favor of the Viennese public. In the majority of these works, Mozart is content to tread a middle ground—between his own instinctive ideas and the expectations of his audience. The *Piano Concerto No. 23*, K. 488 in A major (March 1786), is a careful balance of both of these. It represents a return to a more natural style and contains a truly astonishing wealth of poetic ideas and imagination. Mozart wrote this A major concerto and two others (E-flat major, C minor) while he was working on his opera *The Marriage of Figaro* (1785-86). These three concerti are among his greatest works, although they were written within a few weeks of each other and at the same time he was composing the opera.

For Mozart, the key of A major was associated with tranquil beauty. He also associated it with the sound of the clarinet—an instrument he preferred to the nasal sounding oboe. The *Clarinet Quintet* and the *Clarinet Concerto*, for example, are both in the key of A major. In the *Piano Concerto No. 23*, K. 488 in A major, Mozart omits the usual oboes from the orchestra in favor of clarinets. These were instruments that he had rarely used in his piano concerti.

The first movement is in sonata-allegro form. The orchestra plays both the first and second themes. These two themes return in the soloist's exposition in an ornamented version. The strings present a third theme which becomes the basis of the development section. Mozart wrote a brief cadenza directly into the score. The lyrical quality of this allegro movement and its unusual coloring are due in part to Mozart's replacing of the oboes with clarinets in the orchestra.

The adagio movement is deeply introspective and profoundly sad. The finale is an explosion of light to dispel this gloom. In a series of rondo forms, the finale has the character and energy of music from a comic opera. The sudden and unexpected contrasts contribute to an overall mood of lightheartedness.

Piano Concerto No. 23, in A Major, K. 488.
  composed in 1786

I.   Allegro
II. Adagio
III. Allegro assai

Piano Concerto No. 23 by Mozart. (I. Allegro)

Piotr (Peter) Ilich Tchaikovsky

The Romantic concerto placed an emphasis on virtuosic displays. Romantic concerto composers followed tradition only as far as the tradition suited their immediate needs. This is certainly the case with the Russian cosmopolitan composer, Tchaikovsky.

The *Piano Concerto No. 1* by Tchaikovsky is the most popular of his three piano concerti. It was composed in 1874, orchestrated in 1875, and premiered by the Boston Symphony Orchestra in October of 1875. Although it has a typical three movement design, it is an unusual work that caused Tchaikovsky much pain and anguish in its early stages of composition.

In December of 1874, Tchaikovsky played the solo piano part for his friend Nicolai Rubinstein—a prominent Russian pianist and conductor. After hearing the entire work, Rubinstein went on to tear the piece apart saying it was "worthless and unplayable . . . with passages so fragmented, so clumsy, so badly written, they were beyond rescue . . . " Rubinstein would no doubt be very surprised to find out that it was destined to become one of the most popular piano concerti in the world.

Part of the criticism was due to the unusual form of the first movement. After the dramatic horn passage at the beginning of the concerto, the introductory section that follows is based on huge chords in the piano over a beautiful lyric melody in the strings. This truly "romantic" and memorable melody never returns after the introduction. Although the rest of the movement is full of other lyric and beautiful themes, nothing is quite as moving as this introductory section.

The second movement, a combination of a slow movement and a scherzo, and the finale are very short compared to the first movement. Both of these movements are based on alternating themes, and not on extensive musical development. The combined time of the second and third movements is less than that of the first movement all by itself.

Piano Concerto No. 1 in B-flat minor, Op. 23
    composed in 1874

I.   Allegro non troppo, Allegro con spirito
II.   Andante semplice, Prestissimo, Andante semplice
III. Allegro con fuoco

☐   *Piano Concerto No. 1* by Tchaikovsky. (I. Allegro non troppo, Allegro con spirito)

The Concerto in the 20th Century

No new type of concerto has developed in the 20th century. Many composers have been interested, however, in reviving the procedures of concerto composition from prior eras. Since World War II, the basis for concerto composition has been a dramatic solo-ensemble relationship. Each side is a musical character involved in anything from a calm discussion to a violent argument, or even with independent development. The term concerto has lost any formal implication and now refers to any solo-ensemble composition. Belá Bartók's *Concerto for Orchestra*, for example, is a concerto for more than one hundred soloists.

Joaquín Rodrigo

Born in Spain in 1901, Rodrigo has been blind since the age of three. He studied music with Francisco Antich in Valencia before becoming a pupil of Paul Dukas (composer of the *Sorcerers Apprentice*) in Paris.

As a composer, Rodrigo is similar in style to an Impressionist. Musically, he is content to create attractive melodies and rhythms that evoke the generally bright and sunny atmosphere of Spain. In 1946 Rodrigo was appointed to the Manuel da Falla chair at the University of Madrid as both a teacher and a composer. His most famous composition is the *Concierto de Aranjuez*. This work is infused with an underlying nostalgia for an older and more chivalrous Spain, perhaps reminiscent of Cervantes' *Don Quixote*.

The concerto takes its inspiration from the royal town and gardens of Aranjuez as they looked during the 17th and 18th centuries. Aranjuez was the springtime royal residence built around the year 1800 on the plateau of New Castile, to which the Spanish kings retired from the summer heat. The composer and his wife had visited them during their honeymoon.

The famous middle movement of the concerto is a finely crafted balance between the subtle sound of the solo guitar and the rich colors of the chamber orchestra. After its initial sorrowful introduction, the movement is like a grand serenade. It eventually fades away into a magnificent solo guitar cadenza over a soft tapestry of orchestral colors. This is the most emotional movement of the three. It was inspired by the death of his first child and the near death of his wife after childbirth. The composer has added many personal images (impressions) to this movement. For example, the use of harmonics at the end of the movement represents the soul of their deceased child ascending into heaven.

Concierto de Aranjuez, for guitar and orchestra
   premiered in 1940

I.   Allegro con spirito
II.   Adagio
III.   Allegro gentile

☐   *Concierto de Aranjuez* by Rodrigo. (I. Allegro con spirito, II. Adagio)

Dimitri Shostakovich

Born in September of 1906, Shostakovich was under scrutiny from Soviet commissars for most of his career. Shostakovich and his music were frequently 'out of favor' after World War II. However, after the death of Josef Stalin in 1953, his music began to return to favor in Russia.

The *Concerto No. 2 in F major*, Op. 102, was written in 1957 for Shostakovich's son Maxim. Born in 1938, Maxim was an advanced student at the Moscow Conservatory when he premiered this concerto on his nineteenth birthday. The piano writing in the first allegro suggests both the types of pieces that professional pianists have to master (études, fantasies, toccatas) and the devices they must master (playing in octaves, scales, arpeggios, chromatic scales). The second theme (sonata-allegro form) resembles the traditional British song "What Shall We Do with a Drunken Sailor" – purely a coincidence. The middle movement is scored almost exclusively for piano and strings and contains one of the composer's most romantic and moving themes. The final allegro, with its brilliant and tricky 7/8 time passages, is based on two themes. The first theme seems to get stuck on a single note while the second is a dance-like 7/8 time passage that leads immediately into a solo passage from the Charles Hanon five-finger exercises that all pianists endlessly practice and simultaneously dread. This is obviously a joke shared by both father (composer) and son (performer) as the movement at this point begins to sounds like a piano exercise gone wild!

Piano Concerto No. 2 in F Major, Op. 102.
   composed in 1957

I.   Allegro
II. Andante
III. Allegro

☐   *Piano Concerto No. 2* by Shostakovich. (I. Allegro)

John Adams

The American composer John Adams, who received a Grammy Award (1988) and a Pulitzer Prize in Music (2003), first learned how to play the clarinet as a young boy. His father, who had played clarinet in swing bands in New England, was his "first and most important teacher." Although Adams did not write for the instrument until he was nearly fifty years old, the piece *Gnarly Buttons* was composed after he re-discovered his deceased father's clarinets many years later in his California home.

The piece is scored for solo clarinet, English horn, bassoon, trombone, banjo (also mandolin and guitar), piano, two synthesizers, and five strings (2 violins, viola, cello, bass). This unusual combination of instruments underlines the folk and vernacular roots of this piece. According to Adams, "Gnarly - means knotty, twisted or covered with gnarls... In American school kid parlance it takes on additional connotations of something to be admired: awesome, neat, fresh, etc. The 'buttons' are probably lingering in my mind from Gertrude Stein's *Tender Buttons*, but my evoking them here also acknowledges our lives at the end of the 20th century as being largely given over to pressing buttons of one sort or another."

Each of the three movements has a programmatic title with the first movement, *The Perilous Shore*, coming from a 19th century Protestant hymn. The second movement, *Hoedown*, is usually associated with horses, but according to Adams, "this version of the traditional Western hoedown addresses the fault lines of international commerce from a distinctly American perspective." *Put Your Loving Arms Around Me* is "a simple song, quiet and tender up front, gnarled and crabbed at the end."

Gnarly Buttons, for solo clarinet and ensemble
   premiered in 1996

I.   The Perilous Shore
II. Hoedown (Mad Cow)
III. Put Your Loving Arms Around Me

☐   *Gnarly Buttons* by Adams. (II. Hoedown)

"Where Mozart is, Haydn cannot appear."

F.J. Haydn, when invited to the Coronation of Emperor Leopold II

"Keep your eyes on that young man. Someday he will give the world something to talk about."

Mozart, after hearing Beethoven play piano for him

Mozart said, "Papa, you have no education for the great world and you speak too few languages." To which Haydn replied, "Oh, my language is understood all over the world."

Conversation prior to Haydn's departure to London in 1790

"Here is Beethoven, the working-man in his shirt sleeves, with his great Herculean breast bared to the elements." Wagner then straightened himself up and, giving a swing of his baton, brought it down with an abrupt "Ta-ta-ta-tum!" as his orchestra began Beethoven's <u>Symphony No. 5</u> in C minor.

A description of Richard Wagner conducting Beethoven's Fifth Symphony

The Symphony

A symphony is a large-scale orchestral work of serious aim, normally in four sections called movements, with at least one of the movements in sonata-allegro form. The effect on the audience, from a philosophical viewpoint, is to make the listener forget their own concerns and live for the time being on a plane of musical experience.

Today, it is a term that means an extended work for orchestra in multiple movements, or in one movement with multiple sections. While usually abstract in content, many examples have somewhat explicit programs. It became the major vehicle of orchestral music in the late 18th century. From Beethoven on, it was regarded as the highest form of orchestral music. The adjective "symphonic" implies extensive and thorough development.

The term symphony comes from the two Greek words syn (together) and phone (sounding). It was used by Giovanni Gabrieli (Chapter 4) and others for concerted motets. In the 17th century, the terms sinfonia and symphony were used to denote introductory movements for operas, cantatas, and oratorios. They were also used to designate an instrumental introduction to an aria or an ensemble piece. The common factor between the two was that they were usually part of a larger framework, such as an opera or church service. Instrumental music written for its own sake arises from the practice of playing music that was originally written for voices.

The term "symphony" was first applied to large-scale works by the Mannheim composers in the mid-18th century. The Mannheim school flourished under the Elector Karl Theodor (1724-99). The definition was borrowed from the Italians, including Sammartini of Milan (1701-75), who wrote seventy-seven symphonies. At this time, symphonies were still in three movements (fast, slow, fast). One of the major symphony composers during this era was Johann Stamitz. His musical innovations included the use of subtle dynamics for effect (crescendo and decrescendo), the use of dynamic markings within the phrase, a precision-like use of tutti strings, and contrasting themes (stylistically, tonally, dynamically) within a single movement.

Most symphonies today have a conductor. Depending upon the size of the ensemble, one may not be necessary though. Certainly during the time of Bach, and even Haydn and Mozart, the orchestra was generally not large enough to warrant one. In the 17th century, the first chair violinist (concert master) often stood by his seat and indicated the tempo with his bow while the composer sat at a keyboard. If the composer was not at the keyboard, he was the first chair violinist and may have directed the orchestra from his chair. The modern-day conductor came into existence at the end of the Classical era. As the orchestra continued to grow during the Romantic era, the need for a conductor became a necessity.

The job of the conductor is to coordinate the ensemble's performance, to interpret the music of the composer, and to lead the orchestra in that musical interpretation. Another important position in the orchestra is that of the concert master. The first violinist holds this position and is second in importance to the conductor. This is why the concert master makes a separate entrance from the rest of the orchestra. The duties of this person include assisting the conductor, establishing the bowings for the string section, and making decisions regarding personnel, touring, etc. The concert master also has the responsibility of tuning the orchestra and in playing the solo passages in the music.

The Classical Symphony

Classicism is perhaps best understood by studying the evolution and development of the symphony. The sheer volume of symphonic production (more than 12,000) makes it the basic standard of achievement and comparison. During the Classical era there was an uninterrupted continuity in the development of the symphony. At first, the symphony had only the skeletal necessities of instrumentation and tempo contrast. Through gradual experimentation, it became a balanced array of procedures that ultimately defined the Classical style. In all of its phases, the form dominated the musical life of the 18th century.

There were no public concert halls in Europe at this time. In Mozart's time the public concerts took place in theaters, palace salons, and in the large rooms of taverns or other commercial buildings. The nobility and court held private concerts for which symphonies were required.

From studying the orchestras of the 18th century we can see that there was no real Baroque or Classical orchestra. At this time there were no national or international orchestral standards. There were local, regional, and national traditions and preferences, some of which were widespread and long-lived. There were also constant changes and experimentation. The size of an orchestra was often related to changes in the economy. In the late 1780's when Austria was involved in war, the orchestras dramatically declined in size. The size of the orchestra was also related to the size of the theater or hall, the generosity of patrons, local customs and preferences, political changes, and even political revolutions.

F.J. Haydn

The composers Franz Joseph Haydn and Wolfgang Amadeus Mozart represent the highest achievements of Classical style. While Mozart assimilated the procedures of many composers, Haydn intensified his own compositional processes. In many ways, Haydn created the model of the symphony. In his hands it became a four-movement composition for strings, woodwinds, brass, and percussion. The typical pattern is Allegro, Andante, Minuet and Trio, and Allegro. In short, the modern day symphony orchestra and the symphony as a form both have their roots in the works of Haydn.

As a composer, Haydn is difficult to categorize. His output does not fall neatly into various "periods" since his works often reflect the circumstances of their composition. He was, after all, a subject of the patronage system.

Appointed to the court at Esterházy (Hungary) in 1761, he began a steady output of symphonies. In his music he began an internal expansion. He also enlarged his thematic ideas as a new manner of development and experimented with remote key modulations. Haydn extracted many interesting sounds from a group that was as small as twenty musicians. Here is an example of one of his earlier symphonies, the *Symphony No. 29 in E major*, composed in 1765.

The first movement opens with a flowing melody. The emphasis moves easily from strings to winds and back, and creates a mood of contentment that remains essentially undisturbed. The second movement is scored for strings alone—typical of this period. The melody is shared between first and second violins.

Contrasts in dynamics help underline the playful phrasing patterns in the third movement. The trio section of this movement uses a minimal amount of material. The symphony finale features pulsating bass lines and sequential patterns in the violin passages.

Symphony No. 29 in E major
   composed in 1765

I.   Allegro di molto
II.   Andante
III. Menuet and Trio
IV.   Presto

Symphony No. 29 by Haydn. (Complete)

From Haydn's *Symphony No. 31* (1765) onwards, the four-movement scheme, with the minuet standing third, became the traditional outline of the symphony. In July of 1776 he wrote an autobiographical sketch. Credited with being the "Father of the symphony," he had already composed more than sixty symphonies by this time, and many were enjoying success throughout Europe. Yet Haydn, in his autobiography, never even mentions his symphonies—only some of his sacred and secular vocal music. Symphonies were music for use and lacked the prestige of either vocal or instrumental music intended for court or aristocratic gatherings.

Haydn's career then took a dramatic turn in 1790. His patron, Prince Nicholas Esterházy, died at the age of seventy-six. After his death, Haydn left the court and traveled to Vienna where, after visiting Mozart, he left for England and arrived in early 1791. During the years 1791-95, Haydn wrote his last symphonies (No. 93 to 104). These "London Symphonies" were written in two groups of six for J.P. Solomon's concerts in London. This was Haydn's first contact with a large orchestra. Although hand picked, his Esterházy orchestra only had between sixteen and twenty-two players.

In May of 1795 his final symphony, No. 104, was introduced at a concert that was perhaps his greatest triumph. Haydn subtitled it the "London" symphony in honor of the city. Not only did the audience love the music on the program, but the reviews were ecstatic. Two months later he returned to Vienna. Soon after he returned, Haydn conducted his *Symphony No. 104* in Vienna. His music never received the kind of popular acclaim in his homeland that it had in London.

The "London Symphonies" use development techniques in the exposition and recapitulation sections that show the revolutionary potentials of the sonata-allegro form. This strongly influenced Beethoven and, to a lesser degree, Mozart. With an emphasis on structure rather than on melody, motivic development in the music became more important than the melody itself.

The finale of the *Symphony No. 104* is based on an English folk tune. This melody is introduced by the violins with a simple accompaniment from the horns and celli. It is similar to a London street song known as "Hot Cross Buns." Here you can see how the development of the melody is more important than the actual melody itself. This symphony premiered in London on 4 May 1795. Haydn himself conducted the premier of the "London" symphony.

Symphony No. 104 in D Major, "London"
    composed in 1795

I.   Adagio, Allegro
II. Andante
III. Menuetto
IV. Spiritoso

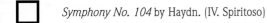 *Symphony No. 104* by Haydn. (IV. Spiritoso)

Mozart and the Symphony

Mozart began writing symphonies at the age of eight or nine, and his compositional activity spans twenty-five years. His symphonic writing was sporadic since he was not required to compose as many for a permanent appointment as Haydn was. Mozart wrote for specific circumstances, namely upon being commissioned. His style is a blend of Italian lyricism and graceful rhythmic movement. This is coupled with an Austro-Germanic harmonic depth, textural interest, subtly of phrasing, and orchestral virtuosity.

Like those of his contemporaries, his early symphonies were written as curtain-raisers or fanfares to herald the beginning of plays, operas, cantatas, oratorios, and public and private concerts. In these settings, they were sometimes used as introductions and finales. Symphonies were also heard in churches punctuating the High Mass.

In Salzburg and Vienna they even appeared as outdoor serenades on many of the warm Austrian summer evenings. These early symphonies were, with few exceptions, intended to be witty, charming, brilliant, and even touching. They were not meant to be works of great musical significance. The vocal and instrumental solos they introduced were the main attractions at concerts. At the theaters, the main attractions were the plays, operas, or oratorios. In church, attention was focused on the liturgy and the accompanying vocal music. At dinner parties or outdoor occasions the interests were social, at occasions of state they were political and ceremonial.

Mozart's most important symphonies were those written between 1782-88. These break new ground in emotional content, key center inventiveness, and formal originality. Included in this group are the "Haffner" (D major) K.385, "Linz" (C major) K.425, "Prague" (D major) K.504, the G minor K. 550, and the "Jupiter" (C major) K. 551 symphonies.

The influence of Haydn and Mozart on each other seems to have extended little beyond matters of technique. Their differences in personality, however, stand out with great clarity. Life was harder for Mozart, and at times his difficulties gave an edge to his music. While Haydn's music shows more meaning after he went through his "Storm and Stress" period, his music remained essentially for the enjoyment for his audience. Some of the compositional differences in the Mozart symphonies, as compared to those of Haydn, include:

1. More wind assignments and more idiomatic writing.
2. Counterpoint heard for textural color.
3. A rich chord vocabulary with ingenious modulations.
4. The use of color, often in development sections, with little thematic change.

Symphony No. 40 in G minor

The last three symphonies of Mozart were composed within the amazingly short period of two months. 1788 was a productive year for the composer, but even so the composition of three symphonies of major proportions during the summer months was extraordinary.

A certain mystery surrounds the creation of this music. It was unusual for Mozart to write orchestral pieces during the summer, since performances were not likely to be scheduled outside the regular concert season. Furthermore, the composer received no commission and no payment for these works, and at least two of them were never even performed during his lifetime. Why, then, did he write them?

A likely explanation is that Mozart wrote the symphonies for concerts projected for the following winter that never materialized. His practicality is shown by the fact that, once a performance opportunity finally presented itself three years later, he revised the Symphony No. 40 in G minor by adding clarinet parts and changing the oboe parts, and permitted an orchestra four times the intended size to play it.

Nothing is known of the audience reaction to the first performance of the G minor Symphony at the 1791 premiere, when Antonio Salieri conducted an orchestra of 180 musicians. Indeed, it is not even definitely confirmed that this performance took place.

Mozart, though trying to write music specifically for audiences, was inexorably drawn in his late works toward complexities and deep emotions that often puzzled his listeners. The soft opening, for example, is exceedingly rare for a classical symphony without a slow introduction. The pervasive insistence in the first movement on short motivic figures rather than full-blown melodies contributes to the work's intensity, a feature that would surely have made for difficult listening in the late 18th century.

What was really unprecedented about this piece was its many levels of subtlety. The intense mood of the work is created by an almost excessive amount of time spent in the minor key, and by certain powerfully abrupt changes of tonal area. Three of the four movements are in G minor, and even within the first movement the music hovers around G minor more than expected. The lyrical second theme (winds and strings alternating), cast at first in B-flat major, comes back in the recapitulation not in the expected G major but, with surprising poignancy, in G minor.

Symphony No. 40 in G minor, K. 550
   completed in 1788

I.   Molto allegro
II. Andante
III. Menuetto
IV. Allegro assai

☐   *Symphony No. 40* by Mozart. (I. Molto allegro)

Early 19th Century Symphony

The symphony, as a genre, is full of strong attachments and expectations. While designed for the concert hall, during the 19th century it retained much of the regal structure of court times. The addition of the minuet always reminded audiences of its royal ancestry and helped to retain an air of festivity in the genre.

Performed as part of miscellaneous concerts with many other works, the 19th century symphony became the most important part of the program. As the composer's status changed from that of a hired servant to one of a creative artist, the symphony rose in importance. Beethoven was the first truly independent composer. He was initially ignored in favor of those continuing in the Haydn-Mozart symphonic tradition. In the long run, however, Beethoven has overshadowed all other symphonic composers.

Music historians tend to classify Beethoven as the culmination of the Classical era. He retained the Classical ideal of the symphony based on the Haydn-model, and greatly expanded the sonata-allegro form. Virtually all the sections and movements of the symphony were expanded by him. His third and ninth symphonies have experimental structures while the first, second, fourth, and seventh symphonies use a Haydn-esque slow introduction.

Beethoven began the use of a theme as a source for inventive thematic development. This takes place in all sections of the composition, including the coda section. He also adds other instruments into the orchestra, including the piccolo, trombone, and contrabassoon. With the addition of these instruments he also began to give many instruments a new independence—especially the separation of the cello and bass line.

Beethoven and His Time

With the music of Beethoven, the listener is seized by the music's intense emotional struggle, and is forced to listen to its conflict and resolution. Most listeners can relate to the element of "struggle" in this music on either a symbolic, personal, or technical level. Beethoven confronted the personal, social, and ethical problems of his time, and searched for an answer in his music. He took the forms that had been developed for polite entertainment and stretched them to contain and externalize his feelings. In doing so, Beethoven began to use music for "self-expression" and to emotionally involve his audiences.

The *Symphony No. 3*, "Eroica," is a departure from the Haydn symphony style. At first dedicated to Napoleon, and then later "to the memory of a hero," Beethoven showed that his music celebrated the human spirit rather than the evils of the monarchy. In doing this, he composed the second movement in the style of a funeral march to indicate the end of the monarchy. The third movement is no longer a minuet, but a scherzo (joke). The joke is that it is too fast to dance to and it is in a duple meter, not triple. The extended tonic confirmation at the end of the final movement represents the triumph of the common man over the aristocracy.

Symphony No. 3 in E-flat major, Op. 55, "Eroica"
  completed in 1803

I.   Allegro con brio
II.   Marcia funebre
III. Allegro vivace
IV.   Allegro molto, Andante, Presto

☐   *Symphony No. 3* by Beethoven. (II. Macria funebre)

Certainly Beethoven's *Symphony No. 5*, Op. 67 from 1808, is one of the masterpieces of the symphonic literature. The first movement has no introduction. The opening motive is frequently described as "fate knocking at the door." It also represents the composer's confrontation and struggle with his impending deafness. This intense and concentrated first movement went through twenty-six versions before Beethoven was satisfied that it "said" what it was supposed to say. For this symphony, Beethoven added several new instruments, including a piccolo, a double bassoon, and three trombones. He also connected the last two movements to heighten the musical drama. Within the entire symphony there is a unity of form as the main theme from the first movement is quoted in each of the following three movements.

With his *Symphony No. 5*, Beethoven opened the door to the Romantic era and to the possibility of communicating emotions directly from composer to audience. It was instrumental music's vagueness of meaning that made it the ideal art form for Romantic artists to express concepts and feelings that they believed were beyond the ability of words to express.

Symphony No. 5 in C minor, Op. 67
  completed in 1808

I.   Allegro con brio
II.   Andante con moto
III. Allegro con moto
IV.   Allegro

☐   *Symphony No. 5* by Beethoven. (I. Allegro con brio)

8 Oh friends, not these sounds . . .

"By the time I had made his acquaintance, Beethoven had ceased to play the piano either in public or at private gatherings, and my only opportunity of hearing him was when I once chanced to call at his house during the rehearsal of a new trio . . . It was not a treat; for one thing the piano was badly out of tune . . . At forte passages the poor deaf fellow banged the keys so vigorously that the strings twanged, while in the piano passages he played so softly that whole groups of notes went unheard."

Louis Spohr, 1813

As the orchestra grew visibly restless, Brahms stepped up to the director's stand. He said, "Gentlemen, I am aware that I am not Beethoven – but I am Johannes Brahms."

Description of an orchestra rehearsal in Vienna

"I am three times homeless. As a native of Bohemia in Austria, as an Austrian among Germans, and as a Jew throughout the world."

Gustav Mahler, Post-Romantic composer

Beethoven and the Romantic Symphony

His *Symphony No. 9* (1817-23, performed 1824) is a solitary masterpiece that more closely resembles the work of the innovative Romantic composers. The first three movements are on a comparably grand scale. The second movement, a misplaced scherzo, demonstrates Beethoven's ability to organize an entire movement in sonata-allegro form around a single rhythmic idea. The most radical section of the work is the fourth movement, where a full chorus and four vocal soloists are finally heard. The message of the text is one of the brotherhood of man through joy, and the love of an eternal heavenly father.

In this symphony, the orchestra in expanded as Beethoven places even greater technical demands on the orchestra, soloists, and chorus. The fourth movement clearly shows that Beethoven was an emotional volcano and a deep musical thinker. Where Haydn and Mozart addressed a small company of aristocrats and people of wealth, Beethoven addressed mankind. The opening line of the bass soloist sets the mood and dispels the darkness and gloom of the music just before his entrance. The line, written by Beethoven himself to introduce Schiller's *Ode to Joy* poem, is "O friends, not these sounds! Let us sing more cheerful songs, more full of joy!"

Symphony No. 9 in D minor, Op. 125, "Choral"
   completed in 1824

I.   Allegro ma non troppo
II.   Molto vivace
III. Adagio molto e cantabile
IV.   Presto, et. al.

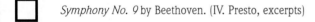 *Symphony No. 9* by Beethoven. (IV. Presto, excerpts)

The Symphony after Beethoven

Although the symphony continued to be a major form during the Romantic era, many composers tended to infuse the form with external meanings and references. As sonata-allegro form continued to expand, the emotions in the music became less restrained. The musical descriptions also became more specific as the musical structures were adapted to fit the composers non-musical references.

Johannes Brahms, who only wrote four symphonies, is considered the most important symphonic composer of the second half of the 19th century. Following in the footsteps of Beethoven, his musical characteristics include the frequent use of cross rhythms, sweeping melodies, and a highly refined emotional style.

Other composers in this traditional Romantic style include Schubert, Mendelssohn, Schumann, and Tchaikovsky. Mozart's *Symphony No. 39* and *Symphony No. 40*, which were almost continuously lyrical rather than architecturally strong, appealed to many Romantic composers and became their models. If the symphony was to follow Beethoven's lead, then you could conclude that further excursions in the form were futile.

Franz Schubert's symphonies were a failure in his own time since they were not his most natural form of musical expression (Chapter 10). Although he wrote nine symphonies, two are considered masterpieces—the "Great" C major *Symphony No. 9* and the "Unfinished" *Symphony No. 8*.

Felix Mendelssohn wrote twelve symphonies in his youth and five mature works. His "Reformation" (1830) and "Lobgesang" (1840) symphonies have religious associations. The "Italian" (1833) and "Scotch" (1842) symphonies are both somewhat programmatic. It is the two overtures, A *Midsummer Night's Dream* and *Hebrides*, that are his strongest works and point the way to the symphonic or tone poem.

Robert Schumann wrote four symphonies beginning in his early thirties. They follow the same lyrical tradition as Mendelssohn. Musically, they are not as innovative as his piano music. He used sonata-allegro form more freely than other composers, often placing the themes in an "incorrect" order or key.

The symphonies of Schubert, Mendelssohn, and Schumann are an escape into the world of pleasant feelings. They are not a symbolic grappling with the difficulties of life, which was the heritage of Beethoven. Romantic music rarely dealt realistically with the lives of the artists or the public. Many of their instrumental melodies defied the musical development established by Haydn and Beethoven. While these composers relied on the beauty of the melody itself, only Brahms was able to skillfully develop the music in the tradition of the Classical masters.

Johannes Brahms

Brahms was much closer to Beethoven and Bach in that he used symphonic methods from another era to channel lyrical and romantic impulses into his own musical compositions. His lyrical melodies are richly harmonized in the tradition of Schubert, Mendelssohn, and Schumann. The musical characteristics of his four symphonies include:

1. The use of the Classical four movement structure.
2. A strict use of sonata-allegro form in the first movement.
3. The rejection of programs or titles.
4. The use of an orchestra of modest size.
5. The use of older compositional devices including the fugue, canon, and passacaglia.

His *Symphony No. 1* (1876) was written after he spent time composing in other mediums like the serenades, *Piano Concerto No. 1* (1859), the *German Requiem* (1868) and the *St. Anthony Variations* (1873). After its premier, it was hailed as the successor to Beethoven's *Symphony No. 9*. As a "renovator" of tradition, Brahms rejected the various modes of progress (programs, extra-musical references). His success as a composer was not due to his adaptation of Beethoven's techniques, but rather in the way he used his own lyrical gifts.

One of his major innovations was the substitution of an "Allegretto e grazioso" for Beethoven's "Scherzo." This movement is one of sheer listening enjoyment and shows a mastery of the symphonic form in the use of extension, variation, and instrumentation. In other words, Brahms demonstrates his consummate skill in the manipulation of his melodies.

Symphony No. 1 in C minor, Op. 68
    completed in 1876

I.   Un poco sostenuto, Allegro
II.   Andante sostenuto
III. Allegretto e grazioso
IV.   Adagio, Allegro non troppo ma con brio

Symphony No. 1 by Brahms. (I. Un poco sostenuto, Allegro)

Nationalism

The domination of the symphonic scene by the German composers made it difficult for composers from other countries to find a voice. In Russia, Modest Mussorgsky was the most radical of the nationalists, also known as the "Russian Five." These five composers bonded together to write music in a distinctly Russian style. They included Borodin, Cui, Balakirev, Rimsky-Korsakov, and of course, Mussorgsky. He, however, never wrote a symphony. His musical style was more suited to piano works or opera.

With the tide of revolutions that swept across Europe in the early 1800's, nationalism became a dominate force in the arts. In Czechoslovakia, three great Czech composers sought a musical language unique to their own identity—Smetana, Janácek, and Dvorák. Of the three, Dvorák is viewed as the most original and influential. His *Symphony No. 9*, from the "New World," was written while he was teaching in the U.S. He was closer to the traditionalists in style and was the most gifted in integrating Czech folk songs into symphonic music.

Gustav Mahler and the 20th Century Symphony

The first decade of the 20th century brought an end to the attempt to pour a Romantic symphony into a Classical mold. The trend was then to create symphonic forms directly from the nature of their materials. Between the years 1901-18, the most important symphonic composers were Sibelius, Neilsen, and Gustav Mahler.

Gustav Mahler completed his first four symphonies by the turn of the century. Mahler the symphonist cannot be separated from Mahler the song composer. These four symphonies are related to his early song cycles. Themes from his "Lieder eines fahrenden Gesellen" (Songs of a Wayfarer, 1883-84) appeared in the First Symphony, while the Second, Third, and Fourth symphonies all incorporated melodies from his "Das Knaben Wunderhorn" (The Boy's Magic Horn, 1888-89). Following the example of Beethoven, Mahler also used voices in his Second, Third, Fourth, and Eighth symphonies.

Mahler told Sibelius in 1907 that, "The symphony must be like the world; it must be all embracing." From this idea, the Fifth (1902), Sixth (1904), and Seventh (1905) symphonies of Mahler form a second group. They are purely orchestral and show a new discipline in thematic and formal craftsmanship.

As is typical of these post-Romantic works, his *Symphony No. 5* in C-sharp minor is long, formally complex, vaguely programmatic in nature, and demands huge performing resources. It also uses a new contrapuntal language as the themes are entirely different from each other in both rhythm and melody.

This Fifth Symphony begins with a funeral march as it "marches" from death to life. Ending in triumph, this symphony is an affirmation of the human spirit. Cast in an unusual structure and vast in scope, the symphony became a vehicle that Mahler used to give voice to the complete man. His lifelong preoccupation with suffering, death, and how to transcend them permeates his works. This work suggests that Mahler had in mind the ideas similar to those of the third and fifth symphonies of Beethoven. His *Symphony No. 5* moves from the gloom of the opening "Trauermarsch" (funeral march) to the triumph of the Scherzo and the joy of the Finale. For Mahler, it symbolically addresses the question "Is there a heaven, and am I going there?" The Finale answers with a definitive YES!

Symphony No. 5 in C-sharp minor
   premiered in 1904

I.   Trauermarsch
II.   Stürmisch bewegt (Stormy motion)
III. Scherzo

IV.   Adagietto
V.   Rondo-Finale

☐   *Symphony No. 5* by Mahler. (I. Trauermarsch)

Epilogue

In 1918, the Russian composer Sergei Prokofiev finished his Symphony No. 1, the "Classical" symphony. His intention was to compose a symphony Haydn would have composed if he had been alive in 1918. According to Prokofiev, "Haydn's technique had become especially clear to me after my studies... It seems to me that, had Haydn continued to live into our time, he would have retained his own way of writing and at the same time added something new... I wanted to compose a symphony in a classical style, and as soon as I began to progress in my work, I christened it the Classical Symphony, first because it sounded much more simple and second out of pure mischief..."

The Classical Symphony takes forms, melodies, phrase structures, and rhythms typical of classicism and twists them in humorous yet graceful ways. We can hear a hypothetical original version of the music lurking beneath the surface.

The piece begins with a two-measure introduction to the main theme. Of the first eight measures this theme sounds as if it could almost have been written by Haydn, except for the violins quintuplet figure. But then the theme is repeated a step lower. In a truly classical piece such a repetition would probably take place a step higher. The difference is subtle, but it gives the movement an unmistakably humorous atmosphere.

The third movement's humor lies primarily in its extreme brevity. In addition, its purposefully clumsy phrases and unexpected twists of harmony create a delightful parody of classical minuets. The fact that this gavotte is in duple meter, rather than the standard minuet's triple meter, adds to the humor.

The effervescent finale abounds with subtle harmonic twists, unexpected modulations, and clever turns of phrases. There is something both enduring and endearing behind the Classical Symphony's parody of classicism. This work anticipates the neo-Classical style of the 1920's-40's.

Symphony No. 1 in D major, Opus 25, "Classical"
completed in 1917

I.   Allegro
II.   Larghetto
III. Gavotte
IV.   Molto vivace

☐   *Symphony No. 1* by Prokofiev. (I. Allegro, III. Gaovtte, IV. Molto vivace)

There are many other famous symphonies by various 20th century composers. These works however, have little in common with the Classical symphony other than the name and the multi-movement format.

Movement III. - Mostly Vocal Music

9 Ancient music, distant voices

"In our times, of all men, singers are the most foolish."

Guido d'Arezzo, theorist, teacher, and monk who reformed music notation

"I have held nothing more desirable than that which is sung throughout the year; according to the season, it should be agreeable to the ear by virtue of its vocal beauty."

Giovanni Pierluigi da Palestrina, Renaissance church composer

"They made the words clear in such a way that one could hear even the last syllable of every word."

Vicenzo Giustiniani, on the music from early Baroque operas

"The end of all good music is to affect the soul."

Claudio Monteverdi, first composer of opera

"As poetry is the harmony of the words, so music is that of the notes."

Henry Purcell, English composer of the early Baroque

Classical Antiquity

Music is not a separate art. At the beginning of recorded history, music was already alive. This chapter will examine the ancient music and distant voices from our past.

As the foundations of Western culture and philosophy came from the Greeks, so did the foundation of our musical ideas. Unfortunately for us, music existed in their society only to accompany poetry or verse. Very few examples of music have survived from Greek and Roman times (Classical antiquity). Since we do not have enough information to give us an accurate idea of how their music actually sounded, we can only make educated guesses. What we do have, however, are their writings concerning their theories and aesthetics of music. In these areas, the Greek contribution to Western attitudes is extremely important. The Greeks wrote about the power music had to influence the listener's emotions, behavior, and morals. They called this "ethos." This ethos made music a powerful force for good or for evil.

Plato, the great ancient Greek philosopher, was born c.427 B.C. and died c.347 B.C. He is considered, in the modern sense of the word, the real founder of a philosophy of the arts. Many of his ideas and methods were derived from the teachings of his master, Socrates.

After Socrates' death in 399 B.C., Plato started on a series of extensive journeys during which he studied with Euclid. He soon returned to Athens and began his career as a philosopher. Later, he founded the so-called "Academy." This academy was a type of school for higher studies. Plato's chief philosophical writings are not written in a systematic form, but take the shape of highly poetic and often dramatically vivid dialogues.

One of the most famous dialogues from Plato's mature period is the one entitled *The Republic*. In this work Plato states his ideas about the organization of the ideal state. He writes that in such a state education is paramount, and that art derives its main value as a means of attaining this educational idea. In this connection, Plato regards music as highly important—its lofty purpose is to serve mankind and not for superficial entertainment. Music is to help in building up a harmonious personality and in calming the human passions. If music was used for only pleasure, Plato saw this as a step towards social chaos. Aristotle, whose ideas were often more down to earth than Plato's, believed that music was useful not only in education and ritual, but also for entertainment and relaxation.

The Greek philosopher Pythagoras (6th century B.C.) is credited with the discovery of the mathematical relationships that dictate the basic intervals of music. To him, music was a mathematical example of the Greek notion of the "harmony of the spheres." This was an inaudible harmony founded on the basic musical proportions or relationships. It was also the basis for the relationship between astronomy and music in Greek education. Greek musical theory was to dominate the West well into the Middle Ages. The entire basis of Western education and the educational system was derived from the Greek model.

From the Greek and Roman times only partial musical fragments have survived. Our first piece of music is the "Hymn to the Muse" (c.130 A.D.). The interpretation for this musical fragment is based on symbols found on a piece of papyrus manuscript. Writings and artworks from the period provide information about the instruments in use at the time.

☐   "Hymn to the Muse." (Greek)

The only surviving musical fragment from Imperial Rome is a four-measure musical excerpt. It comes from the Hecyra by the author Terence. The musical fragment is found in verse 861.

☐   *Hecyra* of Terence. (Roman)

The Middle Ages

The origins of many of the major institutions of Western culture lie in ancient Greece. Education is no exception since the roots of the Seven Liberal Arts, which make up the educational curriculum of the Middle Ages (500-1400), can be traced to Hellenistic culture. For the early Greeks, education consisted of music and gymnastics. The thinkers of the Middle Ages had discovered in the Greek heritage a rich musical tradition that can also be traced back to the Babylonian, Sumerian, Egyptian, and Vedic cultures.

With the refinements made in the secular schools of the Roman Empire, the Seven Liberal Arts of Grammar, Rhetoric, Logic, Arithmetic, Geometry, Astronomy, and Music were gradually adopted as the basis for education in the Middle Ages. Music, which was highly regarded in the ancient world, was gradually accepted into Christian thinking as an instrument of spiritual perfection. Once established with Christian principles, education based on the Liberal Arts was maintained throughout the Middle Ages.

There were two main divisions of the Seven Liberal Arts—the Trivium and the Quadrivium. The literary subjects of grammar, rhetoric, and logic were studied early in a person's education and were considered part of the Trivium. The scientific subjects of arithmetic, geometry, astronomy, and music made up the Quadrivium. Completion of studies in these two areas was considered necessary before one could engage in the study of theology, law, or medicine. That music should be grouped with the scientific studies is rather unusual to the teachers of today. To the Medieval mind, however, it made perfect sense since the other members of the Quadrivium also dealt with measurement, ratio, and proportion.

Arithmetic, the science of numbers, was the key to the Medieval scholar's view of music. Music was the expression of numbers in time. Arithmetic gave pitch, duration, rhythm, stress, and accent to the words of the music. Music was the very essence of the nature of creation, and to sing was to align one's body with the laws of nature, and one's mind and soul with the laws of God.

Music was an important facet of education in the Middle Ages. The roots of Western education are firmly imbedded in Greek culture. In its highest form, music was a speculative study which was necessary for the proper understanding of the Scripture. Music owes its existence as an academic discipline in the schools of the Middle Ages to its membership in the Quadrivium.

Sacred Music

The Middle Ages were anything but homogenous. The state of society moved from the chaos of the fall of the Roman empire to the high point of the 12th century. Then, it fell back in the 14th and 15th centuries into another chaotic period marked by the Black Death, the 100 Years' War, and feudal anarchy. This evolving and dissimilar world was held together by the central force of Christendom. As the light of the Roman Empire dimmed in the 5th and 6th centuries, its congregations and monasteries preserved and nurtured whatever shreds of learning and civilization escaped the onslaught of the barbarians.

The music most carefully preserved from this distant past was the music of worship. Every religion possessed some type of central liturgy—a series of texts outlining their beliefs. These texts formed the basis for the services throughout the year. Spiritual leaders in every great intellectual center carefully guarded their spiritual and liturgical traditions and the music associated with them. These early intellectual centers included Athens, Rome, Jerusalem, Byzantium, and Constantinople (today, Istanbul).

During the Middle Ages, the early Christians acquired their sacred songs from a number of sources, including:

1. Byzantine - earliest, established at the Eastern church by Constantine, Greek Orthodox.
2. Ambrosian - 4th century, Ambrose was the Bishop of Milan.
3. Gallic - used in France until c.800 A.D.
4. Mozarabic - prominent in Spain, appeared c.900 A.D.
5. Gregorian - most common, named after Pope Gregory I (c.540-604).

Most records of music before the year 1000 A.D. pertain to the chants of the Holy Roman Catholic Church. The overthrow of the Roman Empire caused the disruption of the secular centers of learning. Education continued primarily at the monasteries. Quite naturally, the monks were interested in the proper transmission and performance of the music that they used in their daily religious services.

This collection of music is known as "Gregorian chant" and is the single most important Western repertoire of monophonic music. Gregorian chant became widely established in the ninth century in the singing schools (Schola Cantorum) of cathedrals and monasteries. Its continued use was due to the fact that it was the collection used in Rome. When Rome became the center of Catholicism, the Gregorian plainchant spread throughout the Catholic world.

Pope Gregory's main contribution was not work with music per se, but his ability to disseminate the Christian faith throughout the Roman Empire, which traveled as far as London, England. Gregory's many gifts were as a writer, diplomat, administrator, and man of faith.

Today, Medieval sacred music is known as plainchant, or simply chant. Like all music in the church at this time it was monophonic in texture. It featured a melody that was rather "plain" in nature with a wandering, or "free," rhythm that followed the emphasis of the Latin words. The simple melodies were within a range of eight notes, often with no beat or regularly repeating rhythm. They were used to enhance but never to steal attention away from the fullest expression of the Word of God—the Holy Scripture itself. The aim was to praise God through the musical expression of Holy Scripture.

The Mass

The two main rites of the Catholic church are the Mass and the Divine Offices (Canonical Hours). Except for the most important feast days, there is only one Mass per day. The Divine Office consists of a series of eight different services throughout the day—from early morning until evening. For our purposes, we will examine the Mass.

The Mass is a re-enactment of the Last Supper of Christ. The texts for the Mass are divisible into two main groups, the Proper and the Ordinary.

1. Proper - those that are intended for one occasion.
2. Ordinary - those that are repeated throughout the church year whenever the chanting of that text is appropriate.

The chants of the Proper include an Introit, Gradual, Alleluia, Offertory, and Communion. The chants of the Ordinary include the Kyrie, Gloria, Credo, Sanctus, and the Agnus Dei. Since the texts for the Ordinary do not change, composers were most interested in setting these to music. We will listen to two chants of the Ordinary, the "Kyrie" and the "Agnus Dei" from the *Mass for the Feast of the Immaculate Conception* (on December 8). The Greek/Latin original and English translations are listed below.

Greek/Latin		English

Kyrie

Kyrie eleison.	(3x)	Lord have mercy.
Christe eleison.	(3x)	Christ have mercy.
Kyrie eleison.	(3x)	Lord have mercy.

Agnus Dei

Agnus Dei,		Lamb of God,
qui tollis peccata mundi,		who takes away the sins of the world,
miserere nobis.	(2x)	have mercy on us.
Agnus Dei,		Lamb of God,
qui tollis peccata mundi,		who takes away the sins of the world,
dona nobis pacem.	.	grant us peace.

☐ *Gregorian Chants* from the Ordinary of the Mass. (Kyrie, Agnus Dei)

Another musically famous chant that we will discuss later in the course is the "Dies irae." This Gregorian chant is attributed to Thomas of Celano (d.1255). He was a Friar and the biographer of St. Francis of Assisi. The text for the chant comes from the responsory used at the absolution concluding the *Mass for the Dead* (Requiem Mass). Originally, the text came from the prophet Zephaniah. Here is the text as found in the *Liber Usualis*.

Latin	English

Dies irae

Dies irae, dies illa,	O that day, that day of wrath,
calamitatis et miseriae,	of calamity and misery,
dies magna et amara valde:	that great and exceedingly bitter day:
cum veneris judicare,	When Thou shalt come to judge,
saecullum per ignem.	the world by fire.

By the time of Mozart, the "Dies irae" had become the centerpiece of a Requiem Mass. Composers were eager to set this text to music since it was emotional and terrifying. Hector Berlioz, in his autobiographical *Symphonie Fantastique*, used the melody to scare the audience and signify the seriousness of the situation for the "musician of morbidly sensitive temperament." Berlioz was the first composer to use the "Dies irae" outside of the liturgical setting to elicit a sense of death and despair. Other composers that used this chant include Liszt, Saint-Saëns, and Rachmaninov.

☐ *Gregorian Chant* from the Requiem Mass. (Dies irae)

Music and Notation

From the 9th century, because of the study of music historians, we have learned a great deal about the transmission of Gregorian chant. At first, lines (neumes) were borrowed from writers of the time. These lines were used to indicate certain vocal inflections. These neumes were placed over the text so that the monks would have an approximate idea of the pitch to be sung and of the general direction of the melody. There was, however, no indication of rhythm. This was to come much later. Such notation could only serve as a reminder to the singer. Pitch was eventually "fixed" by the invention of the staff and clefs.

Guido d'Arezzo was a Benedictine monk who made important contributions to the development of musical theory in the Middle Ages. He was probably born near Paris around 995 and received his education in the Benedictine abbey of St. Maur-des-Fossès. From there he went to the abbey of Pomposa (Northern Italy), and later to the town of Arezzo. He died around the year 1050.

His reputation as a scholar in the field of musical theory brought him to Rome. There, he convinced Pope John XIX of the quality of the advancements that he had made in the teaching of singing and music.

Guido was one of the first music teachers who devised a way to teach singers how to learn a new piece of music (sight-singing) without having to memorize it. In a letter from 1030 known as the "Epistola de ignoto cantu" (Letter on singing unheard songs), Guido outlined what today we call the "Guidonian Hand." In this system, various notes are assigned to the various joints and fingers of the hand. This eventually evolved into what we today know as the "do-re-me" system of sight-singing. Of course, Guido's reforms did not catch on immediately and the oral transmission of music persisted for quite a long time afterwards.

Early Polyphony

The use of polyphonic devices began in the Late Middle Ages (1100-1400). This marked the beginning of musical freedom from a dependency on chant. This practice was to continue through the Renaissance. While we are not exactly sure when polyphonic music first appeared in Europe, the earliest examples come from the 9th century and a style of music known as "organum." Polyphonic music began with the placement of a freer moving melody above a lower and slower moving Gregorian chant.

The earliest polyphonic schools of music were at the monasteries around France, England, and Spain. The following example is from the 12th century "School of Notre Dame" (Paris) by the composers Léonin and Pérotin. The Parisian musicians at Notre Dame were the first to solve the remaining musical problem of music notation—the notation of definite rhythmic values.

These composers were also the first to develop the basic devices of polyphony (counterpoint). Léonin (c.1159-1201) began experimenting with two-voice organum. His successor, Pérotin (c.1170-1236), used three- and four-voice polyphony with canonic imitation. Listen to the differences between Léonin and Pérotin in the same chant, the *Gradual* for Christmas. Pérotin's version is the earliest known example of four-part music in the history of European music.

☐   *Gradual* by Léonin. (organum)

☐   *Gradual* by Pérotin. (polyphony)

Secular Music

Of course there was also popular, or secular, music during the Middle Ages. However, secular music existed in an exclusively oral tradition. It was not until the 10th century that various systems of notation began to preserve the secular music of the time. Unfortunately, entire secular music cultures were born, flourished, and died out without ever being recorded.

The recording of secular music began when loosely organized groups of traveling musicians wandered across Europe. These "troubadours" and "trouvères" (France) composed, sang, played, and danced their way into various courts and castles. As with most secular music today, the rhythm was lively and they sang about their favorite subject—love. Most of the composers of these pieces are unknown or anonymous (anon.).

Here is an example by a "known" composer, Adam de la Halle, who lived from approximately 1240 to 1287. He was a poet-musician (trouvère) from Northern France. He was one of the only secular composers to use polyphonic textures in his works. The short example we will listen to is a secular composition (song) with the title "J'osè bien a m'amie parler," which loosely translates to "I dare to speak to my friend."

☐   "J'osè bien a m'amie parler" by de la Halle.

Guillaume de Machaut

Like other musicians of the 14th and 15th centuries, Machaut (c.1300-1377) was involved in politics. He served under King John of Bohemia and spent his later years at Notre Dame in Rheims. Machaut is important for his music and poetry. Quite a bit is known about Machaut because there are several large manuscripts of his music and poetry that have survived. During his lifetime, he contributed to all the various secular and sacred genres (pieces) that were popular in France.

Machaut composed twenty-three motets. A motet was originally an unaccompanied choral composition based on a Latin text. The word motet comes from the French language and means "word." During the time of Machaut, however, the text of the motets had become frequently political, moral, and often dealt with the subject of courtly love. Liturgical works were few. Normally these motets are in three, although occasionally in a four part, polyphonic style.

The famous "Hoquetus David" was Machaut's only purely instrumental motet. In this piece you will hear a "hocket" that is a musical "hiccup." This common device was used in vocal writing during this time and is similar to what today we would call syncopation. The featured instruments are two cornettos (wooden trumpets), an alto shawm (ancestor of the oboe), and bells.

☐   "Hoquetus David" by Machaut.

Messe de Notre Dame

Because he wrote the first complete polyphonic setting of the Ordinary of the Mass to have survived, Machaut's place in music history is an important one. Although he was not an innovator, his compositions display a mastery of all the techniques of the era and his natural gift for melody and expression.

Written around the year 1337, all the movements of the *Messe de Notre Dame* (Mass of Our Lady) are for four voices. The "Kyrie" is set in a motet style—there is a Gregorian chant melody that serves as the basis for the composition in the tenor part. This movement is subdivided into large sections separated by brief interludes of monophonic chant.

☐ *Messe de Notre Dame* by Machaut. (Kyrie)

The Renaissance (1400-1600)

The end of the Middle Ages was a time of trouble all over Europe. This era was marked by conflict between nations, social unrest, and the further weakening of the power of the Holy Roman Catholic Church by the Protestant Reformation. Even mother nature, it seemed, was angry at Europe as it unleashed the Black Death—the most horrible epidemic in history that ravaged Europe by the end of the era.

During this time, and reaching into the Renaissance, a division was taking place religiously, politically, and artistically. Secularism was taking hold of the arts, the vernacular in literature was overtaking Latin, and the aristocracy had begun to compete with the Church in the hiring and commissioning of artists (patronage system).

The two major advancements during the Middle Ages were in music notation and literacy. In the Renaissance, the invention of music printing (movable type) by Ottaviano Petrucci was just as revolutionary and very important. By publishing their music, composers were able to reach the general public in a way they never could before. Music was no longer exclusive property of the church or court, since anyone with money could afford to buy whatever music they wanted.

During the Renaissance there were two distinctive schools of composition—the Burgundian and the Flemish (Netherlands) schools. The Burgundian school flourished during the first half of the 15th century and included the composers Dufay and Binchois. The Flemish composers (1450-1600) were from a region now consisting of Northern France, Belgium, and Holland. These composers included Ockeghem, Obrecht, and Josquin des Prez.

Josquin des Prez

Josquin was one of the greatest composers of all time. He was the first composer to really make music a personally expressive art. He was fortunate to have the majority of his musical compositions published during his lifetime. Since his music became well known during his time, Josquin had a great influence on many other Renaissance composers.

His sacred works are usually in a conservative, contrapuntal style. Many of his secular works, however, tend toward a homophonic texture. The example we will listen to is his motet "Tu pauperum refugium" (Thou refuge of the poor). You will hear both a homophonic and a polyphonic treatment of the words in a very moving four-part, a cappella setting.

☐ "Tu pauperum refugium" by des Prez.

The Madrigal

The first real towns and cities began to develop as the common people moved out of the feudal structure of the Middle Ages. In these towns there was a new class of people emerging—the middle class, or the general public. Music soon became important at social functions, weddings, festivals, and in the home as part of a cultured lifestyle. One of the most important types (genres) of music composed for the educated amateur musician was the madrigal—a song in the language of the people that features polyphonic imitation, soprano-dominated melodies, and often a bright dance-type rhythm. These madrigals provided performers, amateurs, and professionals with music for dancing and singing.

Beginning in the 1560's, madrigals soon became a musical vehicle for experimentation and new ideas. This highly sophisticated part-song tried to mirror and intensify the imagery and emotional content of the text.

This sophisticated musical concept is known as word, or tone, painting. In this way the madrigal differs from other Renaissance music in that it tries to imitate and describe human feelings.

The Italian madrigal, which was the source of inspiration for an entire generation of English composers, was an intimate fusion of words and music. William Byrd (1543-1623) seems to have been the first English composer to grasp the importance of the madrigal. He, along with Thomas Morley, represented the earlier period of English madrigal whose style corresponds to the second Italian school. Soon, it acquired native characteristics and peculiarities of the English language. English madrigals appeared under a variety of names, including song, sonnet, and ayre (air).

It was the composer Thomas Morley (1557-1602) who helped to create the style of Elizabethan madrigal. Morley wrote in a light style that reflected a lively grace and a sense of harmonic clarity. In 1595 Morley composed the madrigal "Now is the Month of Maying." This is one of his most well known madrigals and features dance-like rhythms and the typical English "Fa-la-la" vocal chase.

A madrigal in a different mood is his "Farewell, disdainful." Notice in particular, the tone painting of the lines "O come again, return thee" as the voices repeat the word "again," and then the imploring "no, no, false love." This madrigal was published in the year 1593.

☐ "Now is the Month of Maying" by Morley.

☐ "Farewell, disdainful" by Morley.

Palestrina

Of course, religious music continued to flourish during the Renaissance. Perhaps the best known composer of the late Renaissance is Giovanni Pierluigi da Palestrina (c.1525-94). His last name is that of the town where he was born. The town of Palestrina is less than fifty miles from Rome. During his employment in Rome, he wrote over one hundred masses, many motets, hymns, and magnificats. In his sacred works Palestrina developed a polyphonic technique that included seamless counterpoint and an almost constant imitation in the voices. The control of dissonance and melodic motion produced a smooth, flawless, and non-dramatic style that suited the devotional nature of the liturgical texts.

An intriguing legend surrounds Palestrina and the Council of Trent that was held during the Counter Reformation (1545-63). Palestrina supposedly composed a mass that demonstrated to the Cardinals that polyphonic music could stay out of the way of the text and its meaning. Whether this is true or not, Palestrina was undeniably a musician sincerely dedicated to the spiritual goals of the Counter-Reformation by denouncing the effects of secular music on sacred music. He is credited with saving polyphony from being banished by the Cardinals.

In the "Exultate Deo" you will notice the emotional restraint, polyphonic textures, and a balanced melodic flow. Even in this piece, one of his most joyful compositions, there is always a certain amount of serenity and reverence associated with his music. Most of his music is filled with the very essence of chant. Notice the direction of the melodic line in the opening soprano passage on the word "Exultate," which means Rejoice. Palestrina carefully considered the meaning of the word, and then set it to music. This is then followed by the typical Palestrina seamless melody and polyphonic texture.

☐ "Exultate Deo" by Palestrina.

After the <u>Messiah</u> was finished, Lord Kinnoul paid Handel some compliments on the noble entertainment he had lately given. To which Handel responded "My lord, I should be sorry if I only entertained them – I wish to make them better."

Description from the first London performance of *Messiah*

"The world will not have such a talent again in a hundred years."

F.J. Haydn, upon learning of the death of Mozart in 1791

"It is a pity to lose so great a genius, but a good thing for us that he is dead. For if he had lived much longer, we should not have earned a crust of bread by our compositions."

Attributed to Antonio Salieri, in reference to W.A. Mozart

". . . the product of my genius and my misery, and that which I have written in my greatest distress, is that which the world seems to like best."

Franz Schubert, in reference to his art songs

Sacred Vocal Music

Classical music has a rich tradition of sacred choral music. Among the major forms of large scale choral works are the oratorio, mass, and requiem mass. The message of redemption is integral to these works as it is to all Christianity. The title of this chapter is from a line in the requiem mass—the Mass for the Dead. The complete line, in Latin, is "Voca me cum benedictis" which translates to "Call me with the Blessed."

The Oratorio

An oratorio is a composition with a long libretto of religious or contemplative character that is performed in a concert hall or church. As opposed to an opera, it is performed without scenery, costumes, or action. Musically, the oratorio features solo voices, a chorus, and an orchestra. This definition applies to most but not all oratorios. Other features distinguishing the oratorio from opera are a greater emphasis on the chorus, an absence of quick dialogue, and the use of a narrator (testo). The narrator functions to introduce the characters and to connect their parts. The oratorio is distinguished from the sacred cantatas of J.S. Bach by their greater length and the use of a more narrative libretto.

The English oratorio is represented by G.F. Handel. His oratorios *Israel in Egypt*, *Messiah*, *Judas Maccabeus*, and *Jephtha* are the supreme achievements in this genre. In contrast to Bach's devotional attitude, Handel approached the oratorio more subjectively, using it to express his own dynamic personality and incorporating elements of his own dramatic opera style. His oratorios were intended to be performed during Lent, when theatrical performances (opera) were forbidden by law.

Handel became a naturalized British citizen in 1726. His career over the next few years reflected the ups and downs of opera in London and changes in musical taste. Handel's last operas (1740-41) were complete failures, and from then on he did not compose for the London opera audience. In 1741 he accepted an invitation from the viceroy of Ireland to perform at a charity concert in Dublin. For this occasion Handel wrote his sacred oratorio *Messiah* in an amazing twenty-four days. *Messiah* is the story of the coming of Christ, his life and Crucifixion, and the Resurrection.

A servant from Handel's London residence reported that he worked as if he was possessed—hardly eating or sleeping, working until he was so frenzied that he appeared to be going mad. Supposedly, when Handel finished the "Hallelujah Chorus" from the *Messiah*, he said "I did think I saw all Heaven before me, and the great God Himself . . ."

In 1742 the *Messiah* had its premiere in Dublin amidst much excitement and anticipation. The concert hall was completely full, and the newspapers and handbills had requested that women refrain from wearing their "hoop" skirts and men "forgo their swords." Hundreds of people, unable to gain entry to the concert, listened outside as they crowded around the windows and doorways. The performance was a tremendous success. Back in London in 1743, King George II was so moved by the "Hallelujah Chorus" that he stood up to honor the composer. This tradition still continues today.

The *Messiah* is over two and a half hours long and consists of about fifty different musical pieces, including an overture, recitatives, arias, and choruses. Most performances today are of condensed versions. When Handel wrote this monumental piece of music he did not intend it to be a religious or church piece, but rather an entertainment work. However in modern day practice, the first half of the work is performed at Christmas, while the second half receives its performance during Easter.

The *Messiah* brought Handel wealth and fame. In 1752 Handel began to have problems with his eyesight. After a series of operations by the same surgeon that caused Bach's blindness (1750), Handel also lost his sight. In the spring of 1759, 74 years old and blind, Handel was still performing and leading performances of his oratorios. He fainted at a performance of the *Messiah* in April of 1759. Sensing that he was near death, Handel supposedly told his friends that he wanted to die on Good Friday. He missed it by a few hours dying on April 14 (Good Saturday) in 1759. His funeral and burial at Westminster Abbey were attended by many aristocrats, musical patrons, musicians, artists, and lovers of music from all over England. The monument at his grave is marked with a stone tablet that is engraved with a portion of the score to the *Messiah*.

☐ *Messiah* by Handel. "Behold a virgin shall conceive" (recitative), "Oh thou that tellest good tidings to Zion" (aria and chorus), "Hallelujah" (chorus)

Music in Germany

Devastated by the turmoil of the Thirty Years' War, Germany in the late 17th century was made up of over 300 smaller states. Each state had its own ruler and court, and subscribed to different churches. Each ruler tried to provide himself with a suitable palace. All of their ceremonial and extravagant works of art were financed by the taxes from the peasants.

The German-speaking lands were also religiously divided. The Catholic Church still held most of its power in southern Germany. However, over most of the remaining areas Lutheranism (Protestant) and Pietism prevailed. Johann Sebastian Bach, from a family that had been Lutheran for six generations, believed in the God-given nature of talent and creativity in all the artistic disciplines—especially in the field of music. Music was seen as a manifestation of praise, and the more creative and musically fulfilling the composition, the greater the glory offered up to God.

Germany absorbed a number of musical influences into its own tradition of polyphonic vocal music. From Italy, dramatic melodies, the unique style of bel canto singing, and the concerto were assimilated. France contributed the "French overture style" (slow, fast, slow) and the dance suite. While some German musicians preferred one style over another, in the late Baroque these various influences were combined into and became part of a new German style. This new style was to reach its high point in the music of J.S. Bach.

At the end of many of his religious works Bach inscribed "Soli Deo Gloria"—To God alone belongs the glory. Bach was the last of the great religious artists and the all-time master of the fugue. World famous compositions exist in each category of Bach's music—vocal, orchestral, chamber, and keyboard. Although he was not an inventor of new musical forms, he perfected many of them and developed them in ways no one had thought of before.

Mass in B minor

In February of 1733, Augustus II, the Elector of Saxony, died. His son became King of Poland and Elector of Saxony. To impress the new Elector and secure a position as "Kapellmeister," Bach wrote two sections of a liturgical Mass—the "Kyrie" and the "Gloria." Bach wrote the "Kyrie" to open the mass at St. Nicholas' Church to mourn the dead Elector, while the "Gloria" ended the mass in celebration of the new ruler Augustus III.

When Bach submitted these two movements to Augustus III, he also sent a letter complaining of his unjust treatment and low wages in Leipzig. While he did secure the position of Kapellmeister in 1736, it turned out to be an honorary position. This meant that there was no pay involved, only a title.

Bach was, however, encouraged by the new monarch's favorable disposition toward the arts. From 1747-49, Bach adapted music from earlier works and added some newly composed sections to the mass. Eventually he completed the *Mass in B minor*. Although it was eventually presented to Augustus III, it was not performed in Bach's lifetime—Bach died in July of 1750. It was probably better for Bach that it did not receive a performance while he was alive since the Leipzig population of Lutherans would have strongly objected to their musical director composing a Catholic Mass. The form of this masterpiece is greatly enlarged. At just over two hours long, the scale of the work transcends the possibility of any liturgical performance anyway.

The *Mass in B minor* reached into a mysterious remoteness of spirituality. Bach seemed to be working towards a universal statement of Christian faith. This can be seen, for example, in his use of Gregorian chant melodies in the "Credo" section of the mass.

The principal parts of this mass are from the Ordinary of the Mass—the Kyrie, Gloria, Credo, Sanctus, and Agnus Dei. The use of soloists to contrast with the full choir, and the instrumental advantages of an enlarged orchestra, created unique compositional possibilities for emotion and feeling (Doctrine of Affections). We will examine four different sections from this masterpiece of choral music.

Kyrie—The first four measures of the "Kyrie" are the fugue subject for a five- part chorus and orchestra. The orchestra was composed of strings, flutes, oboes, bassoons, and an organ. Frequently, the "Kyrie" settings began with a slow homophonic opening. (See Chapter 9 for the text and the translation.)

☐   *Mass in B minor* by Bach. (Kyrie)

Gloria—The "Glory to God" section bursts into a D major setting that is bright and radiant. Trumpets and flutes add brightness to the vibrant string sound. The second (minor) section, "et in terra pax," is much more solemn. The motive (theme) then grows into an extensive fugal coda in which the trumpets return after having been silent during the middle section. The final section is also in D major.

Gloria in excelsis Deo	Glory be to God on high
et in terra pax hominibus	and on earth peace to men
bonae voluntatis.	of good will.

☐   *Mass in B minor* by Bach. (Gloria)

Crucifixus—The music for this comes from an earlier Bach cantata, *Cantata No. 12*, composed 1714. The original text was "Weeping, Wailing, Worry, Trembling." This movement is full of chromatic notes, suspensions, and a downward motion leading to a sobbing melody. Combined with a slow tempo and a minor key, Bach created a profoundly moving and sorrowful musical setting of the crucifixion. Musically, this is a chaconne (musical form) above a regularly recurring bass figure.

Crucifixus etiam pro nobis	And was crucified also for us
sub Pontio Pilato	under Pontius Pilate.
passus et sepultus est.	He suffered and was buried.

☐   *Mass in B minor* by Bach. (Crucifixus)

Et resurrexit—In contrast to the "Crucifixus," this section deals with the resurrection of Christ. In this movement the entire chorus and orchestra (with trumpets) burst out in D major. After a short introduction, a fugue begins in the bass, alto, tenor, and finally, the soprano voices. Bach seems barely able to contain himself with a great outpouring of excitement and joy.

Et resurrexit tertia	And the third day he rose
die secundum	again according to the
scripturas...	scriptures...

☐   *Mass in B minor* by Bach. (Et resurrexit)

In contrast to Handel, the death of J.S. Bach on 28 July 1750 was not an elaborate affair. His grave in the St. John churchyard in Leipzig was not even marked. No one lined the streets for his funeral procession and no foreign dignitaries were in attendance. His coffin was not moved inside the church until almost 150 years later.

Since his music was not published during his lifetime, Bach's music reached only a limited audience—his immediate church-going parishioners and the various courts that he wrote for (Weimar, Cöthen, Leipzig, etc.). In fact, for nearly 50 years after his death his music was not even published. Bach was just another anonymous servant of God.

Later on in the Classical era, both Mozart and Beethoven studied and admired Bach's music. Yet it was in 1829 that the Romantic composer Felix Mendelssohn revived Bach's music with a performance of the *St. Matthew Passion*—one of his musical compositions that was composed almost 100 years earlier in 1731!

The Requiem Mass

The word "requiem" traditionally refers to the Roman Catholic Mass for the dead. The opening Introit of the mass begins with the Latin phrase "Requiem aeternam dona eis domine" (Grant them eternal rest, O Lord). The first word of the text is where the name of the genre comes from. Many composers wrote musical settings of the Requiem Mass. These liturgical works were intended for actual use in a service as a prayer for the soul of the departed.

Although the movie *Amadeus* did wonders for the sale of Mozart's music, the story of the "gray messenger" and his *Requiem Mass* was changed for dramatic reasons. Well, that's Hollywood for you.

☐   *Requiem Mass* by Mozart. (Confutatis, Lacrimosa)

A German Requiem

This is the largest work by Johannes Brahms in any medium. In this piece Brahms established himself as a mature composer. He created a unique masterpiece of technique and effect that expressed the universal longings of mankind for peace and consolation.

The composition of *A German Requiem*, Op. 45 from 1866, was influenced by the music of past centuries. This was an unusual trend for this time. The primary stimulus for the work was the death of his mother in 1865. Some of the musical materials for this work came from prior manuscripts.

In this piece, Brahms transcends his personal grief to produce a universal statement of acceptance and consolation of death, and of hope. This is a mass for those left behind—those who are in mourning. It leaves out the Christian message of "redemption through Christ only." This probably contributed to the lack of success in his adopted home of "Catholic" Vienna.

The requiem mass has seven movements with the text coming from the Holy Scriptures. Brahms assembled the text himself from Martin Luther's translation of the Bible. With this, Brahms creates a universal text that does not follow any particular church liturgy. In a letter to the director of the Bremen Cathedral, where the piece was premiered, he explained that the "German" referred only to the language it was sung in and that he would gladly have called it a "Human Requiem." Written for soprano, baritone, chorus, and orchestra, A German Requiem is approximately one hour in length.

The first movement is "Selig sind, die da Leid tragen" (Blessed are they that mourn). It is in an overall form of **A B A**. The somber mood of this movement is enhanced by the lack of violins, piccolo, clarinets, trumpets, tuba, and timpani—the bright instruments of the orchestra. The A section is a soft opening with fragments of the melody being presented before the entire melody is heard. It also features an a cappella section. The B section is the "Freuden" (Joy) section. The movement ends as it began, in a mournful atmosphere.

☐   A German Requiem, by Brahms. (I. Selig sind, die da Leid tragen)

A slow march-like passage in triple meter begins the second movement, "Denn alles Fleisch, es ist wie Gras" (For all flesh is as grass). After an orchestral introduction with its lush sound, the timpani (funeral march) enters and the contrast of major and minor tonality begins. The consoling call for patience is brightened by the woodwinds. Note especially the vivid tone-painting of the phrase "the early rain" in the harp and flute. A huge crescendo announces the repetition of the opening paragraph.

☐   A German Requiem, by Brahms. (II. Denn alles Fleisch, es ist wie Gras)

The fifth movement was written for soprano and chorus with orchestra. This movement is entitled "Ihr habt nun Traurigkeit" (And ye now therefore have sorrow). It begins with a short introduction with woodwinds and string pizzicato. Why does Brahms use a soprano in this movement? Because of the line in the text "But I will see you again." The soprano represents an angel from heaven singing down to earth. This is a message of gentle and even personal consolation, as it is the most specific part of the mass that is a memorial to his mother.

☐   A German Requiem, by Brahms. (V. Ihr habt nun Traurigkeit)

The German Lied

A lied (lieder) is an "art song" in the German vernacular. The greatest period of the German lied began with Schubert (1797-1828). After a few preliminary songs in a somewhat traditional style, he opened a new era with "Gretchen am Spinnrade" in 1814 when he was only seventeen years old.

There soon followed a flood of masterworks including the "Erlkönig," "Wanders' Nachtlied," "Der Wanderer," and the song cycles of "Die Schöne Müllerin," and "Winterreise." In his last year, Schubert composed his final song cycle "Schwanengesang." Measured by the artistic perfection of these songs, even the most beautiful lieder of Schumann and Brahms pale in comparison, and only Hugo Wolf's lieder approach Schubert's. Others who significantly contributed to this genre include Mendelssohn, Liszt, Wagner, Mahler, and Richard Strauss.

Franz Schubert

The true Romantic side of Schubert's music can be seen in his art songs. His songs are typical Viennese melodies that came to him quite easily. In the art song, Schubert was able to find success and eventually a reputation for composition. He established himself as a composer by song writing—this was a first in the history of Western music. It was in the lied that his Romanticism could find its most natural and original expression.

As with other composers we have studied, there is a close relationship between the words and the music—the music attempts to portray the meaning (often symbolic) of the words. This musical procedure is called word, or tone, painting. To this end, the piano part is an integral component in the song. It is not just a background accompaniment, but an equal partner with the voice in portraying the drama contained in the story.

Many of Schubert's songs have a simple melodic line. Some are almost folk songs ("Die Forelle" - The Trout), while others are full of Romantic longing and suffering ("Am meer" - By the sea). Still other songs are intense and dramatic ("Der Atlas" - Atlas).

☐ "Erlkönig" and "Der Atlas" by Schubert.

Epilogue

The revolutionary tendencies of the 20th century found their clearest expression in Arnold Schoenberg's suite *Pierrot Lunaire*, Op. 21 from 1912. *Pierrot Lunaire* is a collection of twenty-one songs for soprano and chamber orchestra. Besides their novel harmonic style and unusual instrumentation, they demonstrate a new type of vocal style called "sprechstimme." The speech-like declamation is distinguished by a rise and fall of the speaking voice. This "hyper-expressive" style of singing is a non-realistic (fantastic) language halfway between singing and speaking. Known as Expressionism, this style of music would eventually lead to Schoenberg's revolutionary 12-tone, or Atonal, style (see Chapter 16).

☐ "Mondestrunken" from *Pierrot Lunaire* by Schoenberg.

William Walton was a composer from the 20th century English school. Walton was catapulted to fame with his 1923 composition *Façade*, a witty and fantastic setting of the abstract poetry (symbolism) of Edith Sitwell.

A "Fanfare" is used to introduce the piece and is followed by a "Hornpipe." The "Hornpipe" is an English dance that has a nautical flavor to it.

☐ *Façade* by Walton. (Fanfare, Hornpipe)

In England, Benjamin Britten was perhaps the most eminent of the 20th Century composers. His most important works were his operas and choral works. In terms of musical style, he was a Classicist and rejected the Wagnerian principle of endless melody. His most dramatic work was *The War Requiem* (1962). This piece combines Latin texts with the anti-war poetry of Wilfred Owen, a British soldier who was killed at the end World War I.

☐ *War Requiem* by Britten. (Dies irae)

I went on stage for Papageno's aria with the Glockenspiel . . . I played a joke on Schikaneder (Papageno): where he has a pause, I played an arpeggio, he started - looked off-stage and saw me. When the second pause came, I did nothing - so he waited and would not go on. I guessed what he was thinking and played another chord - whereat he hit the Glockenspiel and yelled "Hold your tongue!" at which everybody laughed. I think this joke made many people notice for the first time that he does not play the instrument himself.

Mozart, in a letter to his wife on 8 October 1791

Caruso was dragging out his arias, singing slowly, "Chi son? Chi son?" (Who am I?). "Sei un imbecile!" (You're a fool) shouted Puccini.

Description of Puccini at an opera rehearsal

"When I arrived here all these organs were playing airs from Rigoletto, Travatore, and my other operas from morning till night. I was so annoyed that I hired the whole lot for the season."

Verdi, when asked why his villa was full of portable organs

What did you expect, a happy ending?

Well, let's start with what opera is not. Opera is not "concert" music. Opera is theatrical music. Its origins go back as far as ritual (tribal) music and the sacred plays of the Middle Ages (*The Play of Daniel*). Opera is bound by convention. It is a sung, instead of spoken, drama that also features acting, costumes, dancing, recitatives, arias, choruses, scenery, and a story (libretto).

Opera is not a realistic form of art and the listener or viewer should not expect it to be! Often times the enjoyment of an opera is further complicated by a language barrier. Until the time of Mozart, most operas were almost exclusively sung in Italian. Even today, the majority of the great operas are either in Italian, French, or German.

The form of opera itself includes almost every musical medium. Accompanied by a symphony orchestra, it features solo voices and a chorus (a vocal ensemble of sopranos, altos, tenors, and basses). The character of the piece may be serious, light-hearted, or have elements of both. Some of the music is music for its own sake (absolute), while most of the music is there to convey the story (programmatic). An opera also may contain dance (ballet) and drama. Add to these elements the lighting, set designs, and costumes, and you end up with a magnificent, spectacular display that is unique to the theatrical world of opera.

Opera composers tend to fall into two categories: those that have given the words and their meaning the dominate role, and those that have used the words and the plot as the means to their musical aims. Stated another way, composers either emphasize the words or the music in an opera.

Around the year 1600 opera as a major genre had its beginnings. During this time certain composers and poets met at the palace of Count Bardi (Florence) to discuss the revival of Greek drama. These Renaissance intellectuals were attempting to recapture the spirit of the Greek theater that blended music and poetry. At least they tried to recreate what they believed took place in a Greek play. In doing so, they came up with a new form of musical composition—the opera. This new art form was designed to change vocal music from a highly polyphonic and complex style into music where the words could clearly be understood (homophonic).

The first great opera composer was Claudio Monteverdi who was born in Cremona in 1567. His opera *L'Orfeo* (1607) is considered the first real opera. The first operas were designed for the aristocrats, and not the common people. It would, however, be thirty years before the first public opera house opened in Venice—the Teatro San Cassiano. Opera became a public institution early on in the history of Western music. It spread from Florence to Venice, then to Vienna, Paris, London, and Hamburg. These cities became the main centers of opera during the 1700's.

After the mid-19th century, opera became a virtually seamless structure designed to deliver the music-drama in the most striking and effective manner. Some still used arias, recitatives, ensembles, choruses, and the like, while others began to use spoken dialogue as well (*Carmen*, by Georges Bizet).

Today, opera is one of the grandest stage spectacles, full of some of the most beautiful music ever written for the voice. It may also be the greatest art form invented so far in the history of the Western world.

Opera's reality is not that of the streets, but of the emotions and of the mind. It is about music and how, through music, we examine our common humanity—how our deepest desires and longing affect our behavior, and the consequences of these actions for our lives and the people around us.

The music in an opera has two levels of meaning going on simultaneously. The words and the music of the singers drive the action of the story, while the music from the orchestra often comments as a narrator on this action. This gives us an insight into what is really going on and what is about to happen. It allows us to examine the personality, motivation, thoughts, and dreams of the characters in a dramatic manner.

An opera begins with an overture. The function of the overture is to set the mood and build up a feeling of excitement and expectation before the curtain goes up on the dramatic action. In the overtures of some operas you will hear the important themes and melodies from the opera itself. This is often done to familiarize you with the music to come.

Where and how do you begin to study an opera? First pick an opera. Then read up on it—the libretto, reviews, books, etc. Get a recording or video of the performance and listen to it before you go. Knowing the libretto ahead of time is crucial. This will allow you to concentrate on the music.

Die Zauberflöte
The Magic Flute, Wolfgang Amadeus Mozart

An opera in two acts by Mozart, with a libretto in German by Emanuel Schikaneder. It is based on the story "Lulu" in Wieland's *Oriental Fairy Tales* (1786).

Principal characters (cast):
Tamino - Egyptian prince, tenor
Papageno - a bird-catcher, baritone
Sarastro - high priest of Isis and Osiris, bass
Queen of the Night - coloratura soprano
Pamina - her daughter, soprano
Monostatos - chief of the temple slaves, tenor
Papagena - soprano
3 ladies in waiting to Queen of the Night - two sopranos, one mezzo-soprano

Time: reign of the Pharaoh Ramses I
Place: Egypt
First performance: Theater an der Wien, Vienna
30 September 1791

The Magic Flute is a singspiel (singing play), or a play with much singing. Schikaneder, an actor, friend, and fellow Freemason, commissioned the work from Mozart during a time in his life when the composer badly needed money. Mozart wrote the score with particular singers and actors in mind. Schikaneder was a baritone of limited vocal talent who played the role of Papageno, while Josefa Hofer, Mozart's sister-in-law, was the brilliantly pyrotechnic coloratura for whom the Queen of the Night's arias were written.

This opera was written for the popular theater in Vienna and not the opera house. By all accounts, it was well received by the audience, and Mozart enjoyed its success. This success, however, did not help Mozart very much financially. He died about two months after the premier of the opera, which he had conducted.

Despite the inconsistencies in the plot (for example the Queen of the Night is a good woman in Act I, but a villain in Act II), *The Magic Flute* is a fairy tale and was a huge success from the very beginning. The opera shows us the humanist side of Mozart since it is an opera about real people with real emotions.

The notions that a prince (Tamino) and a commoner (Papageno) are equal human beings, that light will triumph over darkness, and that good will overcome evil, are typical ideals from the Age of Enlightenment. While these figures did rise above the normal everyday life, they remained recognizable to the Viennese. Papageno is the traditional Viennese clown "Casperl" that certainly would have been known to every 18th century person. The concepts of human dignity and of the rights of man were also found in the works of Montesquieu, Voltaire, and Rousseau.

Papageno and Papagena, two of the main characters, are common people into whose music Mozart poured his celebration of love between man and woman. The story deals with the nature of love (Tamino and Pamina, Papageno and Papagena), sympathy for a person's mistakes and character flaws (Papageno), and a desire for freedom (Pamina), justice (Sarastro), and happiness (Tamino). In this opera, as in all good fairy tales, good triumphs over evil. There is also plenty of comic relief along the way.

Libretto Synopsis

The overture to the opera begins on a solemn note. The music from the opening of the overture will later appear in reference to the rites of passage at the temple. Then it becomes light and happy, as a fairy tale should.

In the opening of Act One, Tamino is saved from a serpent by the Queen of the Night's three attendants. Having fainted, Tamino believes his rescuer to be Papageno—the comic bird-catcher. For not admitting the truth, Papageno is punished by the attendants. The attendants then give a picture of Pamina to Tamino and, of course, he immediately falls in love with her picture. Her mother, the Queen of the Night, arrives to tell Tamino of Pamina's capture by Sarastro.

For their rescue mission, Tamino is provided with a magic flute, and Papageno with magic bells. Pamina is guarded in Sarastro's palace by the evil Moor, Monostatos. Meanwhile, Tamino learns that Sarastro is a wise priest and that it is the Queen who is evil. Papageno and Pamina are caught trying to escape by Monostatos and his slaves. Papageno uses the magic bells to set the evil Moor and his slaves dancing helplessly. Tamino and Pamina meet and fall in love.

In order to become members of Sarastro's sect, Tamino and Papageno undergo a vow of silence that the latter finds unbearable. Tamino resists the temptation to speak to a hurt and bewildered Pamina. Papageno wishes for a wife, but an old woman shows up instead. As Papageno reluctantly accepts, she turns into a beautiful woman, Papagena. Then she immediately disappears. Meanwhile, protected by the magic flute, Tamino and Pamina pass the initiation rites of fire and water.

The dejected Papageno tries to hang himself. He is advised to use the magic bells and finally brings his Papagena back. The Queen, her attendants, and Monostatos make a last attempt to destroy Sarastro and rescue Pamina, but flee at the sound of thunder. Both couples are united and all live happily ever after.

▭   *The Magic Flute* by Mozart. (excerpts)

La Bohème
The Bohemians, Giacomo Puccini

An opera in four acts by Puccini, with a libretto in Italian by Giuseppe Giacosa and Luigi Illica. It is based on the novel *La Bohème* by Henri Murger.

Principal characters (cast):
Marcello - a painter, baritone
Rodolfo - a poet, tenor
Colline - a philosopher, bass
Schaunard - a musician, baritone
Benoit - the landlord, bass
Mimi - a seamstress, soprano
Musetta - Marcello's old girlfriend, soprano

Alcindoro - Musetta's admirer, bass

Time: about 1830
Place: Paris
First performance: Teatro Regio, Turin
  1 February 1896

Puccini studied composition at the conservatory in Milan. While he lived in Milan he had a roommate by the name of Pietro Mascagni, who composed the opera *Cavalleria Rusticana*. At this time they led the life of starving artists. Many of these experiences were of great use to him in writing *La Bohème*. Like the opera's character Colline, Puccini once had to sell his coat for money!

Puccini was a song and theater man. His music was of the theater; sensuous song and melodic melodrama. He was the end of a long line of Italian opera composers that included Rossini, Donizetti, and Verdi. As an opera composer he was part of the late 19th century school of "verismo." These were operas that dealt with the real world in real settings, rather than with history, legend, or traditional heroes. While the characters and events were the kind found in everyday life, the music made them seem larger than life.

This opera is about four starving young artists on Paris's Left Bank in the 1830's. Puccini's particular genius lay in the successful blending of arias, dialogue, action, and orchestral continuity. All of these contribute to the forwarding of the dramatic action to produce a captivating theatrical experience.

The realism in this opera abounds at virtually every level. The dialogue, for example, contains humor, wit, anger, frustration, love, and other emotions in a realistic manner. The recitatives suggest patterns of speech, while the orchestration, which is often understated, is very supportive of the text. You will notice, for example, how Mimi's death is introduced in the orchestra (Act IV) and lets the audience know what has happened even before the characters on stage know!

The musical dynamics are mostly within the range of a realistic performance and are not excessively loud and powerful (which would indicate shouting). Most of the dynamics are actually at a piano to pianissimo level. At the symbolic level, poverty, illness, death, and solitude (loneliness) are all associated with coldness, while love is associated with spring. This is certainly a novel attempt at realism within a genre that has always been associated with fantasy and fiction (*The Magic Flute*, for example).

La Bohème is one of Puccini's most popular operas. Each act has great music and features a wonderful dramatic highlight.

Libretto Synopsis

The opening act paints the vivid descriptions of four starving artists (Bohemians). We can also see their Romantic illusion—they live for their art and they are in love with the idea of being in love. This is especially true for Rodolfo. Love, for the Bohemians, is the release from the tragedy of day to day life (love can conquer all). At the end of Act I, Rodolfo and Mimi are searching for her key on the floor of his freezing cold apartment. It is in this scene that the two fall in love with each other and with the ideal of love.

In Act II, the Bohemians have a night out on the town at the comic expense of Musetta's spurned admirer, Alcindoro. The tensions and conflicts (love and jealousy) of the two pairs of lovers provide the basis for the musical and dramatic action of Act III. In the final act, Act IV, the Bohemians sell off their possessions to buy medicine for Mimi. Unfortunately it is too late, as Mimi dies of consumption (pneumonia).

☐   *La Bohème* by Puccini. (excerpts)

Aïda
Giuseppe Verdi

An opera in four acts by Verdi, with a libretto in Italian by Antonio Ghislanzoni. It is based on the French prose of Camille du Locle.

Principal characters (cast):
Radames - captain of the guard, tenor
Amneris - the Pharaoh's daughter, mezzo-soprano
Aida - Amneris's Ethiopian slave, soprano
The Pharaoh - bass
A Messenger - tenor
Ramphis - high priest of Egypt, bass
Amonasro - Aida's father and king of Ethiopia, baritone

Time: reign of the Pharaohs
Place: Memphis and Thebes
First performance: Teatro Italiano, Cairo
  24 December 1871

Aida was commissioned by the Khedive of Egypt to celebrate the opening of the Suez Canal. While the canal opened on schedule, the opera did not—the costumes and sets were still in Paris because of the Franco-Prussian war. The premiere of *Aida* took place in 1871 at the opening of the new opera house in Cairo.

Because of the delay, Verdi was able to review what he had written, and the result was one of the grandest of grand operas—one that has completely withstood the test of time. *Aida* is not a patchwork of show pieces, but rather a fully integrated opera. Into this rather remote story of ancient Egyptian battles, Verdi created real characters with human feelings and qualities. Verdi concentrated on this depiction of his characters. The result is that from the prelude to the final duet at the end, the listener becomes completely involved in the characters of the opera. The drama grows and flows inevitably as the spectacular scenes are a logical part of the dramatic work. The arias and recitatives are a seamless whole, and are always motivated and blended into the evolving dramatic action.

Libretto Synopsis

The dramatic action of Act I revolves around Radames and the two women who are in love with him, Amneris and Aida. The Pharaoh and various priests announce that Isis has spoken and has named Radames as the new Egyptian commander. Only Aida is unhappy, since Radames will be going into battle against her father and her people—the Ethiopians. While she wishes Radames well, she feels as though she has betrayed her own people. She prays to the gods to take pity on her situation.

At the beginning of Act II, Amneris tries to get her slave girl (Aida) to reveal her true feelings for Radames. In tricking her, Amneris reminds her of her place. She orders Aida to accompany her to witness the triumphant return of Radames. At the victory celebration the Pharaoh decides that Amneris and Radames will wed. This casts both Radames and Aida into despair.

In Act III Aida and Radames meet along the banks of the Nile at night. They reveal their true feelings for one another and discuss their desperate situation. During the conversation Radames innocently gives away the secret route of the Egyptian army. As he does so, he is overheard by Ramphis and captured.

In the final act, Ramades is sentenced to death and is to be buried alive in a tomb. Amneris begs for mercy but goes unheard. As Radames prepares to meet his death, he notices another figure in the tomb with him. It is, of course, Aida. Finally united, the lovers sing their last duet. Amneris, in the temple above, prays and sings to the gods to forgive Radames and to give her peace of mind.

☐   *Aida* by Verdi. (excerpts)

"Opera is passion before everything."

Giuseppe Verdi, composer of *Aida*

When I asked her why she had never sung any of Wagner's roles, she looked at me with her beautiful eyes, and simply asked me, "Have I ever done you any harm?"

British throat specialist Sir Felix Simon, on the singer Adelina Patti

Hans Richter stopped the 'cellos in the passionate cantilena in the Prelude to <u>Tristan</u> with the words, "Gentlemen of the violoncellos, you play that like married men."

Description of an opera rehearsal for Wagner's *Tristan and Isolde*

"I know of no more admirable occupation than eating, that is, really eating. Eating, loving, singing, and digesting are, in truth, the four acts of the comic opera known as life . . ."

Gioacchino Rossini, Romantic opera composer

The Music Drama

"Gesamtkuntswerk," or total art, was Wagner's term for the synthesis of music, text, acting, and scenery into a new musical form. His idea was to raise the opera to a new level, and to combine and synthesize all of its elements into a total work of art. In doing so, Wagner called his operas "music dramas"—a term that is generally used in reference to the four operas that make up the *Ring Cycle*.

In his music dramas, Wagner made several important musical changes. As a way of organizing the music, he used a thematic device called a "leitmotif." These leitmotivs were themes that represented a person, place, feeling, etc. He also used another musical device called "unendlich melodie" (unending melody). This style of melodic composition did away with arias and recitatives in favor of a continuous flow of music and melody. Complete cadences and resolutions are delayed in favor of continuous action. As for the words, the Wagnerian musical style became a declamatory style with a clear and correct enunciation of the words. In the music dramas the words are as important as the music. This is the opposite of the Italian "bel canto" style.

Tristan and Isolde, the darker side of eroticism, is in a class by itself. It is full of torrid, erotic, and intoxicating music. The overwhelming concern of the music is Isolde's passion. This opera was the summation of all the virtues and sins of the entire Romantic age. Musically, it was the epitome of the "dissolution of tonality," as Wagner used an all-dissolving chromaticism. His approach to music carried romantic harmony to the extreme with its fantastic orchestral polyphony and obsession with instrumental color. Harmonically based on the chromatic scale, Wagner used the leitmotivs for structural unity.

Tristan and Isolde
Richard Wagner

An opera in three acts by Wagner, with a libretto in German by the composer.

Principal characters (cast):
A young sailor - tenor
Isolde - an Irish princess, soprano
Brangäne - her attendant, mezzo-soprano
Tristan - a Cornish knight, tenor
Kurwenal - his retainer, baritone
King Marke - ruler of Cornwall, bass
Melot - a courtier, tenor

Time: legendary time of King Arthur
Place: Cornwall, Brittany, and the oceans
First performance: Royal Court Opera, Munich
10 June 1865

Libretto Synopsis

The opera is set in the legendary Celtic world of the early Middle Ages. The opera begins with a famous "Prelude"—one that can be heard in many concert halls around the world without its opera. It features the "liebestod" (love death) leitmotif that represents the fate of the star-crossed lovers. Wagner repeatedly draws upon this theme (leitmotif) and its fragments. This is one way of adding musical unity to the opera.

Death hangs over the first act. The setting for the act is Tristan's ship, which is carrying Isolde back to Cornwall to marry King Marke. The many significant events that have taken place before the opera are recounted by Isolde in her aria to Brangäne "Wie lachend sie mir Lieder singen" (As they laugh and sing their songs at me). Through her aria we discover that Isolde has the power to heal. Not knowing who he was, Isolde healed Tristan—the very man that defeated and killed her betrothed, Morold (an Irish knight). Isolde plans to poison Tristan. She manages to get him to drink a goblet of wine in a toast of reconciliation. The poison, however, was substituted for a love potion by Brangäne. The act ends with the two "hopelessly" in love.

Act II captures the scent of a glorious summer night. In a rapturous duet, Tristan and Isolde pour out their love for one another amidst the garden in King Marke's stronghold. As daybreak nears, the two lovers ignore Brangäne's warnings until it is too late. King Marke arrives and catches the lovers together. In the skirmish that follows, Tristan is mortally wounded by the treacherous Melot. The scene ends as Isolde throws herself on the body of her wounded lover.

In Act III the bleak seas and burning sun lead us into Tristan's inner suffering. He is delirious as he awaits a ship bearing Isolde. Tristan, alone without his lover, experiences great mental and physical pain. He longs for death to unite them both. Upon hearing that Isolde has arrived, Tristan deliriously tears off his bandages and then collapses. Isolde enters and holds Tristan in her arms. She sings of how she has come back to die with him. Then, almost in a trance, she sings her long farewell to Tristan and to life. As the liebestod (love death) reaches the climax, Isolde dies and falls on the lifeless body of Tristan.

☐   *Tristan and Isolde* by Wagner. (excerpts)

Carmen
Georges Bizet

An opera in four acts by Bizet, with a libretto in French by Henri Meilhac and Ludovic Halévy based on the novel by Prosper Mérimée.

Principal characters (cast):
Carmen - a gypsy, soprano
Don José - a corporal, tenor
Escamillo - a toreador, baritone
Micaela - a peasant girl, soprano
Zuniga - the lieutenant, bass
Morales - a sergeant
Frasquita - a gypsy, soprano
Mercedes - a gypsy, soprano

Time: about 1820
Place: Seville and nearby
First Performance: Opéra Comique, Paris
    3 March 1875

The audience was understandably puzzled by a tragic opera at the Opéra Comique, and a complex story at that (a love triangle is always complicated). There were also several major problems on opening night: the soprano (Marie Galli-Marié) lost her castanets and had to use a broken dish instead, the tenor sang uncontrollably flat, and the timpanist miscounted and went into a loud timpani roll in the middle of a soft, delicate aria. And on top of that, the Parisians were expecting a lavish ballet section in the opera and all they got were some gypsy girls dancing around in a tavern. (Also, in its original form, there was spoken dialogue between the arias and not recitatives.)

This opera has many great tunes in it including the "Habañera" and the "March of the Toreadors" — but it is also full of drama. In fact, it was probably too real and not acceptable by the Parisian audience (i.e., working-class girls smoking on stage).

But as with the "Habañera," it is the music that drives the drama. Today, it is unquestionably one of the world's great operas. (After having written more than ten opening arias for Ms. Galli-Marié, Bizet got so frustrated that he went to the library and pulled out a book on Spanish tunes. He borrowed the "Habañera" from the Spanish composer Sebastian Yradier. This was the one that Ms. Galli-Marié found acceptable.)

Libretto Synopsis

Act I opens up in Seville Square. A shy young country girl (Micaela) is looking for her fiancée — Don José. Not finding him there, she departs. Soon Don José enters the square. This is followed by the cigarette factory workers (girls) entering the square to go to work. As Carmen enters the square, she sings to a group of admirers the celebrated Habañera aria "L'amour est un oiseau rebelle" — Love is like a wild bird. This, in many ways, is a signal of things to come. (Eventually we witness the spell that Carmen has over Don José.)

Both Zuniga (soldier) and Escamillo (matador) have their eye on Carmen in Act II. But she, at least for the moment, is looking forward to seeing Don José. This is the scene that sets up the love triangle between Don José and Escamillo. And later, because of a conflict with Zuniga, Don José ends up becoming an outlaw and running off with Carmen and a band of smugglers. Although he chooses love over duty, Don José does so only when compelled to as a consequence of jealousy and uncontrollable temper. These are character flaws that will set off the final tragedy.

In the final act, Act III, Carmen has tired of Don José. Although Don José has tried to control her, Carmen is a free spirit. She warned men with her "Habañera" that her love is like a wild bird. Escamillo now has come looking for Carmen upon hearing that she is through with Don José. When he shows up at their camp, a confrontation between the two rivals begins. Carmen throws herself between the two men, saving Escamillo.

Later she turns the cards to see her future. Every time she does, the ace of spades keeps turning up — the death card. She sees death for herself and for Don José. She begins to believe that her fate is bound up with his. This musical "fate motive" will come back at the end of the opera. In the second scene from Act III, the love triangle is resolved as Carmen and Don José confront each other outside of the bullring as Escamillo fights the bull inside the ring. Notice the musical and visual parallels between what is going inside of the ring and outside.

☐   *Carmen* by Bizet. (excerpts)

Salome
Richard Strauss

An opera in one act by Strauss, based on the play by Oscar Wilde and adapted by the composer.

Principal characters (cast):
Salome - daughter of Herodias, soprano
King Herod - step-father of Salome, tenor

Jokanaan - John the Baptist, baritone
Herodias - wife of Herod, mezzo-soprano
Narraboth - guard, tenor

Time: c.30 AD.
Location: Judea
First performance: Dresden, Germany
   9 December 1906

Richard Strauss was a renowned composer of tone poems by the time he wrote his opera *Salome* (see Chapter 14). This is a work of not only orchestral brilliance but of seething sexuality and raw passion. Salome was banned for a time in both London and New York.

The characters become so engaged in a desperate struggle that, unrestrained by moral judgment, they destroy others as well as themselves. Consequently, they come across as somewhat less than human and unnatural. The music, in conveying this internal and external conflict, is often wild and brash. This creates the necessary tension and conflict (dissonance). The quality of the music is so overwhelming, and it carries the dramatic action so well, that the words become secondary to the music.

Full of harsh expressionism and approaching atonality, Strauss carried Wagner's ideals to the extreme. He may have even stepped over the edge a bit. Musically, Strauss uses the Wagnerian principles of continuous music and leitmotivs to represent both persons and actions. The wide leaps in melody, restless and conflicting rhythms (to convey various emotional states), and complex harmonies, were all ideas that influenced the composers who eventually abandoned tonality altogether (Schoenberg, Webern, Berg).

Kaiser Edward VII supposedly said, "I like this fellow Strauss, but *Salome* will do him much damage." The scandal (and of course success) of *Salome* allowed him to build a new villa in the resort town of Garmisch. So much for the Kaiser's prediction! After *Salome* and his other shocker *Elektra*, Strauss stepped way back to the 18th century with the opera *Der Rosenkavalier*—a deliberate throwback in both story and music.

Libretto Synopsis

Salome is fascinated by the prophet Jokanaan (St. John the Baptist), a prisoner of King Herod's. After seeing him, Salome becomes physically infatuated with him and decides that she must have him. Her opportunity comes when Herod, who is lusting after Salome, bids her to dance. She agrees to dance for him only if he promises to grant her one wish. This being done, Salome dances the famous "Dance of the Seven Veils." As her reward, she demands the head of Jokanaan.

Herod is shocked by this and offers her half of his kingdom. She, however, will not yield. She demands that he fulfill his promise. Herod finally agrees. As he watches Salome sing to, and eventually kiss, the head of Jokanaan, he is both fascinated and repulsed. As she becomes increasingly more sexual and graphic, Herod is finally overcome with revulsion. With her mother no longer in the scene, he orders her crushed to death by the shields of the on-looking guards.

▢   *Salome* by Strauss. (excerpts)

Nixon in China
John Adams

An opera in three acts by John Adams with a libretto in English by Alice Goodman.

Principal characters (cast):

Premier Chou En-lai - baritone

President Richard Nixon - baritone

Dr. Henry Kissinger - bass

Nancy T'ang - mezzo-soprano

Second secretary to Mao - alto

Third secretary to Mao - contralto

Chairman Mao Tse-tung - tenor

Mrs. Pat Nixon - lyric soprano

Chiang Ch'ing - coloratura soprano

Time: Monday, February 21, 1972   Place: Peking, China

First performance: Grand Opera, Houston, Texas - October 22, 1987

According to the composer, "The idea was that of the stage director Peter Sellars, whom I'd met - in New Hampshire, fittingly enough - in the summer of 1983. I was slow to realize the brilliance of his idea, however. By 1983 Nixon had become the stuff of bad, predictable comedy routines, and it was difficult to untangle my own personal animosity - he'd tried to send me to Vietnam - from the larger historical picture. But when the poet Alice Goodman agreed to write a verse libretto in couplets, the project suddenly took on a wonderfully complex guise, part epic, part satire, part a parody of political posturing, and part serious examination of historical, philosophical, and even gender issues. All of this centered on six extraordinary personalities: the Nixon's, Chairman Mao and Chiang Ch'ing, Chou En-lai, and Henry Kissinger. Was this not something, both in the sense of story and characterization, that only grand opera could treat?" It took another five years after Nixon's visit to China to reestablish formal diplomatic relations between the U.S. and China – an event that neither Chairman Mao nor Chou En-lai lived to see. This opera won a Grammy Award in 1988 for the "Best Classical Contemporary Composition."™

Libretto Synopsis

The composer, John Adams, has provided this information on his opera: Nixon's 1972 trip was in fact an epochal event, one whose magnitude is hard to imagine from our present perspective, and it was perfect for Peter Sellars' dramatic imagination. *Nixon in China* was for the sure the first opera ever to use a staged "media event" as the basis for its dramatic structure. Both Nixon and Mao were adept manipulators of public opinion, and the second scene of Act I, the famous meeting between Mao and Nixon, brings these two complex figures together face to face in a dialogue that oscillates between philosophical sparring and political one-upsmanship.

In Act II we see each in major female figure in their public role: Pat is the perfect diplomatic guest, being treated to a whirlwind tour of the city and 'loving every minute of it.' The shrill, corrosive Chiang Ch'ing interrupts the ballet to shout angry orders at the dancers and sing her credo of power and violence, 'I am the Wife of Mao Tse-tung.' But in the final act, the focus of both text and music is their vulnerability, their desperate desire to roll back time to when life was simpler and feelings less compromised. Indeed, all five of the principals are virtually paralyzed by their innermost thoughts during this act. In the loneliness and solitude of his or her own bed, no one can avoid the feeling of regret, of time irretrievably lost and opportunities missed. It falls to Chou En-lai, the only one with a modicum of self-knowledge, to ask the final question: 'How much of what we did was good?'

☐   *Nixon in China* by Adams. (excerpts)

"What is the so-called New Russian School but the cult of varied and pungent harmonies, of original orchestral combinations and every kind of purely external effect? Formerly there was composition, creation; now there is only research and contrivance."

P.I. Tchaikovsky, to his patroness Nadezhda von Meck

"You might think this strange, but I have never seen the ballet. The night of the première, I kept my eyes on the score. As you know, the public acted in a scandalous manner. The gendarmes arrived at last. . . Well, on hearing this near riot behind me I decided to keep the orchestra together at any cost, in case of a lull in the hubbub."

Pierre Monteux, the first conductor of Stravinsky's *Rite of Spring*, writing about the opening night "riot" at the ballet in Paris

"The most invigorating sound I heard was a restive neighbor winding his watch."

A music critic's description of the Stravinsky piece composed in memory of Claude Debussy

History of the Ballet

A ballet is a stage display whose principal artistic element is the dancing. It is a blending of the arts: dance, drama, set design, costume design, music, and choreography. As an art form dance started in Greece. A related form, the pantomime, started in the Greek theater at Rome. This featured an actor on stage that had his lines chanted by a singer.

During the Middle Ages and Renaissance, dancing was frowned upon by the church because of its corrupt associations with paganism, although many popular religious festivals and processions had dance in it. It also flourished in popular life and was accompanied by secular music.

The Renaissance was an age of "spectacles," especially at court and in the houses of the nobility. Hardly any festivity passed without a "masque," or display, in which dancing had an important place. Ballets came to form the interludes in operatic pieces or poetic plays. This impulse came from Italy, the home of the "comedy of masks" and many other types of drama. In 1489, for example, the marriage of the Duke of Milan to Isabella of Aragon was such a spectacle that it was a landmark in the history of the ballet. It was talked about all over Europe and set a fashion, particularly in France, where such interludes had been popular since the Middle Ages.

At the Court of Louis XIV the most talented dancers devoted themselves to the art of ballet, as it was in such royal favor. Moliére furnished comedy-ballets and Lully composed music for them. It was from the court that the ballet passed to the opera, to be developed by composers like Lully and Rameau.

At first the ballet in the public theaters lacked one important advantage—an advantage that it had enjoyed at court. The female dancers at court were of the highest rank and danced at the all the festivities. In the theaters there were no professional ballerinas—only male dancers wearing masks. Lully changed this as the 18th century became the age of the French ballet. This era saw a succession of great dancers, and almost every one left behind an important innovation (i.e., changes in costume, new steps, pirouette).

During the 19th century Romanticism, and later Realism, dominated the ballet. The transformation in sentiment, taste, and costume brought on by the French Revolution completed the reforms of the 18th century. Both the Republic and the Empire were based on the models of Classical antiquity. In particular, the Empire set the fashion of copying Grecian modes in architecture, furniture, and dress. This change in aesthetics allowed the dancers to move more gracefully. The grand age of ballet dancing was at hand. Its interpreter was Carlo Blasis whose *Code of Terpsichore*, published in London in 1828, was a manual of dancing and pantomime based entirely on the Classical ideal.

Some of the major developments of this era included flesh-colored tights and shorter skirts (not above the ankles) which spread out from the waist. What was more important was the introduction by Taglioni of "pointes" on the extreme tip of the toe. New ballet shoes were then developed for this style of dancing that gave the ballerina the illusion of floating. This appealed to the Romantic age with its passion for sylphs and disembodied spirits. It also lowered the status of the male dancer who could not achieve this effect because of the shape of the male instep.

Dance began to change from a Classical discipline into one of technical virtuosity. The flowing skirt of the Classical fashion was gradually cut away to a mere wisp (tutu) encircling the waist of the dancer. This was done so that the audience, like judges at a gymnastic competition, could appreciate the degree of exactness with which the steps were performed. Concurrently with this elaboration of technique there preceded a change in the character of ballets. This change reflected the transition in literature from the Romantic to the Realistic style of the early 20th century.

The Orchestral Suite

The music from ballet often became so popular that it existed independently of the dancing. Often referred to as "extract" or orchestral suites, these pieces featured the most popular music from the ballet in a setting for the symphony orchestra. Two of the most famous ballets, *The Nutcracker* and *The Firebird*, are also popular and well known in their concert settings as orchestral suites.

From *The Nutcracker* ballet, the March, Dance of the Sugar Plum Fairy, Russian Dance (Trepak), Arab Dance, Chinese Dance, Dance of the Toy Flutes, and the Waltz of the Flowers are the most popular musical moments. These pieces comprise the "orchestral suite" performed in concert halls without the ballet. For the *Firebird Suite*, Stravinsky extracted three main sections from the ballet. From Tableau (Act) I he used the Infernal dance of Kashchei and the Lullaby (Berceuse). In Tableau II, Stravinsky extracted the Finale or "Disparition" (Disappearance) section.

The Nutcracker

completed in 1892

Music by P.I. Tchaikovsky
Story by E. T. A. Hoffmann
Premiered in St. Petersburg
    17 December 1892

Tchaikovsky had a natural affinity for composing ballet music. Although his three ballets (*Swan Lake, The Nutcracker, Sleeping Beauty*) are considered important parts of the dance repertoire, during his time they were not very successful. Many of the dancers, for instance, complained of the difficulty of the rhythms. Shortly after he died, these three ballets entered the repertory of the Russian ballets.

Ballet Synopsis

The Nutcracker is a Classical ballet in two acts, with three scenes. It begins with an overture that is both delicate and bright. Act I takes place on Christmas Eve early in the 19th century. The story revolves around Clara, a young child, who falls asleep and has a vivid dream. In her dream she sees her Christmas tree grow to an enormous size. Then a swarm of mice arrive and try to capture her favorite Christmas present—a Nutcracker. Once the mouse king is killed, the Nutcracker magically transforms into a handsome, young Prince.

Act II takes place in the "land of sweets." This magical place is ruled by the Sugar Plum Fairy. An enchanted grotto changes into Clara's own theater where many of her favorite dolls have come to life. They all dance for her and the Nutcracker—now her handsome prince. As her dream ends, Clara is awoken by her parents. At the end of the ballet she remains immersed in the memory of her adventures.

Some of the most memorable music and dances come from Act II as the various dolls come to life. These pieces include a March, the Dance of the Sugar Plum Fairy, Russian Dance (Trepak), Arab Dance, Chinese Dance, Dance of the Toy Flutes, and the Waltz of the Flowers.

☐   *The Nutcracker* by Tchaikovsky. (excerpts from Act II)

The Russian Revival

Starting in 1735, Peter the Great introduced many aspects of European culture into Russia. One of the results of this introduction was a passion for Western dancing. The old school was replaced with a new style. The foundation of this new Russian school is dated from the alliance between Sergei Diaghilev and the dancer Mikhail Fokine. This resulted in the formation of a company that gave its first season at Paris in 1909, and acquired in western Europe the infamous title of "The Russian Ballet."

Igor Stravinsky, Alexandre Benois, and Mikhail Fokine were brought together and combined their efforts under the watchful eye of Sergei Diaghilev. Diaghilev was the impresario of the Russian Ballet and a man of artistic genius. The Russian Ballet seasons in Paris before World War I are the most well known and celebrated in the history of ballet. Diaghilev commissioned composers like Igor Stravinsky and Manuel da Falla. He adapted existing music like Schumann's *Carnival* and pieces by Chopin and Rossini. His employment of artists like Benois, Bakst, and Picasso resulted in the creation of scenery and costumes that set a new artistic standard in ballet.

Ballet is a combination of the arts of music, drama, and painting. One of the elements that give value to a picture, and that differentiates a great painting from an average one, is the successful representation of movement. The great choreographer Fokine blended these elements and, in doing so, elevated them all.

The Firebird

completed in 1910

Music by Igor Stravinsky
Scenario by Mikhail Fokine
Premiered in Paris
25 June 1910

Sergei Diaghilev and the Russian Ballet had an enormously successful debut in Paris in 1909. Diaghilev conferred with his chief choreographer, Mikhail Fokine, and they agreed that the 1910 season would include a ballet on a Russian folk subject. After reading some Russian folk tales, Fokine decided that the legend of the Firebird would be adapted for the ballet. Diaghilev and Fokine commissioned Stravinsky to write the music for the ballet, after having heard a concert by this relatively unknown composer.

While the music was in the tradition of Stravinsky's teacher, Rimsky-Korsakov, the *Firebird* was also bold, original, and extremely colorful. In trying to musically distinguish the real characters (Ivan and the Princess) from the magical ones (Firebird and Kashchei), Stravinsky borrowed an idea from his teacher. For the real or "natural" characters, Stravinsky composed diatonic music—major and minor scales. The supernatural characters were given chromatic music.

Ballet Synopsis

The story begins when Prince Ivan, in pursuit of the Firebird, enters the magic garden of the green-taloned demon Kashchei. After catching the bird, Ivan releases her and is rewarded with a fiery feather that will allow him to call upon the Firebird whenever he gets into trouble. Ivan then falls in love with one of the princesses who are under the spell of Kashchei. He breaks open the gates to follow her into the demon's castle. After a wild dance by Kashchei's guardian monsters, Ivan is captured. As Kashchei prepares to turn him into stone, Ivan suddenly remembers the Firebird and waves the magic feather. The Firebird appears and causes the demon and his monsters to dance until they collapse from exhaustion. Then she guides Ivan to a casket that holds the soul of the evil Kashchei in the form of a giant egg. After Ivan smashes it, the demon's captives are released from enchantment. At the end of the ballet the prince and princess are united.

Musically, the colorful orchestration and the rhythmic drive of the "Infernal Dance" foreshadow the primitivism of Stravinsky's 1913 ballet the *Rite of Spring*. In between these two works is yet another masterpiece of ballet and music from 1911, entitled *Petrushka*. While *Petrushka* is virtually a suite of dances with an explosive finale, the *Rite of Spring* is an exploration of rhythm. Stravinsky was the first composer for whom rhythm was as exciting as melody. In both of these ballets Stravinsky used his imagination to explore rhythm and, in doing so, created a revolution in musical composition.

Stravinsky returned to *The Firebird* ballet three times later in life. In 1911, 1919, and 1945 he extracted three different orchestral suites from the full ballet version. These suites are performed more frequently than the ballet. Today, *The Firebird Suite* remains his most popular piece.

☐   *The Firebird Suite* by Stravinsky. (excerpts)

The Ballet Music of Aaron Copland

One of the most important American composers of ballet was Aaron Copland. In the 1930's-40's Copland wrote three ballet scores, all of which were enormously successful and popular. *Billy the Kid* (1938) drew upon the American folk legend of William H. Bonney. Not only was Bonney a western killer and desperado, but he was loved and admired as much as he was feared. The ballet tried to capture this larger than life legend in a way that shows us many aspects of his heroic myth.

The second of his ballets was *Rodeo* (1942), which was subtitled "The Courting at Burnt Ranch." The original choreography and book were by the legendary Agnes de Mille. This love story of the American Southwest centers around an American cowgirl who tries to get herself a man (a ranch cowboy). This was followed by *Appalachian Spring* (1944). This ballet was commissioned by the modern dance pioneer Martha Graham. The story is about a young couple and how their love for one another holds them together during their first year of marriage.

Copland's music embodied a rough and ready spirit and the upbeat optimism of America before World War II. His music was confident, assertive, sentimental, and sometimes nostalgic. His greatest contribution was his ability to convey a wide range of emotion and to write music that was easily recognized as American.

Both *Rodeo* and *Billy the Kid* were "westerns" in their use of actual cowboy songs and ballads. This use of borrowed melodies adds to the unmistakably American character of Copland's musical style. Since Copland had not written this kind of music before *Billy the Kid*, he modeled his music on Virgil Thomson. In his two documentary films, *The Plow that Broke the Plains* and *The River*, Thomson used cowboy songs, traditional southern spirituals, and old popular tunes.

Copland borrowed from other American sources, including music of the church and minstrel shows. The tunes may have been presented "straight" once or twice, and then were reused with significant musical changes to them. New musical phrases were often formed so that the flow of the music was never determined by the original tune. It was in this way that Copland's music differed from Thomson's.

☐   *Aaron Copland - A Self-Portrait*.

Rodeo

completed in 1942

Music by Aaron Copland
Scenario by Agnes de Mille
Premiered in New York
   16 October 1942

On October 16 of 1942, the first performance of *Rodeo* was an unqualified success. It was a gala event at the sold-out Metropolitan Opera House in New York. Many performances since then have established *Rodeo* as a classic of the indigenous American dance repertory. In 1945, the composer arranged the ballet score as a symphonic suite, and it thereupon entered with equal security into the indigenous American concert repertory.

Ballet Synopsis

In his ballet *Rodeo*, Copland is much closer to writing a musical comedy. It bears the subtitle "Courtship at Burnt Ranch." The story centers around a cowgirl who tries to show assembled cowboys she can match them. She has a crush on head wrangler and wants to impress him, but she is thrown from a bronco and embarrassed. She is then teased by the city girls who have come to watch the weekly rodeo.

   At the dance that evening she is out of place in her ranch clothes. She then leaves the dance, gets all dressed up and returns. Now, the head wrangler wants to dance with her, but she turns him down in favor of the one cowhand who was friendly to her all along. She then dances with this friendly cowhand.

   The music of *Rodeo* is divided into four sections: Buckaroo Holiday, Corral Nocturne, Saturday Night Waltz, and the Hoe-down. This last section, the Hoe-down, makes use of an old fiddle tune known as a breakdown.

☐   *Rodeo: Four Dance Episodes* by Copland. (Hoe-down)

"I felt really sorry for the poor horns and trumpets. They blew until they were blue in the face."

Richard Strauss to his father, after a rehearsal of his tone poem *Don Juan*

"Gentlemen, I would ask those of you who are married to play this as though you were engaged!"

Richard Strauss, during an orchestra rehearsal of *Don Juan*

"The first one to bring this filthy score into my class, the first to make these errors of harmony, I will - - him to the door of my class and - - him to the gate of the Conservatory."

A teacher at the Paris Conservatory of Music in reference to Debussy's opera *Pelléas et Mélisande*

"It would be tedious for you to learn the causes of the moral sickness from which I am by no means cured as yet. My existence up to now has been a strange, romantic tissue of adventures and distressing emotions."

Hector Berlioz, in an 1832 letter to Gasparo Spontini

Program Music

One of the revolutions of the Romantic era was the development of program music. This is narrative or descriptive music. The term "program" refers to any music attempting to represent non-musical ideas without using words. As composers tried to develop new forms that the public would understand, they turned away from the symphony and towards a new type of descriptive music. For the orchestra, composers wrote program symphonies, symphonic poems, and tone poems. All three of these are essentially large scale dramatic works for an orchestra. The basis for the musical composition often was derived from the field of literature and was influenced by the plays of Shakespeare. The title of this chapter, "To sleep, perchance to dream," comes from Hamlet, Act 3.

The term program music was first used by Franz Liszt, who also originated the idea of a symphonic poem. Liszt defined program music as "a preface added to a piece of instrumental music, by means of which a composer intends to guard the listener against a wrong poetical interpretation, and to direct his attention to the poetical idea . . ." This program was designed to put the listener in the same frame of mind as the composer so that the objects being described could be understood. The term should only be used when describing instrumental music that has a narrative or descriptive meaning.

In program music, the composer depicts objects and events. The musical form is derived from following the story line (dramatic form). The development of the music is related to the poetic idea, as musical ideas are secondary to the action of the story.

Franz Liszt was aware that he did not invent the idea, only the term. The Baroque composer Vivaldi, Classical composer Beethoven, and the Romantics Berlioz and von Weber all wrote programmatic music. With Liszt, however, the symphonic poem replaced the symphony. This new genre, beginning in 1854, was adopted by many Romantic composers. His twelve symphonic poems are based on plays, myths, poems, pictures, or ideas. As enthusiasm for literature grew during the second half of the 19th century, other composers experimented with literary-based music. It was Richard Strauss that changed the name of the genre from symphonic poem to "tone poem."

The adjective "symphonic" came to mean a work of a serious nature for a large orchestra with a development and transformation of themes. These works took on the importance and scale of the symphony while avoiding its basic structure.

It was Hector Berlioz who took the biggest step towards true program music. He introduced the distinction between subject and object in his composition *Harold in Italy*. In his *Symphonie Fantastique* (1830), Berlioz introduced the revolutionary concept of an "ideé fixe" (fixed idea) at the outset of this program symphony. This melodic representation of the main character, his beloved, was to undergo changes throughout the work. To convey to the audience what was happening dramatically, the changes in the story are paralleled by changes in the musical theme(s).

Literature and the tone poem (program symphony) provided the organizational basis for many of the works of Czech and Russian nationalism. Additionally, the symphonies of Mahler and French orchestral music were affected by literature. Famous works in this style include Mussorgsky's *Pictures at an Exhibition* (orchestrated by Maurice Ravel), Smetana's *Má Vlast*, and Dvorák's *Slavonic Dances*. While these ideas led to Impressionism, this form of music cannot be regarded as program music. Impressionism is considered to be music of an expressive atmosphere rather than a descriptive nature. Knowledge of the subject is not essential for understanding the music of these composers. A good example of this is Claude Debussy's *Prelude to the Afternoon of a Faun*, composed in 1894.

This genre survived as a major musical force well into the 20th century. Many composers turned to this genre as a way of continuing the innovations of Romanticism. For example, Gustav Holst's programmatic composition *The Planets* musically describes each planet according to a program that he provided.

Hector Berlioz

Berlioz created the modern symphony orchestra. He gave real meaning to the term "tone color" through his experimentation with instrumental combinations.

Literature, the theater, and the music of Beethoven also had profound influences on Berlioz. He was the first composer to really make a break with the harmonic rules of the past as his music becomes the music of the future. Berlioz was also a critic and writer whose music was studied by Liszt, Wagner, and all of the later Romantic composers. He was a revolutionary musician who was uninhibited, highly emotional, self-expressive, and often bizarre.

The invention of the program symphony was also an accomplishment of his. The five movement *Symphonie Fantastique* is an autobiographical piece of music - yet another first in music history. It is based on his feelings and emotions, as well as several significant events from his life.

Symphonie Fantastique, Op. 14a
    completed in 1830

I.   Reveries, Passions
II. A Ball
III. Scene in the Country
IV. March to the Scaffold
V.   Dream of a Witches' Sabbath

Symphonie Fantastique by Berlioz. (V. Dream of a Witches' Sabbath)

Modest Mussorgsky

Mussorgsky was the only member of the Russian nationalists (Russian five) who did not visit the West. In fact, he never even left Russia spending almost his entire life in St. Petersburg. As a composer, he was the most original of "the five" who did not believe in art for art's sake. In his music, he avoided writing "development" sections as he tried to directly address the listener.

Although he was a member of the Russian five, he was not a professional composer but an office worker for the government. One of his most famous and original pieces was composed in 1874, *Pictures at an Exhibition*.

Although this piece was originally written for the piano, the most well known version is the one that was orchestrated by Maurice Ravel in 1922. This piece was written as a homage to Victor Hartmann - a Russian architect, painter, and a friend of Mussorgsky.

When Hartmann died at the age of thirty-nine, Mussorgsky set out to compose a memorial piece for Hartmann. In its original form, it is a piano suite in ten movements - each of which represented one of Hartmann's works. The piece is linked by the "promenade" theme which depicts the composer moving from one picture to the next.

We will listen to the following four sections: *Promenade* - this is a portrait of Mussorgsky and his impressions while walking in a gallery showing the Hartmann exhibit. This theme will link many of the other pictures. *The*

Old Castle - this painting is a watercolor of a troubadour singing in front of a vast medieval Italian castle. Notice the use of the alto saxophone — this was Ravel's choice for the theme. *Hut of Baba Yaga* - the home of the witch Baba Yaga in Russian fairy tales. She lives in a hut mounted on the legs of a giant chicken. Hartmann designed a clock face that represents Baba Yaga's ride on a broomstick. *The Great Gate of Kiev* - Hartmann's architectural design for a structure to commemorate the day Alexander II escaped assassination in Kiev. The gate, which was never built, is pictured with a giant helmet on top.

☐　　*Pictures at an Exhibition* by Mussorgsky/Ravel.
　　　(Promenade, Old Castle, Tuileries, Hut of Baba Yaga, Great Gate of Kiev)

P.I. Tchaikovsky

The original performance of the *1812 Overture* took place outdoors at the Cathedral of the Redeemer in Kremlin Square. This was the same setting for the "Coronation Scene" from *Boris Godunov.* At the premier, rifle and cannon fire from the Czarist troops were added to the ringing of the huge cathedral bells.

Overture 1812

completed in 1882

Tchaikovsky used Russian folk songs in this work. The Russian "Czar's Hymn," as well as the French National Anthem, "La Marseillaise," are in this piece. The overture opens with a Russian hymn "God Preserve Thy People." In an agitated section that follows, Napoleon's troops advance toward Moscow. The horns introduce a slow march as the Russians prepare for battle. The armies clash and fall back to the French "La Marseillaise."

A Russian lullaby and folk song are heard during the next section where the troops are freezing in the bitter winter's evening. The next morning, the French advance and, after another day of war, the armies retreat. Again, the Russian folk song and lullaby are heard. Then a new battle begins—this furious battle scene features the use of cannons and rifles with the themes of the French and Russian armies. When the opening music from the Czar's Hymn returns, this indicates that the Russians have won the battle. The piece ends in triumph to the sound of bells, cannon and rifle fire (celebrating the victory), and the "Czar's Hymn."

☐　　*Overture 1812* by Tchaikovsky.

Richard Strauss

Don Juan was the legendary seducer of women. His "crimes" were two-fold. First he mocked the conventions of man by taking any woman for his pleasure. Second, he taunted God by ridiculing a dead man, and then inviting his statue to dinner. The tale was first written and set in a full dramatic form in 1630. Later, the legend changed so that Don Juan was to become something of a hero who rose above the pettiness of society. The opera *Don Giovanni* was a dramatic opera in two acts by Wolfgang Amadeus Mozart. The libretto was written by Lorenzo da Ponte and is based on this Don Juan legend. It was premiered in Prague on 29 October 1787.

Richard Strauss used the Don Juan legend as the basis for his third tone poem. It was his first work of great daring and genius. In it, Strauss does not tell the legendary story, but rather seeks to evoke the youthful and passionate nature of Don Juan. It was more of a psychological study than a representational piece. The subject of Don Juan came not from Lorenzo da Ponte or from Mozart's opera *Don Giovanni*, but from Nikolaus Lenau's unfinished drama of 1851 entitled *Don Juan.*

129

Don Juan, Op. 20

completed in 1888

Strauss was twenty-four years old when he composed Don Juan, a symphonic poem (tone poem) with four thematic groups. The work is cast in a rondo-like structure. The main theme is the hero (horns), and the alternating sections represent his female conquests. The opening of the piece represents "youth's fiery pulses" racing off in search of the first conquest. Theme number two is stormy and beautiful, while the third theme (oboe solo) is tranquil and represents Don Juan having to work at seducing this third woman. After his amorous conquests, the four horns announce a new heroic musical theme that Strauss called "Don Juan triumphant."

Following this is a "Masked Ball" at the end of which his morale has reached rock-bottom. The ghosts of his three former mistresses dance across his consciousness. In despair, he wanders through a graveyard and mockingly invites the statue of a distinguished nobleman he has killed to dine with him. While the statue does not come to dinner, the nobleman's son Don Pedro does. As they duel, Don Juan, with Pedro entirely at his mercy, realizes that another victory is worthless. So Don Juan gives up and allows himself to be run through by his revenge-seeking opponent. At the end, when the horn theme returns one last time, the strings begin a thunderous descent suggesting that the end is near for our hero. A replaying of the various female themes precedes a broken-up pianissimo chord that symbolizes the approach of death. This then leads to the silence at the end of the work and the death of Don Juan.

Three quotations from the drama can be found in Strauss's score and obviously provided much of the inspiration for his musical descriptions. The first is a statement of Don Juan's philosophy, "Would that I could fly through every place where beauty blossoms . . . and, were it but for a moment, conquer." The second is his reply to his brother's warnings about his life, "I keep myself fresh in the service of beauty . . . the breath of a woman that is as the odor of spring today may perhaps tomorrow oppress me like the air of a dungeon . . . then, to triumphs ever new, so long as youth's fiery pulses race!" The third quotation is of Don Juan awaiting his fate, "It was a beautiful storm that urged me on; it has spent its passion, and silence now remains . . ."

▢   *Don Juan* by Strauss.

Impressionism

A landmark piece in the style of French Impression was *La Mer* by Claude Debussy. This piece was about Debussy's "impression" of the sea, and not just facts and figures about it. It is full of color, movement, and suggestion, and is not a realistic description of the sea. The French believed that you could make a deeper effect by suggestion than by the German procedure of realistic description. Impressionism was a type of program music that was very atmospheric and general in nature. Musically, Impressionism is distinguished by vague and hazy (colorful) harmonies with a wisp of a melody. Another name for this is "melodic suggestion."

The sounds of Impressionism, as compared to the sounds of Bach, Beethoven, or Brahms, were new and considered unusual by the audiences of the late 1800's. To create this different sounding music, Debussy invented new harmonies, evocative melodies, and avoided a marked rhythmic drive. In terms of harmony and melody, Debussy created the whole-tone scale. This scale weakened the home-base concept of tonality.

In his piano piece "Voiles" (Sails), Debussy used the whole-tone scale in the opening melody. The picture he painted was one of dreamy, graceful sailboats in the afternoon sun off in the distance. The piece comes from his *Préludes*, Book I, of 1910. This is a *character piece* – a descriptive piece for solo piano.

☐   *Préludes*, Book I, "Voiles" by Debussy.

Debussy also turned to pentatonic scales that he had first heard at the International Exhibition in Paris (1889-90). He was greatly influenced by the performances of the Javanese gamelan orchestras from Indonesia. Also from his *Préludes*, Book I, is this piano piece entitled "La fille aux cheveux de lin," or "The girl with the flaxen hair." It features the use of pentatonic scales.

☐   *Préludes*, Book I, "La fille aux cheveux de lin" by Debussy.

In attempting to reject the Austro-Germanic dominance in music, Debussy (and Ravel) set out to create a French national school of composition. As the painters living in Paris were attracted to exotic places (Rousseau, Gauguin), Debussy was musically attracted to exotic colors from far away places– especially Spain, Greece, the United States (jazz), and Asia.

In 1903, Debussy published a set of piano works entitled *Estampes*. In "Pagodes," he evokes sounds of exotic Asia through his use of: a variety of bell-like imitations that create a shimmering surface quality, pentatonic scales, combinations of different crossing rhythms, and exotic piano washes all of which are suspended over a long pedal point.

There is also a "Western" aspect to this music since he uses an evolved type of sonata-allegro form. By the early 20th century, sonata-allegro form had become virtually free from all the structural rules that were initiated by Haydn, Mozart, and Beethoven. This piece establishes a feeling of timelessness and is very sonorous.

☐   "Pagodes," from *Estampes* by Debussy.

The Nocturnes

In 1894, Debussy wrote in a letter to a Belgian violinist: "I am working on three nocturnes for violin and orchestra that are intended for you . . . an experiment in the different combinations that can be achieved with one color - what a study in gray would be in painting."

When he finished the work in 1899, no solo violin part was found. It ended up being a piece just for the orchestra, and in three parts - Nuages (clouds), Fêtes (festivals), and Sirènes (the Sirens from Greek mythology).

Here is the program for each of the three movements as written by Claude Debussy:

I. Nuages - Clouds renders the immutable aspect of the sky, and the slow, solemn motion of the clouds. The clouds fade away in gray tones lightly tinged with white.

II. Fêtes - Festivals gives us the vibrating, dancing rhythm of the atmosphere with sudden flashes of light. There is also the episode of the procession (a dazzling fantastic vision), which passes through the festive scene and becomes merged in it. The festival continues throughout the day. Off in the distance the procession can be heard (muted trumpets). It will get closer and closer until it merges with the festive scene, and then disappears into the distance. The disappearance is again represented by the muted trumpets.

III. Sirènes - depicts the sea and its countless rhythms, and presently, amongst the waves silvered by the moonlight, is heard the mysterious song of the Sirènes as they laugh and their song passes on. (For this movement, Debussy uses a choir with the orchestra, but not the whole choir - just the women. They do not sing any words, they are a "wordless" chorus that does not appear on the stage in a performance. The undulating rhythms and dynamics are used to portray the ocean and create a sense of forward motion.)

The *Nocturnes* display three typical influences on Debussy: Russian music, the imagery of poetry, and Impressionism in painting. In fact, the title of the work derives from the "Nocturnes" of James Whistler, whose paintings the composer knew and loved. Debussy's *Nocturnes*, like Whistler's paintings, are about psychological states. Thus, despite the descriptive titles and program notes, *Nocturnes* is not really program music. Vague harmonies, wisps of melody, sensitive colors, ethereal sonorities – these qualities are the essence of Debussy's impressionism, and nowhere are have they been beautifully given shape than in his *Nocturnes*.

Nocturnes

completed in 1899

I.   Nuages
II. Fêtes
III. Sirènes

 *Nocturnes* by Debussy. (III. Sirènes)

Recent Works

The Odyssey by the Greek poet Homer was the inspiration for the 4-part extended art song *Odusseia*. The *Prologue* opens with a passage on the wooden flute, representing the voice of Homer, as 3 scenes from the "tale of the man of twists and turns" unfold. *Fire and Sea* is a musical depiction of the storm that was sent to punish the Greeks on their voyage home. *Call of the Sirens* describes the women on the rocks that enchanted the sailors with their songs. *Sirens of Ulysses* (Ulysses by James Joyce) is set at the Ormond Hotel (Dublin) as people eat, drink, and listen to an Irish musical *session*. Baritone Anthony Moreno commissioned this for his 2013 Senior Recital (*Cole Conservatory*) with Kenner Bailey accompanying. It was orchestrated in 2014 for the *LA SuperNova Ensemble*.

Odusseia

1. Prologue – The Oracle, The Muse
2. Fire and Sea
3. Call of the Sirens
4. Sirens of Ulysses (or Dublin)

The Cask of Amontillado (Edgar Allan Poe, 1846) is a story of 2 men. Montresor, insulted by Fortunato, has planned revenge involving a cask of rare Amontillado wine deep in the vaults of his palazzo. When they finally reach the crypt, however, it is empty and Fortunato is chained to the wall and left to die! The composer adapted the original story for Anthony Moreno (2015 Masters Recital, *USC Thornton School of Music*) and scored it in one continuous movement for baritone (Montresor), tenor (Fortunato), the *LA SuperNova Ensemble*, and Kenner Bailey (piano).

 *Odusseia, The Cask of Amontillado* both by William E. Doyle (excerpts).

"A father who had decided to send his sons out into the world at large thought it his duty to entrust them to the protection and guidance of a man who was very famous at the time and who, furthermore, happened to be his best friend. Similarly, I send my six sons to you . . . Please receive them with kindness and be to them a father, guide and friend."

W.A. Mozart, the dedication attached to his six "Haydn" string quartets for F.J. Haydn

"I tell you before God, and as an honest man, that your son is the greatest composer whom I know either personally or by reputation. He has the taste and, what is more, the greatest knowledge of the technique of composition."

F.J. Haydn, to Leopold Mozart after hearing W.A. Mozart's "Haydn" quartets in 1785

"Yes, my friend, you were right; works like yours ought not to be meddled with; other people's alterations only spoil them. You are a true poet."

Franz Liszt, spoken to Frédéric Chopin

Music for Entertainment – The Suite

A suite is a collection of dance movements. The term first appeared in 1557 and originally referred to a set of dances known as "branles." By the late 17th century, the suite had become a prelude followed by a group of paired dances that were all in the same key. These instrumental pieces (movements) can be in any order and are meant to be performed in a single sitting.

In the Baroque era, a suite was an instrumental genre with several movements in the same key. Most of the forms originated as dance styles of music. The terms partita and overture were also used to indicate a suite. By the late 19th century, the term suite also came to mean a group of pieces extracted from a larger work, especially from a ballet or an opera. While the term was not in general use until the late 17th century, the pairing of dances had a long history.

Beginning in the year 1650, the French ballet and the music of Lully were very popular. From this popularity the practice of excerpting dances and airs from stage works, and presenting a collection of them as a suite, began. J.S. Bach's four *Orchestral Suites* (BWV 1066-69), and Handel's *Water Music* (c.1717) and *Music for the Royal Fireworks* (1749), are the most famous (Chapter 4). Most orchestral suites begin with an overture. This explains why the term overture may be found as the title of an entire suite. Dances were in no particular order, and the choice of dances in the suite depended upon what the popular dance styles were.

With the exception of the orchestral suites mentioned above, Handel's suite writing was limited to the keyboard. J.S. Bach wrote approximately forty-five suites. At the peak of his use of this genre are the *Cello Suites*, the *English Suites*, and the *French Suites*. (Bach did not name them English and French; these titles were added later.) His *Harpsichord Partitas* were perhaps the climax of his output of suites. Each of his suites did something unique for the medium that they were composed for.

Baroque Orchestral Suite

There are four orchestral suites composed by Bach. These suites were designed for public entertainment. They all begin with an overture that is composed of three separate parts in three different tempi—slow, fast, slow. The fast middle section is characterized by a polyphonic, fugal style. *Orchestral Suite No. 3*, in D major (BWV 1068), was written for a string ensemble, basso continuo, two oboes, three trumpets, and two timpani. This suite did not follow the typical Baroque suite formula of dances of Allemande, Courante, Sarabande, and Gigue. This one is written to include an Overture, an Air, two Gavottes, a Bourrée, and ends with a Gigue.

This orchestral suite was probably composed at the court of Cöthen for an outdoor celebration given by Prince Leopold around 1720. The prince was a great connoisseur and patron of music. He was also a competent violinist and a good bass singer.

There is also the possibility that this piece was first performed in connection with Bach's position at the Leipzig Collegium Musicum. Bach directed and composed for this group from 1729 until the 1740's. The cafe proprietor, Zimmermann, presented regular musical performances in his coffee house (winter) on Fridays and at his coffee gardens (summer) on Wednesdays. The performers at these concerts were university students. These concerts had become one of the most important musical traditions in the concert life of Germany. By the time Bach was directing the Collegium, the music performed was of various types—anything from light works and compositions for special occasions (trumpets and timpani), to various orchestral and chamber works.

Orchestral Suite No. 3 in D major, BWV 1068
  composed c.1720
I.   Overture

II.   Air
III. Gavotte
IV.   Bourrée
V.   Gigue

☐   *Orchestral Suite No. 3* by Bach. (II. Air, III. Gavotte)

The disappearance of the suite during the Classical and Romantic eras was a matter of several independent processes. Many of the functions of the suite were now fulfilled by the sonata, symphony, and concerto. In Vienna, for example, the divertimento functioned as a piece of light music, as did the suite. The divertimento, however, was not tied to the popular dance forms of the day. In the late 1800's, the "extract" suite became popular— *Carmen Suite*, *The Nutcracker Suite*, and later *The Firebird Suite*.

In the 20th century a re-emergence of the suite was intensified by the experimental interests of composers. An interest in older forms caused the suite to be in vogue with the composers Hindemith, R. Strauss, Stravinsky, Respighi, and others. There were also the characteristic suites that were nationalistic in content, and the "program suites" like *The Planets* by Gustav Holst and the *Grand Canyon Suite* by Ferde Grofé. However, these did not appeal to all the 20th century composers. The suite also served composers in many other ways and for many different reasons; from Arnold Schoenberg's *Five Orchestral Pieces* to Karlheinz Stockhausen's *Momenté*, the relationship of the parts of the suite to the whole is not tied to a reliance on dance forms.

The Serenade

In the late 18th century there was no clear distinction between popular and "Classical" music. Distinctions did not exist between music intended for indoor or outdoor entertainment, nor between chamber and orchestral music. For performances at social occasions, Mozart wrote pieces with such titles as serenade, cassation, and divertimento. The forms of each of these pieces are similar—they are a series of loosely related, light-hearted, often lengthy movements. Some of the movements are dances (minuets), some are marches, some are for solo instruments (similar to a concerto), and some are extended symphonic movements. These serenades were generally used to fill the gaps between festivities. Therefore, Mozart was not concerned with formal unity since the serenades were seldom played straight through from beginning to end.

Serenades were a favorite type of music in the 18th century, especially in Germany and Austria. In the time of Mozart, every member of the aristocracy employed an orchestra to play this music. They could be heard in parks, in the streets, and in the gardens of the wealthy. They accompanied many parties, dinners, weddings, and anniversary celebrations.

Usually an evening party began with a march. This was performed by those instruments that could play while walking into the party. At the end of the festivities, the musicians exited while playing a concluding march. During the evening, certain instruments would be featured (concerto) while the rest of the orchestra provided the accompaniment.

The "Posthorn" Serenade

The *Serenade No. 9* in D major, "Posthorn" was completed on 3 August 1779. Although nothing is known of its first performance, it was heard at an outdoor festival in Salzburg that summer. This particular Serenade has a series of seven movements. In the sixth movement Mozart calls for two unusual instruments for the time—

a piccolo and a posthorn. The posthorn, a predecessor of the modern day trumpet, is only found in this one composition by Mozart. He probably added these two instruments to surprise and to entertain his audience. In the second Menuetto (minuet) movement there are two trio sections—in the first trio section the piccolo is used, while the second trio features the posthorn.

Serenade No. 9 in D major
  composed in 1779

I.   Adagio maestoso, Allegro con spirito
II.   Menuetto: Allegretto, Trio, Allegretto
III. Concertante: Andante grazioso
IV.   Allegro ma non troppo
V.   Andantino
VI.   Menuetto, Trio I, Menuetto, Trio II, Menuetto
VII. Presto

◻   *Serenade No. 9* by Mozart. (VI. Menuetto, Trio I, Menuetto, Trio II, Menuetto)

The String Quartet

Chamber music was originally intended as music to be played in the king's chambers. This was intimate music best heard in a close setting, not in a large concert hall or public theater. It is one of the cornerstones of Classical music. As a genre, it includes everything from a sonata for a solo instrument to a large, multi-movement work for twelve to twenty players.

The most important early composers of string quartet music were Bach, Haydn, and Mozart. These composers were not content to write simple works that were just fun to listen to. Instead they applied their musical talents so that the music would be formally inventive and musically challenging to the performers and audiences alike.

It was Haydn who almost single-handedly established the string quartet as the most important type of chamber music. The string quartet consists of a first violin, a second violin, a viola, and a cello. The Italians were the first to explore this medium (remember Vivaldi?). In the late 1700's the emphasis shifted to Austria and to Haydn. Mozart later refined and improved upon Haydn's string quartet style in his six famous "essays" dedicated to his elder master and friend.

The "Dissonant" Quartet

The six string quartets which Mozart composed between December 1782 and January 1785 in Vienna were dedicated to Franz Joseph Haydn. They are in a fully mature style and reflect much of the wisdom of the elder master's quartets. From the beginning, these works were planned as an integrated group of quartets. *String Quartet No. 19*, KV. 465 is the last of the six quartets dedicated to Haydn. It is commonly referred to as the "Dissonant" quartet.

The first twenty-two measures of the opening Adagio are what gave this quartet its nickname. This material also serves as the basis for much of the harmonic and melodic tension for the remainder of the work. After such a dissonant opening, the Allegro section is full of energetic melodies in the first violin. To these melodies, the second violin and viola add a steady accompaniment. The intensity and dissonance of the opening introduction return during the development with jagged melodic lines and dissonant intervals being featured.

The second movement is nearly operatic in its duet between the first violin and cello. It provides a relief to the tension of the first movement. The Menuetto is in an energetic and bright C major tonality, with a trio section in the dark and somber key of C minor. The finale is again a tribute to Haydn with a virtuoso display of melodic invention and development.

String Quartet No. 19 in C major, KV 465
   premiered in 1785

I.   Adagio - Allegro
II. Andante cantabile
III. Menuetto - Trio
IV. Allegro

☐   *String Quartet No. 19* by Mozart. (I. Adagio - Allegro)

Programmatic Piano Music
Franz Liszt - Concert Etudes

Perhaps no other composer evoked as much controversy as Franz Liszt. That was because Liszt was so many things to so many people. He lived through practically the entire Romantic era (1811-86) and touched the lives of many artists, including Hector Berlioz, Frédéric Chopin, Victor Hugo, and Eugène Delacroix.

As a piano performer, Liszt was without peers. In style, he was flamboyant, poetic, emotional (often to the point of excess), self-indulgent, inventive, lyrical, and sometimes even demonic. His music was often described as a triumph of substance over form. As he was reported to have said "Le concert c'est moi," or "The concert is me." People went, and still go, to watch the pianist perform the music of Liszt.

The two *Concert Etudes* (concert studies) we will examine were written for pianists with the highest technical command. They were not intended for struggling students! During Franz Liszt's time, his contemporaries had the impression they were listening to four, or even six, hands involved in the playing of these works. Liszt's piano playing acquired the qualities of a truly symphonic instrument, something that amounted to a revolution in piano playing. His approach to the piano was very athletic and brought into play the arms, elbows, and even the entire body. Liszt considered the ideal sound to be that of a full orchestra metamorphosed into the piano. This accounts for his transcriptions of Beethoven symphonies and even a Mozart opera!

From the *Three Concert Etudes*, S. 144 of 1848, we will listen to No. 2 in F minor, "La Leggierezza" (lightness). This is an etude based on chromatic figures. It has been described as "a marvel of subtlety of light and shade."

In 1862-63 Liszt wrote his *Two Concert Etudes*, S. 145. The first one in D-flat major is known as "Waldesrauschen" (rustling woods). The English author Sitwell described this movement as "the wind in a pine wood . . . with the prospect of a knight in armor to ride by." The shimmering musical texture points the way to the revolutionary and Impressionistic piano works of Debussy and Ravel.

☐   "La Leggierezza" from *Three Concert Etudes*, S. 144, by Liszt.

☐   "Waldesrauschen" from *Two Concert Etudes*, S. 145, by Liszt.

Frédéric Chopin - Mazurka, Polonaise, and Nocturne

A visit to Vienna in 1830 was important in motivating Chopin to leave Warsaw, Poland. In Vienna, he was commended at two musical academies and praised for his "extreme delicacy of touch, his indescribable mechanical dexterity and consummate grasp of nuance that sprang from the deepest feeling."

When Poland fell to Russia in 1831, Chopin had already left for a tour of Vienna and Paris. Throughout the remainder of his short life, he was haunted by the thoughts of his suffering native people under Russian rule. Sometimes his music became an outlet for his emotions. This was typical of the Romantic era, and the polonaises and mazurkas were his most explicitly Polish works. Both of these are dance forms of his native country. His piano compositions are often known as piano miniatures, or character pieces. Unlike Liszt, his music was written essentially and intrinsically for the piano.

Some of Chopin's most intimate and nationalistic pieces were his mazurkas. In these works, Chopin took the elements of this Polish dance form and transferred its essence into a great work for his instrument, the piano. Musically, they are characterized by a triple meter, basic rhythmic feel, use of Lydian mode, and the drone of the bagpipes. Chopin wrote over fifty mazurkas, far more pieces than in any other genre.

Quite unlike the polonaise, the mazurka is a Polish dance of rustic character. However, the mazurkas of Chopin were not intended for dancing, but for listening in the salons of the aristocrats and nobility of Paris. The roots of the mazurka as a peasant dance can be found in the "stamping" rhythmic pattern—with the second beat of the triple meter often accented by rhythm, inflection, melody, or dissonance. Chopin typically grouped three or four mazurkas together in a published opus, and sometimes established subtle connections between the works.

☐   *Mazurka* in C-sharp minor, Op. 30, No. 4 by Chopin.

☐   *Mazurka* in F minor, Op. 7, No. 3 by Chopin.

The polonaises (literally, to process) capture the proud spirit of the Polish people. These piano works have a noble and aristocratic air to them. The *Polonaise* in A-flat major is composed of three sections, **A B A'**. The opening A section features chromatic scales. Then, in the right hand, the main theme enters with its uneven, Polish dance-like rhythms. The repeat of the theme is slightly decorated and there is an extensive use of rubato throughout. The B section suddenly modulates to a new key. The return to A' is shortened and concludes with a dramatic coda.

☐   *Polonaise* in A-flat major, Op. 53 by Chopin.

The original composer of the nocturne (night-piece) was John Field. Field was an Irishman who published a set of nocturnes in Paris during the years 1812-36. Built in the same manner as his Ballads, they are full of dramatic contrasts with aspects of ternary or sonata-allegro form fused as required to fit his purpose of drama and mood. No two pieces are quite the same and therefore the exact form is never repeated.

At a time when rapid changes in fashions and trends reflected the social and political changes of the age, the nocturne held all of Paris in rapture. Exploiting the Romantics' obsession with night, in the hands of Chopin it grew to include the vocal elements of Italian opera—trills, arpeggios, ornamental turns, flourishes, and other spectacular effects. The nocturne became a piece at the salons through which the Romantic composers could express their emotions and feelings. The nocturnes of Chopin span almost the entire length of his mature musical career, from the years 1827-46.

The *Nocturne* in C-sharp minor Op. 27, No. 1, is one of his greatest and certainly most complex nocturnes. It was a powerful and personal outcry from this deeply sensitive Romantic composer. The beginning, with its intense clash of tonalities, sets the mood for the work. This nocturne is not just a dreamy, moonlit piece of night music. The middle section features a rumbling bass line and a huge crescendo into chordal sonorities that are fiercely passionate. A return to the opening A section completes this ternary **A B A** form.

☐   *Nocturne* in C-sharp minor, Op. 27, No. 1 by Chopin.

Maurice Ravel - Alborada del gracioso

Shortly after Maurice Ravel was born in 1875, his family moved from a Basque village near the Spanish border to the Montmartre district of Paris, France. It was here that the painters Cézanne, Monet, Renoir, and Pissaro all had their studios. It also was in this fertile environment that Ravel began to study music. He eventually entered the Paris Conservatory at age fourteen.

Alborada del gracioso, composed in 1905, is one of the five piano pieces from his work entitled *Miroirs* (Mirrors). Each of the pieces in *Miroirs* is dedicated to a member of the "Apaches," a group of avant-garde poets, painters, and musicians. The name Apache is a French slang word for "rowdy young men." This piece was dedicated to M.D. Calvocoressi—a newspaper critic and a member of the Apaches. The pianist Ricardo Viñes, another Apache, gave the first performance of this work in 1906.

The title can be translated as "Morning Serenade of the Jester." A "gracioso" is a jester in Spanish comedy, analogous to the fool in Shakespeare's plays. This jester assisted musicians in performing an "alborada," a serenade by a lover to his sleeping sweetheart. With its passionate rhythms, Spanish guitar effects, repeated notes, and glissandi, the work is a demonstration of Ravel's harmonic evolution. It was also an experiment in writing music that would sound improvised. Ravel orchestrated this work for a symphony in 1918. Today it is popular in both its original piano version and as an orchestral transcription.

☐   *Alborada del gracioso* by Ravel.

Isaac Albéniz and Music for the Guitar

A genuinely Spanish instrument, the guitar was slow to establish itself in northern Europe. In Spain, a gentleman playing the guitar was considered the epitome of a nobleman. Musical compositions for the guitar draw from over four centuries of music and musical composition, although many of them are arrangements of works for other instruments—especially Spanish piano music.

The composer Isaac Albéniz (1860-1909) was born in northern Spain but developed a keen interest in the music of the southern region of Spain—Andalucía. Albéniz, who was also a talented pianist, was considered the founder of the modern Spanish school of composers after having studied in Belgium and Germany. A child prodigy on the piano, Albéniz turned to composition which, with the exception of several operas, was almost entirely for the piano. He often used popular dance rhythms in his works and was very gifted at capturing the feeling of a particular dance or location.

Because the sound of the guitar often seems to appear in his piano music, many of these pieces have been transcribed for guitar, including his famous *Sevilla* and *Asturias*. These works are two of the eight descriptive pieces from Albéniz's piano suite, *Suite Española*, Op. 47.

Sevilla is based on the "Sevillanas" dance. The middle section of the dance is particularly evocative of the Moorish history of Sevilla's past. *Asturia* is another of Albéniz's impressionistic pieces. This piece is descriptive of a region on the northern coast of Spain. Sometimes this piece is known as *Leyenda* (legend).

□   *Sevilla* and *Asturia* by Albéniz.

Johann Strauss, II and the Waltz

The waltz is a dance form in a triple meter that probably came from the German dance "Ländler." In the last part of the 18th century, the waltz became popular with composers and in the ballrooms of Vienna. Beethoven, Schubert, Chopin, Berlioz, Tchaikovsky, Ravel, Richard Strauss, and Johann Strauss Jr. all used this form to some extent.

The Blue Danube Waltz, (*An der schönen blauen Donau*, Op. 314), embodied the essence of the waltz in form and spirit—from its softly mysterious beginning to its majestically flowing melody. As with many works that are well known and admired today, it was not a success when it was premiered in Vienna in 1867. Originally written for a band with a men's chorus singing a patriotic text, Strauss composed the piece to help raise the spirits of Austria after their defeat by Prussia in 1866. It was a musical depiction of the Danube river as it gracefully flowed through Vienna, Austria.

When Johann Strauss II rewrote the piece and performed it at the Paris Exposition of 1867, it became extremely popular in Europe and throughout the world. Edward, the Prince of Wales, became so obsessed with it that he invited Strauss to come to London to perform. Strauss accepted and gave six highly acclaimed concerts at Covent Garden. The waltz became so popular that his publisher in Vienna could not keep up with the demand for the sheet music. During the first printing of the waltz, over 100,000 copies were sold! When Johannes Brahms autographed the fan of a young lady with a few bars from the *Blue Danube Waltz*, he wrote next to the music "Not by Johannes Brahms . . . unfortunately." In 1872, Strauss received $100,000. to conduct the waltz fourteen times on a tour of the United States.

Johann II, also known as the Younger (of no relation to Richard Strauss), credited Vienna for his success and unique musical genius. He wrote, "If it is true that I have talent, I owe it above everything else to my beloved city of Vienna . . . in whose air float the melodies which my ear has caught, my heart has taken in, and my hand has written down."

The waltz was also used in the movie *2001, A Space Odyssey.* The film director, Stanley Kubrick, used the musical "flow" of this waltz to represent the weightlessness of outer space.

□   *An der schönen blauen Donau* by J. Strauss II.

Leos Janácek

A diligent collector of folk music, Janácek rejected the styles of western Europe and used the inflections of the Czech peasant language and music in his compositions. He preferred to create his own unique organization of music often based on what he called "speech-motives." These are short rhythmic motives based on the speech patterns of his native language. That is why his music is composed of short rhythmic-melodic cells (ideas).

Although Janácek was influenced by Debussy's use of novel instrumental colors and timbres, they are incorporated into his music in a truly Czech style. His *Sinfonietta* is a nationalistic composition that makes use of Czech folk tunes throughout the piece.

Sinfonietta

This composition is more of a suite than a "little symphony" as the term sinfonietta indicates. This youthful and energetic work was composed by Leos Janácek in 1926 when he was seventy-two years old! In it, each movement features a different group of instruments.

The music was requested by a local newspaper for the Sokol gymnastic festival of 1926, an important event to be celebrated by the newly forged Czechoslovak Republic. Each movement is meant to portray the city of Brno, which had been under German occupation until the founding of the republic in 1918. Later he dropped all the titles, and it was eventually dedicated to the Czechoslovakian Armed Forces.

The first movement, "Fanfares," opens the work and returns at the end of the final movement, "The Town Hall." The first movement is scored for brass and timpani with a fanfare theme coming from nine trumpets. It is mono-thematic and unfolds utilizing one of his favorite devices—mixing variations of a theme with its continuous repetition. This movement also uses highly complex rhythmic superimpositions, harmonies of unresolved chords, quartal harmony, and the use of whole-tone scales. Many of these ideas can be found in the music of the early 20th century.

In the final movement, the fanfare themes are played by the entire orchestra with trills being performed throughout the strings and woodwinds. It is only at the very end of the work that the two ensembles play together.

Sinfonietta
composed in 1926

I.   Allegretto - "Fanfares"
II. Andante - "The Castle" (Brno's Spilberk Castle)
III. Moderato - "The Queen's Monastery" (Cloister)
IV. Allegretto - "The Street"
V.   Andante con moto, Allegretto - "Town Hall"

◻   *Sinfonietta* by Janácek. (I. "Fanfares" and V. "Town Hall")

Ralph Vaughan Williams - Fantasia on Greensleeves

Ralph Vaughan Williams (1872-1958) was the foremost English composer in the first half of the 20th century. One of the main motivations for his music was national—the English folk song. The English folk song style is one that gave Vaughan Williams' music its own individual and immediately recognizable flavor. This piece is a direct quotation of an English folk song. Vaughan Williams adapted it from the "Greensleeves" music in his Shakespearean opera *Sir John in Love*, which was completed in 1928. There are many arrangements of this music available—the one we will hear is for flute, harp, and strings. It dates from the year 1934.

◻   *Fantasia on Greensleeves* by Vaughan Williams.

English Folk Song Suite

Although Vaughan Williams was known throughout the world as one of the most important English composers of choral and orchestral music, he also composed for the contemporary wind, or concert, band. This ensemble is composed of brass, woodwind, and percussion instruments. His most important piece for the wind band is the English Folk Song Suite from 1924. The musical subjects are all traditional, originally written for the wind band, and reflect the composer's lifelong studies in the field of folk music.

English Folk Song Suite
  premiered in 1924

I.   March - "Seventeen Come Sunday"
II.   Intermezzo - "My Bonnie Boy"
III. March - "Folk Songs from Somerset"

  English Folk Song Suite by Vaughan Williams. (March - Folk Songs from Somerset)

John Adams - Chamber Symphony

One of America's most admired and frequently performed composers, John Adams was born in Worcester, Massachusetts, in 1947. After graduating from Harvard University in 1971, he moved to California where he taught and conducted at the San Francisco Conservatory of Music for ten years. In 1978 he began a long and fruitful association with the San Francisco Symphony. Adams' works have received numerous awards, among them the 1994 Royal Philharmonic Society Award for his *Chamber Symphony*.

Completed in December of 1992, the *Chamber Symphony* of John Adams was commissioned by the Gerbode Foundation of San Francisco for the San Francisco Contemporary Chamber Players. The world premier of this piece was given in Holland in January of 1993.

The piece is written for 15 instruments including 4 strings, 6 woodwinds, 3 brass instruments, synthesizer, and drum set (often played by 2 percussionists). The first movement, entitled "Mongrel Airs," begins with a short introduction. This is then followed by the first melodic 'theme' introduced by the violin over a Stravinsky-like ostinato. The rest of the ensemble will eventually pick up this musical material creating a dense, polyphonic structure that Adams states "bears a superficially suspicious resemblance to its eponymous predecessor, the Opus 9 of Arnold Schoenberg." He further comments on a moment of inspiration for this piece; "I was sitting in my studio, studying the score to Schoenberg's *Chamber Symphony*, and as I was doing so I became aware that my seven year old son Sam was in the adjacent room watching cartoons (good cartoons, old ones from the '50's). The hyperactive, insistently aggressive and acrobatic scores for the cartoons mixed in my head with the Schoenberg music, itself hyperactive, acrobatic and not a little aggressive, and I realized suddenly how much these two traditions had in common." The title of the first movement was chosen "to honor a British critic who complained that my music lacked breeding."

According to Adams, "despite all the good humor, my *Chamber Symphony* turned out to be shockingly difficult to play." The instruments in this piece are often asked to play extremely difficult passages at a very fast tempo. The titles of the movements give a general indication of the mood of the music. This piece is musically more complex than his minimalist composition *Shaker Loops* (1978) that is discussed in Chapter 16.

Chamber Symphony
  composed in 1992

1. Mongrel Airs
2. Aria with Walking Bass
3. Roadrunner

  Chamber Symphony by Adams. (1. Mongrel Airs)

The conductor was losing his temper. Finally, at the uncomprehending opera singer, he yelled "I know it's the historical prerogative of the tenor to be stupid, but you sir have abused that privilege."

Attributed to Leonard Bernstein, at an opera rehearsal in Vienna

"The only person who can help poor Schoenberg now is a psychiatrist . . . I think he'd do better to shovel snow instead of scribbling on music paper."

Richard Strauss, in reference to the music of the Second Viennese School of composers

"When I compose I feel like I am Beethoven. Only afterwards do I realize that I am at best only a Bizet."

Alban Berg, referring to the composer of *Carmen*, Georges Bizet

"No I haven't heard any Stockhausen, but I believe I have trodden in some."

English conductor Sir Thomas Beecham, on the music of Karlheinz Stockhausen, a 20th century composer

Folk Music and Concert Music

Folk music expresses the nature of a particular nation or race. You can usually tell something about the "people" by simply listening to their folk songs. Sometimes these songs reflect the climate of a certain country, tell us something about their geography, or even describe what the people do and how they live. Most of all, folk songs reflect the rhythms and accents of the way a particular group of people talk. Their language, especially the language of their poetry, grows into musical notes. These are passed on from folk music into the art music, or opera, of the people. This is what makes Tchaikovsky sound Russian, Janácek sound Czech, Verdi sound Italian, and Gershwin sound American. These patterns flow from speech, to folk music, to the concert music of a particular group of people.

The Symphony According to Ives

One of the greatest and most original American composers was Charles Ives (1874-1954). Ives was a total American and one of the first composers not to follow the musical traditions of central European music. His symphony entitled *New England Holidays* is a perfect example of this.

Each movement in this work is based on, according to Ives, "Something from the memory that a young man might have from his holidays as a boy." The first of the movements to be played was "Washington's Birthday, Winter" during a private run-through in 1913. Its first public performance was in San Francisco in September of 1931. The final movement, "Thanksgiving and Forefather's Day, Fall," did not have its first performance until a month before Ives' death in 1954. About this work, Ives wrote:

> "To the younger generation, a winter holiday means action! And down through 'swamp hollow' and over the hill road they go . . . to the barn dance at the Center. The village band of fiddles, fife, and horn keep up an unending 'break down' medley, and the young folks 'salute their partners' until midnight. As the party breaks up, the sentimental songs of those days are sung half in fun, half seriously, and with the inevitable 'adieu to the ladies,' the 'social' gives way to the gray bleakness of the February night."

Following the slow opening "to give the picture of the dismal, bleak, cold weather of a February night," the famous barn dance section begins. You will hear quotations and the interplay of a number of American folk tunes including "Turkey in the Straw," "Camptown Races," and "Garyowen." The final section, with the "adieu to the ladies," incorporates another old song "Good Night Ladies." Notice the use of an unusual instrument—the mouth harp. It is, after all, the symphony according to Ives!

A Symphony: New England Holidays
composed during 1897-1913, first public performance in 1954

I.   Washington's Birthday, Winter
II. Decoration Day (now Memorial Day), Spring
III. The Fourth of July, Summer
IV. Thanksgiving and Forefather's Day, Fall

A Symphony: New England Holidays by Ives. (I. Washington's Birthday, Winter)

American Music and Jazz

After World War I there was something that was a part of American folk music and belonged to all Americans. In its many forms it was called "jazz." Throughout its chronology, jazz has been a melting pot, taking diverse cultural elements and forming them into a music that has been accepted as American. It is both indigenous to this country and the most democratic music ever devised. Jazz is a way to shape musical material. The word jazz is believed to have derived from the French verb "jaser," to chatter and have animated conversation among diverse people. The first usage of the word was in 1917 in a New Orleans newspaper.

There are many misconceptions as to what jazz is, or is not. There are certain elements that distinguish it from other types of music, although all of these elements may not be equally present in any one jazz performance. These elements include interpretation, improvisation, rhythm, syncopation, musical form, and the sounds associated with jazz.

The **interpretation** of music in the jazz style originally came about when Afro-Americans attempted to express themselves on European musical instruments. In jazz interpretation, the player restricts interpretative ideas to their conception of the melody. This is then colored with rhythmic effects, dynamics, and any other alterations that occur to the musician during the performance.

☐   *Example 1*, without jazz interpretation (straight).

☐   *Example 2*, with jazz interpretation.

Improvisation is similar to interpretation, but without melodic restriction. The melody is the basis for original ideas that must still fit with the harmony.

☐   *Example 3*, same as Examples 1 and 2, but with improvisation.

An emphasis on **rhythm** has always been an integral part of jazz. One reason is that for many years jazz was considered primarily music for dancing. While most jazz is in a duple meter, much has been composed in other meters as well.

Jazz often shifts the melody so that it does not always align itself with the basic beat. This shifting of the accented beat to a weak beat (or weak part of a beat) is called **syncopation**. We will hear this when we listen to specific examples.

In jazz, like Classical music, music is composed in certain forms. One of the most common **forms** is the **A A B A**, or song, form. You probably know this by the terms verse, verse, chorus, and verse. Many contemporary jazz musicians have experimented with some of the familiar Classical forms, including the theme and variation, fugue, and rondo. Perhaps the most important form, especially in early days of jazz, is the twelve-bar blues progression.

☐   *Examples 4A and 4B*, 12-bar blues progressions, hymn-like. (Example 4A is without jazz interpretation and 4B is with jazz interpretation.)

The final category is **sounds associated with jazz**. There are certain sounds peculiar to jazz that are a consequence of it having originated from an "oral" tradition. Many of the sounds are the results of instrumentalists attempting to imitate vocal techniques. Jazz singers and instrumentalists use a variety of techniques that include slurs, vibrato, and bending tones. We will listen to a few of these when we discuss work and field songs.

So what is jazz music? In summary, a listener must decide whether a specific performance contains enough recognizable jazz elements to make it a jazz piece. In contemporary Classical music, the composer remains the focal point, as the performers try to achieve the composer's ideal. In jazz music the performer is the focal point, and tries to integrate something of their personality and background into the music. The audience, which is considered an important part of the performance, would be missing out on the heart of jazz if this did not happen. The jazz composition is never really as important as the way in which it is played.

The clearest definition of jazz that I have found is from the author Bruce Jordan. He wrote that jazz ". . . is not a composer's art. The particular melodies and harmonies which form the basis of a performance, improvised or arranged, are of secondary importance. Rather jazz is the art of the performer, the performing ensemble, the arranger. And the quality of the art is dependent upon their creative ideas."

Jazz Heritage

The beginnings of jazz came about through a blending of the musical cultures of Africa and Europe. From the merging of these heritages, American jazz was born. This blending is still taking place. The addition of more complex rhythms from Africa in the 1940's and the innovations of present day third-stream music with its use of European musical forms (Stravinsky and Bernstein), are two examples.

Music was by far the most vital and unrestrained form of expression in the life of Africans. From morning until night, everything was done to the rhythm of their music. The art form was passed down by word of mouth (oral tradition), from generation to generation. It was a means of preserving tribal traditions, history, and folk lore. Music performed a vital role in maintaining the unity of the social group. Whether religious or secular, improvised or traditional, the music of the Africans was a powerful influence in their lives.

One common misconception about the origins of jazz was that its rhythms came from Africa. Actually it was only the emphasis on rhythm that was truly African. This again relates to their use of music in religion and rituals.

The melodic feature of jazz was inherited directly from European music. The harmonic progression of the blues, for example, was based on the European concept of organization. The tonality that was used derived from European composers too. As I have already mentioned, many of the forms of the Classical composers became standard in jazz works.

What would some of the early "jazz" pieces have sounded like? Here are several examples that were collected by musicologists and those interested in folk music in the 1920's. First we will listen to a work song entitled "Katie left Memphis," sung by Tangle Eye.

☐ *Example 5*, the work song "Katie Left Memphis."

Next is a call and response song. In this example a group of prisoners sing in response to the first "caller." Any harmony that you hear is being improvised. It is being sung by Leroy Miller and a group of prisoners.

☐ *Example 6*, the call and response song "Berta, Berta."

Now we will isolate a few of the melodic elements of jazz that differ from Classical music. They include "blue" notes and bending tones. These are some of the unique sounds that are associated with jazz music.

☐ *Examples 7 to 10*, flat 3rd to major 3rd (bend up), fifth to flat fifth (bend down), a "rip" going up, and a drop (going down).

Religious Music

The impact of Christianity on the Afro-Americans was the origin of the spirituals, hymns, and gospel songs. With the influence of the southern missionaries on the blacks, the European concept of melody and words was imparted. It was in these hymns and church songs that they became acquainted with a more highly organized sense of musical form. The main reason that Christianity took hold so fervently was, of course, due to the poor conditions the blacks lived in and the promise that Christianity held for a better life in the here-after.

The next example is a song called "Gospel Train." It is being sung by the Golden Gate Quartet. Notice the train-like musical effects and the a cappella singing style.

☐   *Example 11*, "Gospel Train."

The blues style was originally a vocal style that developed in late 1800's from these work, field, and call and response songs. Our next example is the song "Stormy Monday" as sung by Junior Wells. In a rhythm and blues style (slow blues), this piece tells his story and asks "Lord have mercy." The blues, as a type of jazz music, is a personal statement. Usually the subject matter is one of personal importance to the song writer. In this song you will notice the use of a blues progression (form), blue notes (bending), and the dialogue between the vocalist and his instrument.

☐   *Example 12*, "Stormy Monday."

Early Jazz

At first, black music in this country was vocal and accompanied by a rhythm of clapping, stomping, and beating on anything available. Then gradually, after the Civil War (1865), the blacks were able to make some instruments and to buy pawned and war surplus ones. Marching bands began to influence black music. Military bands, important in French settlements like New Orleans, also influenced the beginnings of instrumental jazz.

The most common instrumentation for this type of band was a cornet, trombone, clarinet, tuba, banjo, and drums. Buddy Bolden is credited with being the first to lead a jazz marching band. This would eventually lead to the beginnings of New Orleans Dixieland in the early 1900's. The music that is most typical of this era is that of Joe "King" Oliver. In the band with King Oliver was a young trumpet player who would eventually become one of the great musical ambassadors of jazz music—Louis Armstrong.

☐   *Basin Street Blues* performed by Louis Armstrong.

Edward Kennedy Ellington was born in Washington, D.C. in 1899. In the summer of 1914, while working in Asbury Park, N.J., he heard the Philadelphia ragtime pianist Harvey Brooks perform and this changed his life; "I cannot tell you what that music did to me… the individuality of the man showed itself in the composition… that's how I would like to play a piano, so without being told, everybody would know I was playing."

Everything Duke Ellington did for the next sixty years until his death in 1974 was built upon individuality and creativity and his long career as a pianist, bandleader, composer and arranger is a testament to these ideals. Three of his most well known songs are; *It Don't Mean A Thing, Sophisticated Lady*, and *Take the 'A' Train*.

☐   Duke Ellington; *The Harlem Renaissance* and *Memories of Duke*.

Now let's look at the music of two other great American composers—George Gershwin and Leonard Bernstein. We will concentrate on their specific use of jazz in "symphonic" music and in the other American musical genre, the Broadway musical.

George Gershwin

Gershwin was very successful at bringing together popular song, jazz, and orchestral (Classical) music into a great new style—a musical melting-pot and typically American. As he began taking piano lessons around age ten, he studied the Classical masters and learned how to improvise on the keyboard. He usually tried out various popular songs and ragtime pieces.

While working as a "song plugger" for Harms Music, he wrote a song that was to become a best-seller after being sung by Al Jolson. That song, with lyrics by his brother Ira, was "Swanee." George and Ira were on their way to becoming the toast of Broadway, New York, and the entire United States.

The work that established his international fame was an experimental piece of music entitled *Rhapsody in Blue*. This was commissioned by the jazz band leader Paul Whiteman in 1924. Orchestrated by Ferde Grofé, this piece was to help jazz become respectable. Suddenly, all over the world "Classical" composers were borrowing elements of this new and exciting American art form and incorporating them into their own works. Even composers like Vaughan Williams, Bartók, and Schoenberg admired Gershwin's music.

Other great works by Gershwin include *An American in Paris*, *Porgy and Bess*, *Piano Concerto in F*, and many songs for voice and piano that have become standards in the popular and jazz worlds. In many ways, Gershwin bridged the gap between American popular music and music of the concert hall.

☐   *Rhapsody in Blue* by Gershwin. (excerpts)

Leonard Bernstein - <u>On the Town</u>

Leonard Bernstein was undoubtedly the most talented composer-conductor of the 20th century. Born in 1918 in Lawrence, Massachusetts, Bernstein received a solid education in Boston and showed a natural ability with music and languages, especially German, French, Italian, Spanish, Yiddish, and Hebrew. He graduated from Harvard with an enormous array of musical talents. From 1958 to 1972, he appeared as commentator, piano-soloist, and conductor for fifty-three episodes of "Concerts for Young People" (ages 8 to 18) with the New York Philharmonic. Two of his most popular musicals include *On the Town* and *West Side Story*.

As a composer, Bernstein brought many of the elements of jazz to the Broadway musical. In *On the Town*, you will notice many elements of jazz in the music—both in the instrumental score and in the vocal parts. Right from the opening of "New York, New York," the score is a wonderful blend of orchestral texture and jazz rhythms and expression.

The premise of this musical is simple. Three sailors are on shore leave chasing after women in New York City. All three of the characters are supportive friends, and one of them (Gabey) has saved the lives of the other two at sea. In return, Ozzie and Chip show their gratitude by helping him locate the girl of his dreams (Ivy).

The story focuses on how the three friends try to cram the adventure of a lifetime into a single day. The work is youthful, energetic, innocent, and radiant with hope—it embraces life and love, as well as the highs and lows of the Big Apple. It also shows off New York as an enchanted island (Manhattan) and as the fast, colorful, dynamic town that it was during World War II. The show pokes fun at the sailors' idealism that they can actually "see" New York in a day and at their "mating rituals" on shore leave. At the end of the musical, just before the sailors have to go back to their ship, all three men finally meet the women of their dreams.

The music is by Bernstein, with the book and lyrics by his friends Betty Comden and Adolph Green. The original choreography was by Jerome Robbins, and the set designer was Oliver Smith.

On the Town, Leonard Bernstein
   premiered in 1944

Main characters (cast):
Gabey - sailor, the romantic
Ozzie - sailor, the ladies man
Chip - sailor, the tourist
Claire - Ozzie's girl, studying anthropology
Hildy - Chip's girl, a taxi cab driver
Ivy - "Miss Turnstiles," the N.Y. subway female passenger of the month

☐   *On the Town* by Bernstein. (excerpts)

West Side Story

While *On the Town* is not a part of the main Broadway musical repertory, the other collaboration by Bernstein (music), Jerome Robbins (choreography), and Oliver Smith (set designer) is— *West Side Story*. *West Side Story* (1957) is another classic musical. This is a setting of Shakespeare's Romeo and Juliet in the streets of New York. The conflict between the Sharks and the Jets is the modern day equivalent of the feud between the Capulets and the Montagues into which, as in both stories, the tale of forbidden love unfolds.

Conceived by the choreographer Jerome Robbins, *West Side Story* is not just a love story situated in a fictional family feud. The story takes its drive and energy from the streets of New York and the real life conflicts between the local youths and the new immigrants. The use of jazz and Latin American rhythms, along with beautiful ballads, electrifying dances, and a contemporary look at the problems of urban America, all provide an exciting background for the two would-be lovers. *West Side Story* also enjoyed a triumph in its film version that was released in 1961. We will examine several excerpts from the musical.

☐   *West Side Story* by Bernstein. (excerpts)

Atonality

At the turn of the century, music was deeply affected by the changing art world. Musical versions of Impressionism, Primitivism, and Expressionism could be found in the works of Debussy, Stravinsky, and Schoenberg respectively. Schoenberg, along with Anton Webern and Alban Berg, became known as the "Second Viennese School" of composers. Starting with Expressionism, Schoenberg explored the dark side of the human psyche and soul (see Chapter 10). At the end of this style, Schoenberg held in his hands the elements of a new musical language, a language that needed to be organized. This was to become the revolutionary music known as the "system of the twelve-tone series" (Zwölftonreihe). It is commonly referred to as 12-tone music, Serialism, or Atonality. Berg's opera *Wozzeck*, from 1925, was the first to combine Expressionism and 12-tone music in a musical portrait of a mentally tortured German soldier. While Berg represented the lyric side of Atonality, Webern embraced the non-Romantic side of Schoenberg's teachings. Webern did not write any operas and composed in a miniaturist style. For example, in his composition *Five Pieces for Orchestra*, Op. 10 from 1913, the movements average between 30 and 50 seconds in length.

To Schoenberg, the concept of consonance and dissonance was a false one because it sets the two in opposition with each other. He believed that "between the two there are only degrees of teaching the ear and consciousness to be able to perceive these remote harmonic sounds and combinations." In other words, the more your "ear" experiences the remote sounds of this chromatic (12-tone) music, the less shocking and dissonant it will sound. This revolutionary musical style is still alive today.

At the beginning of a piece of Atonal music, the listener is presented with a 12-tone (chromatic) row. You need to focus on this in its basic form before it undergoes various transformations. The melody, or tone row, is often angular, dissonant, jagged in shape, and generally avoids a symmetry of rhythm. The harmony, often dissonant and striking, is based on the structure of the tone row.

In 1923, Schoenberg wrote the first composition to be built exclusively on the principle of 12-tone composition. This work was his *Suite for Piano*, Op. 25. In this composition, Schoenberg emphasizes the "conservative" aspects of his new 12-tone style. The suite is a collection of 18th century dance forms that revolve around a Brahms-like Intermezzo.

Schoenberg believed that this work was not revolutionary, but rather an evolutionary piece of music that was a natural outcome of the tradition of Western music. After fleeing from the Nazi regime in 1933, he settled in Los Angeles where he was a member of the music faculties at the University of Southern California and the University of California, Los Angeles.

Suite for Piano, Op. 25
  composed in 1923

I.   Präludium
II.   Gavotte
III. Musette
IV. Gavotte (da capo)
V.   Intermezzo
VI. Minuett: Moderato - Trio
VII. Gigue

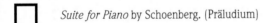 *Suite for Piano* by Schoenberg. (Präludium)

After Schoenberg there was a move towards total Serialism that resulted in an extremely complex and highly organized style of music. Two composers who exemplify this style are Pierre Boulez and Karlheinz Stockhausen.

John Cage, an American composer, took a different direction and experimented with Aleatoric music. He looked for new tone colors in "preparing" a piano by placing screws, erasers, and other objects on and between the strings of a piano. His *Sixteen Sonatas* for prepared piano is an example of this Avant-Garde musical trend.

Minimalism 3

One of the major trends of music that caught on in the 1960's is called Minimalism. The basic concept behind Minimalism is to establish a pattern (rhythm and/or melodic) that will be continually repeated with small and subtle changes along the way. In this field there are three composers that are considered the leading exponents of this style—John Adams, Philip Glass, and Steve Reich.

John Adams

One of the "classic" pieces of Minimalism by John Adams is entitled *Shaker Loops*. The title refers to not only the religious group of the American Shakers, but also to the musical devices of shakes and trills. The "loop" part of the title refers to the looping of the musical phrases as the melody is assigned to different instruments, each playing it at a different time. The result is a constant shifting among the parts. The first and fourth movements are the shaking movements, while the second is composed of "slow languid glissandi." The third movement is essentially melodic and is the emotional high point of the entire composition.

Shaker Loops
  composed in 1978

1. Shaking and Trembling
2. Hymning Slews
3. Loops and Verses
4. A Final Shaking

☐   *Shaker Loops* by Adams. (4. A Final Shaking)

Philip Glass

The minimalist opera *Einstein on the Beach* (1976) was a pivotal work in the life of Philip Glass. It was his first, longest, and the most famous of his thee 'portrait' operas. An opera about the great mathematician who loved music, it was written for the Philip Glass Ensemble of amplified winds and keyboards, a soprano soloist, and a small chorus singing a text comprised of numbers (the actual beats of the music).

In collaboration with Robert Wilson, a prominent New York stage director, the opera was completed in 1976. The two men had decided to collaborate on a theatrical work based on the life of a historical figure. Wilson wanted to stage Chaplin or Hitler, while Glass proposed Gandhi. Eventually, Glass and Wilson agreed upon Albert Einstein with the working title of *Einstein on the Beach on Wall Street*.

In this opera the images of a train, a court trial, a prison, and a spaceship are all juxtaposed to form four scenes. In between the scenes are 'knee-plays' – as a knee is a joint that connects two parts of a leg, a knee-play connects the scenes in this opera. These knee-plays were to become a primary source of musical materials for his other portrait operas, *Satyagraha* (1980) and *Akhnaten* (1983). While *Einstein on the Beach* has been frequently produced since its premiere in 1977, it is, in fact, an opera with very little singing.

☐   *Einstein on the Beach* by Glass. (Knee Five - for two speakers, violin, and organ.)

In 1983, Glass collaborated with filmmaker Godfrey Reggio to produce the most unique mating of cinema and music since *Fantasia* (1940) – *Koyaanisqatsi*. The word Koyaanisqatsi is Hopi for "life out of balance" and this film was the composer's first major popular success. This eighty-seven minute film is completely non-narrative, has no identifiable actor/actress and no dialogue! A myriad of visions – clouds across the sky, the blasting of a housing project, swarms of people moving in and out of Grand Central Station in N. Y., and traffic patterns on the L. A. freeways – *Koyaanisqatsi* is a work that is both musically hypnotic and a philosophical indictment of late 20th century Western society.

☐   *Koyaanisqatsi* by Glass. (Beginning, Vessels)

Steve Reich

Born in New York and raised there and in California, Steve Reich graduated with honors in philosophy from Cornell University in 1957. He also studied at the Juilliard School of Music with William Bergsma and Vincent Persichetti and received his M.A. in Music from Mills College in 1963 where he worked with Luciano Berio and Darius Milhaud.

During the summer of 1970, with the help of a grant from the Institute for International Education, Reich studied drumming at the Institute for African Studies at the University of Ghana. In 1973 and 1974 he studied Balinese Gamelan music and from 1976 to 1977 he studied the traditional forms of chanting of the Hebrew Scriptures in New York and Jerusalem. Many of these diverse musical elements can be found in his music. In 1976 Reich was commissioned by Frankfurt Radio to write his *Octet*. In 1983, he made some changes to the work and added more instruments (8 strings plus 4 woodwinds and 2 pianos) and re-named it *Eight Lines*. According to Reich, "*Eight Lines* is structured in five sections, of which the first and third resemble each other in their fast moving piano, cello, viola and bass clarinet figures..." In composing this work, Reich wanted to have "the transitions between sections as smooth as possible with some overlapping in the parts so that it is sometimes hard to tell where one section ends and the next begins." A hypnotic and mesmerizing work and considered one of the 'classic' minimalist works, Reich's *Eight Lines* takes eighteen minutes to perform.

☐   Eight Lines by Reich. (Part 1)

Reich's *Electric Counterpoint* was commissioned by the Brooklyn Academy of Music's "Next Wave Festival" for the jazz guitarist Pat Metheny. In this piece, the soloist Metheny pre-recorded ten guitar and two electric bass parts, and then played an eleventh guitar part live and against the tape.

The work is in a three movement form of fast, slow, and fast. Each movement is played without pause one after another. The first movement uses a theme from Central African horn music. The slow movement is at half the tempo of the first and features a guitar canon (imitative) in nine parts.

In the final movement the tempo returns to that of the first movement. After a four guitar canon begins (in a triple meter), two bass guitars enter to strengthen the triple meter feel. Then Pat Metheny (live) re-enters with a series of strummed chords and the counterpoint begins again.

Electric Counterpoint
    composed in 1987

1. Fast
2. Slow
3. Fast

☐   *Electric Counterpoint* by Reich. (3. Fast)

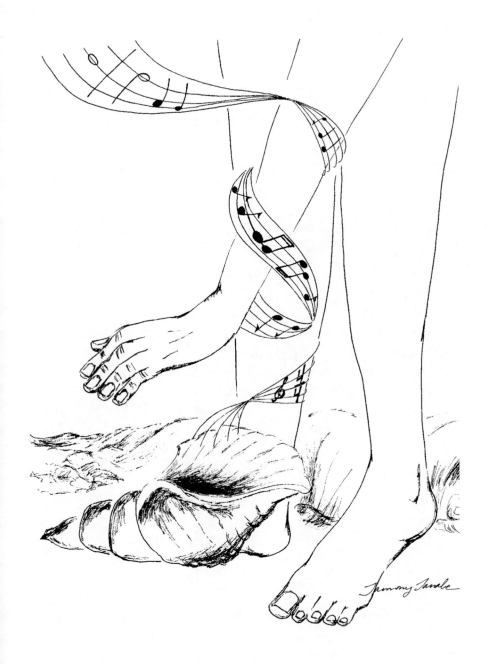

"To stop the flow of music would be like the stopping of time itself, incredible and inconceivable."

Aaron Copland, composer

"It's the songs in the Irish language that are at the heart of the music of Ireland…"

Nuala O'Connor, musician

"Brazilian music is world music in its most literal sense, played across the world, recognized globally, its influence noticeable in the musical output of many other countries from the US to Nigeria."

David Cleary, writer

"The Pacific Ocean covers a third of the earth's surface… It's a region with deep musical traditions, too, buffeted by the regular currents of colonists and explorers and now undergoing dramatic changes."

David Fanshawe, composer/traveler

The Infinite Variety of Music

A limitless variety of music pulses through the lives of the inhabitants of this planet. It is interwoven with the environment and the historical circumstances in which the people of a region live. What is "beautiful" or "good" will vary from region to region. The evaluation of the music by an outside observer may not shed any light as to how the music functions in the society.

Ethnography is the study of music that seeks to provide documentation based on observation and evaluation considered "objective" by an outside scholar from a different culture. At present, there seems to be a shortage of both precise descriptions of music from its performers and of ethnographic materials from outside observers that include the views of the native musician.

Anyone who attempts to describe music within a given culture must be satisfied with focusing on the central or dominant forms of music within that culture. Nations are founded as geopolitical entities, usually with particular ethnicities maintaining a prominent position. Nearly all regions in Asia, for example, are inhabited by combinations of ethnic groups. The cultures which have developed in Asia are made up of complex sets of intermingled elements.

The amount of variety found within a complex society makes assessment of the tradition, in all its forms, quite difficult. Additionally, the factors of the cultural environment including nature and society cannot be overlooked.

The instruments used by people are significantly related to and determined by climate and other features of their respective natural environments (vegetation, forest, etc.). In regions with high humidity, where bamboo flourishes, flutes and many other instruments are made of bamboo while in dryer regions flutes of the same basic shape are often made of reed.

The environment influences not only the materials used in making instruments, but also the manner of vocalization. Due to the open spaces, the singing of rural people in Japanese farming and fishing villages is louder and more coarse than that of the city dwellers. Climatic and ecological zones of the world are useful in providing information on various musical features. The social environment is also a factor in music — the modes of living and occupations which sustain a society are important points of interest in considering the music of that society.

For nomadic or pastoral peoples, rhythm is predominantly based on odd numbers: 5, 7, and 9 beat rhythms. Dance in these groups tends to be vigorous with a lot of turns and leaps. In contrast, among the farming and rice cultivating peoples of the temperate zone, rhythm is based primarily on even beat rhythms: 2 and 4. The dances are slower with the hips low and the feet placed on the ground. The hands and face are also expressively used.

The environment and the function to which music is connected allows us to consider it in the context of society and culture. The development of a "professional musician" appears more in a complex society and is based on talent or musical accomplishment.

Religious practice in Asia ranges from the great and widely practiced religions such as early Zoroastrianism, Hinduism, Buddhism, and Islam, to the indigenous faiths and animistic practices of local tribes and ethnic groups. Recognizing and defining the significance of a religion as a cultural element can help us identify the entire area over which political authority and historical events have been shaped or influenced by that religion. With this information, we can recognize the influence of a particular religion and the specific musical features of that religion. Language or languages are another important determinant in world music. Distinctions regarding language as an aspect of culture are just as significant as religion.

Whether music is fixed or relative in pitch is another factor in considering the unique identity of a music. The use of fixed pitch instruments and metallic instruments, such as the Gamelan music of Indonesia, is very rare in West Asia or South Asia. Singing in unison (by one or more performers) is a distinguishable tradition from the singing of two or more tones simultaneously (by two or more performers) in multi-part singing.

1. JAPAN

High on a wooden cart, the massive o-daiko (great drum) sits imposingly as if it were the altar of some ancient deity. Its 700 pounds of wood and leather has been fashioned into an enormous barrel-shaped drum. On both ends stand young men wielding baton-like drumsticks, ready to attack.

They slowly begin to hammer out patterns of primordial rhythms that seem to emanate from the womb of the earth. The driving momentum builds relentlessly, intensified by the beating of other taiko.

This is Kodo, a unique Japanese folk performing arts company. Using traditional Japanese drums, or taiko, Kodo continues to explore new musical directions, finding ever expanding possibilities in these ancient instruments.

The Japanese characters for Kodo convey two meanings; first, heartbeat – the sound of the mother's heartbeat as felt in the womb. Secondly, read in a different way, the word can mean "children of the drum" – a reflection of Kodo's desire to play their drums simply, with the heart of a child.

In ancient Japan the area of a village was defined by the furthest distance at which its taiko could be heard. Their *One Earth Tours*, which date back to 1981, take the sound of the taiko to the members of a larger community – the world.

While at the same time preserving and developing Japanese traditional arts, Kodo places great importance both musically and culturally on its worldwide contacts with other artists. The major expression of this is "Earth Celebration," a percussion and arts festival that began with the founding of Kodo Village in 1988, and which now brings performers from all over the world to Kodo's base of Sado Island every summer. The energy and different approaches to life and music-making that all these performers bring to Sado continues to fuel Kodo's enthusiasm for playing their way around the world.

Kodo's repertory is largely based on traditional folk sources: songs of the fisherman, the farmer and the common folk as they work; dances celebrating the coming of spring; praying for an abundant harvest or offerings to appease the wrath of an unruly deity. They use a variety of traditional musical instruments, such as the yokobue and shakuhachi (bamboo flutes), the koto (a stringed zither), shamisen (a fretless 3 string lute), and a wide range of wooden drums and percussion instruments.

Kodo is best known for its exciting taiko pieces. Folk-style drumming is prevalent throughout all of Japan's countryside and is found at virtually every festival. While regional styles differ considerably, Kodo strives to retain the unique qualities of each and bring them to the stage in a choreographed presentation. This piece, *Zoku*, is music "for the group."

☐   *Zoku* (taiko drum music), by Kodo.

2. BALI

Indonesian music is represented here by the gamelan ensemble. The linguistic root form of gamelan is "gamel," which means to hit or manipulate with the hands. Accordingly, the majority of instruments in a gamelan are bronze percussion: suspended bossed gongs and gong kettles laid in a horizontal position form the core of the ensemble, and are supplemented by other instruments such as a double headed drum and a xylophone. Among wind instruments there is a bamboo end-blown flute.

Viewed in terms of their functions, gamelan instruments either have a linear function or vertical function. The melodic, or vertical, instruments include the bronze kettles, xylophones, and flute. To punctuate and emphasize segmentation of the melodies, the gongs and the double headed drum are used. Crashing cymbals add to the overall glitter and a flute often sweetens the melody. The gamelan is carefully tuned so that there are differences in pitch between the same notes of similar instruments, giving its sound a characteristic shimmer.

Comparing the island parts of Southeast Asia yields an interesting fact: in Indonesia, gamelan and other music and performing arts are shared by the people of Java and Bali, although the forms of religious faith and social structure are markedly different - Java is Moslem and Bali is Hindu.

There are four representative regional styles of gamelan music: those of West Java, Central Java, East Java, and Bali. Two pentatonic scales predominate in Balinese music. The first is "selisir" derived from the seven-note pelog scale (e,f,g,b,c). The other scale is called "slendro" (c,d,e,g,a). The music of Bali is often characterized by rapid interlocking parts as in this *Sekar*.

☐   *Sekar*, by a Balinese gamelan ensemble.

3. INDIA

India has the most sophisticated music outside of Western European civilization. It is intertwined with religious belief and practice, and began at least a thousand years B.C. It uses a linear tonal system, unlike the Balinese stratified system

The Hindu musical treatise, <u>Natya</u> <u>Sastra</u>, was written in 200 B.C. and connects the ancient musical heritage of India with forms in use today. North India is Moslem, South India is Hindu - they have different instruments and naming systems. But the music is similar in that it is intimately connected with the spiritual world. The music reflects the order of the universe and contributes to a performer's own spiritual development.
Central to their music are the concepts of the *raga* and *tala*. The raga is a melodic scale with 7 tones, but tuned in microtones (shruti). The notes can be played natural, flat, very flat, sharp, and very sharp. There is a complex system of rules that also allow for improvisation and ornamentation, as most Indian music is improvisational. A drone (played on a tambura) accompanies the *raga*.

The *tala* is the rhythm cycle. It has a fixed number of beats that, once the *alapana* (prelude) is over, is strictly adhered to until the end of the piece. The musical compositions seek to create *rasa* - the "feeling" of the music on both the performer and on the audience. An example of Indian classical art music is the following work *Máru-Bihág*, for sitar (a plucked lute instrument), tabla drums, and a tambura (drone).

Máru-Bihág is an evening raga – quiet and meditative music that is appropriate to be played as the sun is setting and evening comes to the household. The ascending scale pattern of the raga is C, F, E, F#, G, B and C. The descending pattern is C, B, A, G, F#, E, F#, E, D, and C.

After a descending glissando, the sitar presents the *raga* in free rhythm, setting forth its pitches and intended character. Many slides, pitch bending alterations, and ornaments enhance the melody (*raga*) over the background drone played by the tambura. The entering tabla (drums) creates a distinct pulse or *tala*. In this raga, in the Gat, the rhythm is a cycle of 10 Matras (beats) in the pattern of 2 + 3 + 2 + 3 = a 10 beat rhythm cycle.

Concerts in India typically begin slowly, just as ragas themselves do. As *Máru-Bihág* develops, the complexities of the rhythm and melodic improvisation intensify. Again, notice that the melody has a non-Western sound and scale structure.

☐   *Máru-Bihág*, performed and introduced by Ravi Shankar.

4. NEPAL

The various ethnic groups of Nepal are broadly classified as being of the Indo-Aryan language group or the Tibetan-Burman language group. The influence of Hindu religion can be seen in the performance of the *Ramayana* tales.

In Katmandu, instruments are of Indian origin with melody differing little from that in Hindu music. There are also various shamanistic religions with practicing professional shamans (medicine men). The southern area of Nepal, known as the Tarai, is populated mainly by Hindus who are racially and culturally related to the people of northern India.

In the Lamaist ritual music (Katmandu, Nepal), the performers are from the "reformed sect" or "yellow hat sect" of Tibetan Buddhists. A ceremony begins with the shaken bells and the hand-held hourglass drum of the officiating priest. Many instruments are played before, between, and after the reading of Sutras (Buddhist teachings). Large earth-shaking trumpets (2-3 meters in length) are played by 2 young monks. Notice also the double reed shawm, the large cymbals, a vertical flute, and a double-headed frame drum that are also used in the ceremony.

 *Lamaist ritual music*, performed by monks from Katmandu, Nepal.

During a contemplative recitation, recorded in 1988, the Gyuto monks identify themselves with the divine Buddha form Yamantaka ("Terminator of Death"). In focused visualization, they ask for life-giving blessings to all beings. This chant is believed to have the power to exorcise the human afflictions of anger, avarice, lust and envy, and transform them into creative wisdom.

This freedom chant is sacred music for meditation and not for entertainment. It is a chant to end oppression and an elegy for those whose blood was spilled in both Tibet and Beijing.

Yamantaka, chanted by the Gyuto Monks, Nepal.

5. BRAZIL

The country of Brazil extends from the northern hemisphere almost to Antarctica and contains tropical, temperate, and frigid climates. There are coastal areas and highland plateaus, savannas, and forests, big cities and isolated villages. Brazil is the largest country in Latin America, its language is Portuguese, and the population is extremely diverse and complex.

There are essentially three population types in Brazil, with an almost even distribution of each:

1. South American Indians - descendants of the aboriginal dwellers of the continent.

2. Descendants of the Europeans - especially the Spanish and the Portuguese.

3. Descendants of the Africans - originally brought as slaves.

Brazilian music found its modern identity at the end of the 19th century with *samba*, a mixture of West African polyrhythms, Portuguese melodies and Native American chants. In the late 1950's Antonio Carlos (Tom) Jobim and others, notably the poet Vinicius de Moraes and the singer/guitarist João Gilberto, developed the most internationally celebrated variation on *samba* – *bossa nova*, the new wave in Brazilian music.

By the early 1960's, this new music began to reach an international audience, largely through collaborations with American jazz musicians like Stan Getz and Herbie Mann. Getz's recording of Jobim's *The Girl from*

Ipanema (a bossa nova) became the biggest hit in the USA in 1962, two years before The Beatles arrived. The second version, a re-make by Crystal Waters, was recorded in 1996 and is a wonderfully updated version of Jobim's classic hit.

☐ *The Girl from Ipanema*, by Antonio Carlos (Tom) Jobim.

☐ *The Boy from Ipanema*, re-make by Crystal Waters.

6. IRELAND

The conventional, abbreviated approach to European history begins with classical Greek and Roman times and ends with the Renaissance (and the subsequent development of the Austro-Germanic heritage). This has been challenged more recently due to a renewed interest in the Celts, bearers of one of the more highly developed cultures of ancient Europe. The history of the Celts can be traced back to Ireland, to Scotland in Great Britain, and to Brittany in France.

Ireland has been under English domination since the 12th century. Although 750 years of discrimination and suppression have inevitably led to a high degree of Anglicization in such areas as religion and language, one can nevertheless discern a proud and independent Celtic heartbeat in the lands that gave birth to Celtic culture.
At first glance it may seem surprising to find that many American cowboy and railroad songs are set to Irish melodies - a partial consequence of the great potato famine of the 1840's. Irish tunes attained widespread popularity after the great migration of Ireland's poorest workers to the USA.

Many of the ballads of Ireland contain themes of protest. These songs served as a source of news for the independence movements that were constantly spreading in Ireland and were sung by street singers. Of course, the inheritors of the Celtic culture continue to play their jigs and reels for pure enjoyment too!

The original Gaelic version of *Mo Ghile Mear* (Our Hero) was written by the 18th c. poet Sean Clarach MacDomhnaill. It is one of the many Irish Jacobite songs written in honor of Prince Charles Stewart (Bonnie Prince Charles). The air is, appropriately, of Scottish origin. The words were set by Jim Connell, a 19th century Irish poet in exile in Scotland. This version features Sting singing with The Chieftains in an arrangement of this song by Paddy Moloney (the leader of The Chieftains). Traditional Irish instruments that are featured in this 1995 recording include the fiddle, bodhrán (frame drum), uilleann pipes, tin whistle, flute, harp, and keyboards.

☐ *Mo Ghile Mear*, and other examples.

7-11 Africa and the World Beat (Mali, Caribbean, Nigeria, Senegal, & Cuba)

It is customary in the Western world for people to use the term "African music" as if it were a single clearly identifiable phenomenon. Yet when one considers the size of the continent (2nd largest in the world), the enormous differences in climate and terrain producing contrasting ways of life across the land mass and, above all, its extreme multi-lingualism (more than 1000 languages have been identified), one should not be surprised at the diversity of music and the difficulty of isolating distinctly African features to the whole continent.

African musicology began with the invention of the recording machine and the first collection was made in 1905. Still today, much of the music of Africa remains unknown.

The earliest evidence of music in Africa comes from North Africa - the hunting bow from almost 30,000 years ago. In general, the nasal sound of the double reed wind instruments and monophonies sung with a tight throat are features which distinguish North Africa from sub-Saharan Africa, where music is characterized by polyphonies and polyrhythms.

The southern edge of the Sahara is generally regarded as the dividing line between North Africa and the rest of the continent. In North Africa most of the people speak Afro-Asiatic languages, and Arab culture had a profound impact there.

In Sub-Saharan Africa, the general musical trait is percussiveness. The placing of the volume peak of a note at its beginning with the subsequent rapid fading is found in percussion, instrumental, and vocal music. Rhythm is more highly developed in Africa than some other features or elements (such as form and melody). Elements of syncopation are prevalent. The consensus about the use of multiple meter is so strong as to remain unquestioned as the basis for African rhythm. Polyrhythm (rhythmic polyphony) is the superimposition of several rhythmic structures.

In the 20th c., the influences of the West have been paramount, especially the use of a Western melodic idiom with European-derived harmony. Important music for the church, stage, folk opera, and popular culture is now being written by a new generation of composers who strive towards African-derived music, yet address themselves frequently to a listening audience rather than a dancing or otherwise visibly participating audience.

7. MALI

Bamako, the capital of Mali, is a dusty town that hugs the bank of the Niger River. There's one small recording studio and precious few venues for live music, yet it is one of West Africa's most musical cities. In this studio Salif Keita has recorded many times.

Being an albino carries a stigma in most African countries and Salif Keita's youth in a village west of Bamako was not easy. On both of his parent's side he is a Keita (noble class) and there was no precedent for someone of such high lineage to take up singing as a profession. He trained as a school teacher but poor eyesight prevented him from teaching as a profession, so, despite his family's disapproval, he began to sing on the streets and in the bars of Bamako.

This 1995 recording of Africa shows the eclectic style of Salif Keita and the results of his years of work in the dance bands and clubs of Mali, as well as influences from the world music scene and his recordings with both European and American artists. The translation of the song is: "Africa stirs us, makes us dream, makes us dance. It's easy come, easy go, eat a lot, work a lot. That's our strength…"

☐   *Africa*, by Salif Keita.

8. The CARIBBEAN

Caribbean music and dance are vitally important elements of life in the region. The Caribbean region includes several dozen island countries and territorial units ringing the northern and eastern boundaries of the Caribbean sea. It also includes neighboring mainland countries with particularly strong cultural and historical ties to the Caribbean islands namely Belize and the three Guianas on the northeastern coast of South America.

The Caribbean region is ethnoculturally diverse. Four major groupings are generally recognized on the basis of

shared colonial histories and official language usage:
- the Spanish Caribbean (Cuba, Dominican Republic, Puerto Rico)
- the French Caribbean (Haiti, Martinique, Guadeloupe, Guyane)
- the Dutch Caribbean (Suriname and the islands of Aruba, Bonaire, Curaçao)
- the British Caribbean (Barbados, the Bahamas, Belize, Guyana, Jamaica, Trinidad and Tobago, the Virgin Islands)

Most of the population of the Caribbean consists of the descendants of African slaves. The juxtapositions and mixtures of cultures in this region are fascinatingly complex. Each of the population groups has its own historic music and dance traditions. The music of the Caribbean thus comprises a multiplicity of world music practices. In addition, blendings of various practices have occurred over time – particularly between African and European styles – further enriching the plurality.

In the French Caribbean, a number of popular music and dance types have emerged and have achieved popularity abroad, with the most recent being *zouk*. A blend of African styles, Caribbean pop, and American funk, *zouk* was the Caribbean's first really hi-tech dance music. It owes much of its sound to developments in Paris, where French Antillean expatriates set about forging a hot new style that would set the pulses of Europeans as well as Caribbean people racing.

Zouk is a Creole word that used to be slang for a "party." In the case of Déde Saint Prix, he has cast his net wide to pull in a huge range of dance-oriented styles to update traditional music.

☐   *Fuerza E Vigor* (Strength and Vigor) by Déde Saint Prix.

9. NIGERIA

Nigeria, the "giant of Africa," is a country of enormous cultural and musical diversity. The Nigerian musical heritage extends from the 16th century traditional court drumming of the Hausa to the efforts of Fela Kuti. Fela has remained an uncompromising critic of every government Nigerians have suffered under since independence in 1960. His career, spanning more than three decades, has been repeatedly interrupted by government violence against musicians, his family and his person.

Fela Kuti was born in Abeokuta, a Nigerian town established in the 19th century as a home for freed slaves, famous for its rebellious and creative spirit. Fela's grandfather was a celebrated composer, his father a piano-playing pastor and his mother a nationalist leader. In the late 1950s Fela moved to London to study music and stayed four years, studying trumpet and musical theory at the Trinity College of Music in London. But it was under the influence of Geraldo Pino's African pop (close to the James Brown style) that he began to develop his own style. By 1969, blending funk and Afro-soul with highlife, jazz, and traditional African music, Fela had invented the form he calls *Afro-Beat*.

The song *Zombie*, from the 1976 LP of the same name, uses the zombie image to criticize the Nigerian military. In the lyrics, Fela yells out commands – *Attention! Left turn! Right turn! Fall In! Fall Out! Fall Down!* The background singers reply with *Zombie!* Highly critical of the Nigerian government, the LP is thought to have resulted in the murder of his mother and the destruction of his commune.

☐   *Zombie*, by Fela Kuti {excerpt}.

☐   *Zombie*, re-make by Spoek Mathambo on the 2013 LP *Red Hot + Fela*.

10. SENEGAL

In a land with few natural resources, Senegal is a fertile garden of musical talent and energy. Music itself is beginning to be viewed as an exportable commodity, like fish.

Baaba Maal was born into the caste of fisherman. His voice, much appreciated by his peer group, and a childhood friendship with the griot (African hereditary musician, guardian of history and traditions), Mansour Seck, took him into a musician's life. He has been keen to popularize the music and dances of his native Fouta Toro region which lies along Senegal's northern borders with Mauritania and Mali. Maal, who trained at the music conservatory in Dakar and won a scholarship to study in Paris, is regarded as the intellectual among Senegalese artists.

His song *Souka Nayo* (I will follow you), recorded in 1998, has already become a world beat classic. It has also been made popular in four different remixes; a Newsday Remix, a Yard Mix, a Thievery Remix, and a Fila Brazilia Mix.

☐   *Souka Nayo* (I will follow you), by Baaba Maal.

11. CUBA

The Indians of Cuba were wiped out in the 16th and 17th centuries, so the music of this country developed from a blending of Spanish and African elements. (Until 1898, Cuba was a colony of Spain.)

Cuba is the island that gave the world the *rumba*, the *mambo*, the *conga*, the *chachachá* and the *habañera*. These dances have traveled all over the new world, the old world, and even gone back to their roots in Africa thanks to the strong influence of Cuban music on West African bands.

Nowhere in the Caribbean is the African influence on music so pronounced – a fact due to the large slave trade. The slaves came mostly from the West African coast and by the 1840s they constituted nearly half the population.

Son is the predominant musical force in Cuban song and dance and the most influential element in popular Latin dance music. It takes many forms, from simple, rustic bands to the brassy arrangements of New York salsa, a style which it underpins. The term is derived from *sonero*, the improvising lead singer in the band.

Irakere, led by composer-pianist Jesus "Chucho" Valdez, has moved further from *son* and into jazz, and combined it with Afro-Cuban cult music. Their name is Yoruba (West African) for "forest," and refers to a region where the best African drummers lived and contests were regularly held. Their ensemble is a highly sophisticated big band with musical elements of salsa and jazz.

☐   *El Coco* (The Coconut), by Irakere.

12. NEW ZEALAND (The Maori)

New Zealand is a member of the Commonwealth of Nations, and has a population of 3 million people. The earliest inhabitants, the Maori, are believed to have arrived from central Polynesia about the 10th century. Their immediate place of origin is still not known with the Society Islands, the Marquesas Islands and the Southern Cook Islands all as candidates. The ultimate origins of the Maori, in common with other Polynesian peoples, lie with remote ancestors who began their migrations between 5 and 10 millenia ago, most likely from somewhere in Southeast Asia. In recent times most Maori are of mixed (with Caucasian) blood. New Zealanders with some Maori blood constitute about 10 percent of the country's population.

The styles of the old Maori songs can be classified into two types: the chanted *karakia* (incantations, invocations), and the melodic *waiata* (songs). The general term for dance was originally haki, but today this term usually refers to the posture dance haka.

The principal instruments of the ancient Maori were a short wooden or bone flute, and a wooden trumpet. Strangely, they brought no drum on their Pacific voyaging, but the rhythmical stamping of the feet provided percussion for the *haka.*

The *haka* is a posture dance with shouted accompaniment. Some are performed by both men and women but most, especially the *peruperu* (war dance), are nowadays performed only by men. They are strongly metric, in conformity with a beat marked by foot stamping and body percussion. Most are in compound meter with crossrhythms and syncopations running counter to the foot stamp. The form is usually a responsorial alternation of leader solo and choral refrain.

Perhaps the most well-known *haka* is *Kamate*, which is performed by the All Blacks Rugby Team and at many Maori meetings. This haka has become so popular that it is now regarded as an emblem of New Zealand. It speaks of the Maori gathering strength from the earth and the forces of nature.

☐   *Maori Hakas*, (*Utaina, Poutini, Toia Mai, Kamate*), traditional.

13. HAWAI'I

The islands of Polynesia are spread over such a wide area that one would expect to find a highly varied series of isolated cultures. A combination of amazing navigational skills and migrational incentives (war, overpopulation), however, has bound the Pacific cultures together.

Hawai'i was the last major area of Polynesia to be settled. It is nearly 2,000 miles from the closest group of large islands. As in other parts of Polynesia, music in Hawai'i was a complex system of poetry (*mele*), rhythm, melody, and movement which served many functions — from prayer to entertainment.

When the chanted words were accompanied by music and dance, the combined performance was known as hula. Today hula exists in two forms. The first, *kahiko*, is closer to the old style, consisting of chanting to the beat of drums. The dancers wear knee-length skirts of "ti" leaves, with anklets and bracelets of ferns. The other, *'auana*, is a more modern style of hula that features bands of musicians playing western-style instruments.

The first example from Hawai'i is *Lei Hali'a* written by Puakea Nogelmeier and performed by Keali'i Reichel (on the CD of the same title). The song speaks of the heart as a place for remembrance and imagination. When memories rest peacefully in the heart like flowers in a lei, then dreams flourish as well. This performance is from January of 1999 and features Keali'i Reichel, dancers from the hula halau (hula school) Keali'i O Nalani under the direction of kumu hula Keali'i Ceballos, and members of the South Bay Youth Orchestra under the direction of William E. Doyle. The dancing is in the *'auana* style.

☐   *Lei Hali'a*, performed by Keali'i Reichel.

The second example is a *mele* (chant). The name of the mele is *Maika'i Ka 'Oiwi O Ka'ala* which roughly translates to "Splendid is the form of Mount Ka'ala," on the island of O'ahu. The mele has a beautiful melody and poetically compares the peaks and ridges surrounding Mount Ka'ala to the beauty and shape of a woman. It was composed to honor King David Kalakaua – the last king of Hawai'i. (This *mele* is also the subject of our last world music example, *Voyage*. The dancing is in the ancient *kahiko* style.)

☐   *Maika'i Ka 'Oiwi O Ka'ala*, performed by Keali'i Reichel.

14. TAHITI

Little is known about the origins or the original forms of the arts of Polynesia. The people in question were non-literate and, before the arrival of Europeans, their traditions existed only in oral forms. Aggressive importation of Christianity by European missionaries resulted in the undervaluation, distortion, and destruction of native traditions.

Traditional Polynesian society was based on a system of rank and social status. The person of highest rank was thought to possess supernatural power, called mana, which was transmitted to him from the gods who had created the world. The common people were expected to maintain a large number of taboos in respect to such mana. This system is reflected in the arts of the islands. In places such as Tonga and Samoa where a system of rank is retained, the high chiefs and their children perform certain dances.

Recently, the peoples of Polynesia, long forced to endure foreign domination, have undertaken ethnic liberation movements. In many locations independence from colonial rule has been achieved, and the people are now experiencing a revitalization of older forms of their indigenous arts and culture.

French Polynesia, a territory of France, is made up of five island groups: the Marquesas, the Tuamotu, the Gambier, the Society, and the Austral Islands. The total land area of these five island groups is some 1,500 square miles, and the total population is about 170,000. Tahiti, one of the Society Islands, is the site of the capital.

In 1880, Tahiti became a territory of France. July 14th, the date on which the French Revolution is commemorated in France, is the central day of Tahiti's largest annual festival. Many athletic and artistic competitions are held and performing groups from many of the surrounding islands come to take part in the festival. Because the government has supplied money for the winners, the festival has always been a source of great excitement and enthusiasm.

The *ote'a* is danced to the accompaniment of only percussion instruments. The percussion ensemble centers on the to'ere, a slit-drum made of a log that has been hollowed out with a long narrow slit running the length of the instrument. At least three to'ere are used in an *ote'a* and are accompanied by a pahu – a bass drum type instrument.

Each of the rhythmic patterns has a specific name. Some patterns are used by all groups while others are newly created patterns that only one groups uses and has a name to describe. The music in an *ote'a* progresses by constantly shifting the rhythmic patterns and the tempo.

The *ote'a* dance style is physically demanding. In actual stage performances the dance almost always tells a story. Often it is combined with performances of *'aparima*: a hand dance which, like the Hawaiian hula, tells the story by means of the hand movement.

An *ote'a* involves the rhythmic movement of legs and hips to percussion accompaniment. Standing on tiptoe, the male dancers bend their legs and rapidly open and close their knees. Women dancers keep their feet firmly on the ground while rotating their hips energetically. They wear skirts (moere) made of bark and lavishly adorn their heads and breasts.

☐   *Ote'a*, traditional Tahitian dance/music.

15. USA

The idea for *Voyage* came while I was traveling in the Brazilian rainforest in October of 1997. In reflecting on the amount of musical borrowings that exist today between the different world music cultures, I decided to write a piece that would musically convey the voyage of music from Tahiti to Hawai'i. Certainly Tahitian music would have to adapt to the new environment of Hawai'i.

Voyage opens with the sounds of the ocean and conch (pu kani) shells. These shells were sometimes used to accompany chants and/or to announce the beginning of a ceremony. Here it is used to symbolize the beginning of the day and to call these early explorers to their canoes. This is contrasted with percussion instruments (to'ere) and rhythms from traditional Tahitian drum music (*ote'a*). Their odyssey, and the musical voyage, then begins as the full orchestra enters with the main themes.

Beginning with the introduction on the ipu heke (double gourd drum), the middle section of the work is based on a Hawaiian *mele* (chant). This section of the composition represents the landing of the first Polynesians in Hawai'i and the subsequent adaptations that took place in their music.

The name of the *mele* is *Maika'i Ka 'Oiwi O Ka'ala* which roughly translates to "Splendid is the form of Mount Ka'ala," on the island of O'ahu. I chose this *mele* because of its beautiful melody and poetry. It describes the peaks and ridges surrounding Mount Ka'ala which are compared to the beauty and shape of a woman. Composed to honor King Kalakaua, each verse is given a different treatment in orchestral tone color. This section, a *kahiko* (ancient) dance style, features kumu hula (master teacher) Keali'i Ceballos and dancers from his hula halau (school) Keali'i O Nalani. (The original version of this chant is on Keali'i Reichel's recording *Lei Hali'a*.)

The return of the conch blowing and Tahitian rhythms signal the return of the Voyage main themes as the music combines Hawaiian, Polynesian, and European elements. The composition was completed in January of 1998 and was dedicated to Mr. Willie Tokishi of American Honda and to hula halau Keali'i O Nalani and kumu hula Keali'i Ceballos. This recording was made in May of 1998 with the South Bay Youth Orchestra under the direction of Dr. Doyle.

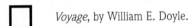 *Voyage*, by William E. Doyle.

16. AUSTRALIA

Australia is home to fourteen species of deadly snakes, poisonous tree and sea snakes, salt and freshwater crocodiles, the box jellyfish (the most poisonous creature on earth), killer sharks, at least five species of deadly spiders, lethal seashells, the cassowary bird (a flightless, man-sized bird with a razor claw on each foot), and other marine 'deadlies' such as the blue-ringed octopus, stonefish, fire-fish, numb ray, and the man-o-war jellyfish to name a few! This continent has one of the most extreme landscapes on earth – from the driest deserts and the wettest rain forests, to the enormously diverse Great Barrier Reef. The reef, which is more than 1,200 miles long, is actually composed of over 3,000 separate reefs and 600 islands. It is longer than the coastline of the west coast of the United States and as important a habitat as the Amazon rain forest. Australia is also home to one of the oldest cultures on earth – the indigenous Aboriginal people.

Aborigines have the oldest continuously maintained culture on earth, and their art and music goes back to the very roots of it. Today the evidence points to an arrival date of the Aborigines of between 45,000 and 60,000 years ago – 30,000 years in advance of anyone else! The historian John Mulvaney believes that the Australian language family may be the world's oldest. This makes their art, stories, and systems of beliefs among the oldest known on earth.

According to my friend David Hudson, "The Aboriginal myths arise from a long time ago, when human beings were believed to eventuate from the stars and supernatural powers were in their possession. These beings were their ancestors and they believed that they created the world around them, the land and the sea. They brought with them the laws, the moral values and the knowledge that they needed to live their life.

They were at peace until changes rocked the land in the form of disasters such as, floods, droughts and volcanoes. To seek refuge against these elements they transformed themselves into animals, birds, insects, plants and rocks in order to hide and protect themselves. It was during this time that the Dreamtime commenced and the multitude of life forms populated the earth in the form we know today."

Dreamtime, or Dreaming, is a term used to describe the Aboriginal system of laws and beliefs. Its basis is their rich mythology about the creation of the earth – their creation stories. Songs and dances, which tell stories of Dreamtime ancestors, have always been a part of the Aboriginal culture. Three instruments that are used in the performance of their music are the clap sticks (pieces of wood that are hit together), boomerangs (also hit together), and the didgeridoo. These instruments, along with clapping the hands and stomping the feet, provide the basis for Aboriginal music performance.

One of the oldest wind instruments in the world, the didgeridoo (yidaki, yigi-yigi) is a ceremonial musical instrument used by many, but not all, Aboriginal people, according to Gavan Flick - owner of *Gavala* Aboriginal Art & Cultural Education Centre in Sydney, Australia. Artists Alanna Rose and Gavan Flick established *Gavala* in 1994 for the Kamilaroi language group located in North-Western New South Wales. "The *Gavala* cultural centre is dedicated to its Aboriginal People and to educating the world about its rich culture and heritage. It is currently the only centre in Sydney which is totally Aboriginal owned and operated, with all its profits returned to the artists." You can visit *Gavala* on the web at: http://www.gavala.com.au

Termites (white ants) naturally eat away at the inside of certain eucalyptus trees making them hollow. After a hollowed out tree is located, the tree is chopped down, stripped of its bark, and cleaned out. Any holes in the bark are plugged up with sugarbag (wax from native honeybees) and a mouthpiece (also made of sugarbag) is formed around the top of the instrument. Once the bark has been scraped off and the finish is smooth, the didgeridoo is painted and decorated with traditional designs in natural (ochre) colors.

Softly vibrating or buzzing the lips in the mouthpiece creates the sound of the didgeridoo. The voice box is used to 'throw the voice' and imitate the sounds of various animals. The secret to playing it, however, is in the 'circular' breathing – a technique of blowing into the didgeridoo and breathing in through your nose at the same time. This creates a continuous sound in the instrument and allows the music to continue uninterrupted. You will notice this technique in David Hudson's solo didgeridoo piece *Emu Chase* and in his more contemporary composition, *Walkabout*. David can be reached on the web at: http://www.davidhudson.com.au

☐   *How to Make and Play the Didgeridoo*, by David Hudson.

☐   *Emu Chase* and *Walkabout*, by David Hudson.

While contemporary Indigenous music is thriving across Australia, many artists have turned to pop music culture (hip-hop, rap, metal, reggae, etc.) bringing traditional and modern elements together. One of the most famous examples comes from the Indigenous group *Yothu Yindi*. The band members are from the traditional owners of North East Arnhem Land – a region of Australia's Northern Territory in which their people (Yolngu) lived in relative isolation until the 1970's. Traditional music performed by this group comes from a people who have lived in, and looked after, their land for more than 40,000 years.

In Yolngu society there is a "complex and elaborate world view, a sophisticated system of kinship, and a rich ceremonial and religious behavior. By attributing human qualities to all natural species and elements, Yolngu people live in spiritual harmony with nature. This is communicated in song and dance," according to the band members. The song *Gapu* (1991), which utilizes traditional instruments, is about the ocean. The lyrics describe the changing tide as it gathers brings in life from the ocean to the shore. *Treaty*, a song from the same album, became an international hit as it called for a treaty and cooperation between Aboriginal and Euro-Australian cultures.

☐ *Gapu* and *Treaty*, by Yothu Yindi.

17. PAPUA NEW GUINEA

Living in small, remote villages, most of the PNG tribe's people (Melanesian) live by subsistence farming growing yams and sweet potatoes. To this day, tribal customs, languages and cultural identities have been retained. But the modern world is nearby – in Port Moresby there are televisions and computers while in the countryside and along the Sepik River, the locals still hunt and fight with bows and arrows and 'bride price' is paid with shells and pigs.

In addition to having over 700 regional languages, PNG has two official languages: English and Pidgin (the most often heard language). In the 1960's the Australian government introduced the original Mount Hagen 'sing sing' as a way for tribes to compete peacefully. Each tribe enters the competition area (a huge grassy patch of land) wearing their traditional costumes while singing and dancing. Many wear grass and leaf skirts, massive shell necklaces, and a variety of huge, multi-colored feather headdresses. This event lasts for two days and is organized so that each group wins some type of award that encourages them to return the following year.

Along the 700-mile Sepik River the tribes speak more than 250 languages making communication difficult between villages. In these villages the people believe strongly in spirits. In the middle region, for example, crocodiles contain the spirits and the ceremonies they perform and carvings they create symbolize their relationship to these spirits. Their huge 'spirit houses' (Haus Tamberans) sit on top of ornamental carved posts and are the focal point of life along the river. The rites that occur here involve initiation, victory celebrations, births, deaths, and other special events. Pairs of flute players (men that have been initiated) perform on the longest flutes in the world. The example you will hear is music to welcome a young initiate into the Haus Tamberan. Dating back thousands of years, these flutes are performed as the men walk slowly around the lodge in a circle.

☐ *Sepik Flutes*, Papua New Guinea.

Bamboo bands are very popular in PNG today. Local villagers create these musical instruments from stacks of varying lengths of bamboo. These bamboo xylophones, erected on ladders, are beaten with rubber flip-flops or tennis shoes. The sound of their voices, the rhythm of their bamboo xylophones, and the guitar (with maximum distortion) all combine to make an exciting and exotic musical performance. This song, sung in Pidgin, was composed in 1985 to celebrate the 10th Anniversary of Independence for PNG.

☐ *Wagi Brothers Bamboo Band*, Papua New Guinea.

Composer Profiles

Adam de la Halle
Dates:	c.1237 - c.1288
Country:	France
Refer to:	Chapter 9
Composition:	"J'osè bien a m'amie parler"
Genre:	secular song
Musical Era:	Middle Ages
Did you know?	He was a French composer (trouvère) from the Middle Ages who worked in Naples, Italy.

Adams, John
Dates:	born in 1947
Country:	United States
Refer to:	Chapter 6, 12, 15, 16
Composition:	*Gnarly Buttons, Nixon in China, Chamber Symphony* and *Shaker Loops*
Genre:	concerto, opera, chamber
Musical Era:	20th century, Minimalism
Did you know?	He received a Grammy award for his opera *Nixon in China*.

Albéniz, Isaac
Dates:	1860 - 1909
Country:	Spain
Refer to:	Chapter 15
Composition:	*Sevilla* and *Asturia*
Genre:	music for guitar
Musical Era:	Romantic
Did you know?	A pianist, he was the founder of the modern Spanish nationalist school of music.

Bach, Johann Sebastian
Dates:	1685 - 1750
Country:	Germany
Refer to:	Chapter 4, 5, 6, 10, 15
Composition:	many instrumental and vocal works
Genre:	everything but opera
Musical Era:	Baroque
Did you know?	The same doctor who ruined his eyesight also operated on and ruined Handel's.

Bartók, Béla
Dates:	1881 - 1945
Country:	Hungary
Refer to:	Chapter 6
Composition:	*Concerto for Orchestra*

Genre:	concerto
Musical Era:	20th century
Did you know?	He died penniless in New York City in 1945.

Beethoven, Ludwig von

Dates:	1770 - 1827
Country:	Germany
Refer to:	Chapter 5, 7, 8
Composition:	*Pathétique Sonata, Symphony No. 3, 5, and 9*
Genre:	sonata, symphony
Musical Era:	Classical, bridge to Romantic
Did you know?	In 1809 when Vienna fell to Napoleon, Beethoven hid in his basement with pillows over his head.

Berg, Alban

Dates:	1885 - 1935
Country:	Austria
Refer to:	Chapter 16
Composition:	*Wozzeck*
Genre:	Expressionism and 12-tone
Musical Era:	20th century
Did you know?	With the coming of Hitler to power, the works of Berg, Webern, and Schoenberg were all banned in Germany.

Berlioz, Hector

Dates:	1803 - 1869
Country:	France
Refer to:	Chapter 9, 14
Composition:	*Symphonie Fantastique*
Genre:	symphonic poem (tone poem)
Musical Era:	Romantic
Did you know?	His "fatal attraction" to Harriet Smithson was the inspiration for his *Symphonie Fantastique*.

Bernstein, Leonard

Dates:	1918 - 1990
Country:	United States
Refer to:	Chapter 16
Composition:	*On the Town, West Side Story*
Genre:	musicals, jazz, American music
Musical Era:	20th century
Did you know?	A modern-day Renaissance man, he was a famous conductor, composer, pianist, and the author of many books on music.

Bizet, Georges

Dates: 1838 - 1875
Country: France
Refer to: Chapter 12
Composition: *Carmen*
Genre: opera
Musical Era: Romantic
Did you know? The opera *Carmen* has been performed in many languages including Russian and Japanese.

Brahms, Johannes

Dates: 1833 - 1897
Country: Germany
Refer to: Chapter 3, 8, 10
Composition: *Symphony No. 1* and *A German Requiem*
Genre: symphony and requiem mass
Musical Era: Romantic
Did you know? Considered the successor to Beethoven, he did not write his first symphony until he was 43 years old.

Britten, Edward Benjamin

Dates: 1913 - 1976
Country: England
Refer to: Chapter 2 and 10
Composition: *Young Person's Guide to the Orchestra* and *The War Requiem*
Genre: orchestral work with narrator, requiem mass
Musical Era: 20th century
Did you know? He is probably the most important 20th century English composer.

Cage, John

Dates: 1912 - 1992
Country: United States
Refer to: Chapter 16
Composition: *Sixteen Sonatas*
Genre: prepared piano
Musical Era: 20th century
Did you know? His piece *Imaginary Landscape No. 4* was written for 12 radios that were set to predetermined wavelengths, and played whatever was "on the air" at the time of the concert.

Chopin, Frédéric

Dates: 1810 - 1849
Country: Poland
Refer to: Chapter 15
Composition: mazurkas, polonaises, and nocturnes

Genre:	character pieces, solo piano works
Musical Era:	Romantic
Did you know?	His lover was a woman who took the pen-name of George Sands. She dressed like a man and smoked cigars.

Copland, Aaron

Dates:	1900 - 1990
Country:	United States
Refer to:	Chapter 13
Composition:	*Rodeo*
Genre:	ballet
Musical Era:	20th century
Did you know?	He is considered the "Dean" of American music. He won an Academy Award for his film music to the movie *The Heiress*.

Debussy, Claude

Dates:	1862 - 1918
Country:	France
Refer to:	Chapter 5, 14
Composition:	*Sonata for Flute, Viola, and Harp, Prelude to the Afternoon of a Faun*, "Voiles," "La fille aux cheveux de lin," and *Nocturnes*.
Genre:	sonata, piano music, program music (tone poem)
Musical Era:	20th century, Impressionism
Did you know?	In 1889 he heard the gamelan orchestras from Java and became fascinated with their scales (pentatonic), unusual timbres, and textures.

Dvořák, Antonin

Dates:	1841 - 1904
Country:	Czech
Refer to:	Chapter 8
Composition:	*Symphony No. 9*
Genre:	symphony
Musical Era:	Romantic
Did you know?	He had a fascination and passion for steam engines and trains.

Gabrieli, Giovanni

Dates:	c.1556 - 1612
Country:	Italy (Venice)
Refer to:	Chapter 4
Composition:	"In ecclesiis"
Genre:	motet, sacred vocal work
Musical Era:	Renaissance
Did you know?	He worked for St. Mark's Church in Venice, Italy.

Gershwin, George

Dates:	1898 - 1937
Country:	United States
Refer to:	Chapter 16
Composition:	*Rhapsody in Blue*
Genre:	combined jazz and symphonic music
Musical Era:	20th century
Did you know?	Started out as a song plugger on Tin Pan Alley and ended up writing for Broadway musicals and Hollywood movies.

Glass, Philip

Dates:	born in 1937
Country:	United States
Refer to:	Chapter 16
Composition:	*Einstein on the Beach* and *Koyaanisqatsi*
Genre:	opera, film
Musical Era:	20th century, Minimalism
Did you know?	He was the film score composer for the movie *Koyaanisqatsi*, which is a Hopi (native American) word that translates to "life out of balance."

Grofé, Ferde

Dates:	1892 - 1972
Country:	United States
Refer to:	Chapter 15, 16
Composition:	*Grand Canyon Suite*
Genre:	suite (20th century)
Musical Era:	20th century
Did you know?	Born in New York, he wrote nine suites based on various locations in the U.S., including a *San Francisco Suite* and a *Hollywood Suite*.

Guido d'Arezzo

Dates:	c.995 - c.1050
Country:	Italy
Refer to:	Chapter 9
Composition:	none
Genre:	music theorist
Musical Era:	Middle Ages
Did you know?	The first "music educator," he invented sight-singing.

Handel, George Frideric

Dates:	1685 - 1759
Country:	Germany
Refer to:	Chapter 4, 10
Composition:	*Messiah* and *Music for the Royal Fireworks*

Genre:	suite and oratorio
Musical Era:	Baroque
Did you know?	He conducted a performance of the *Messiah* one week before he died. Completely blind (unsuccessful cataract operations), he was put to bed thoroughly exhausted after the performance. He never got out of bed, and died on April 14th, 1759.

Haydn, Franz Joseph

Dates:	1732 - 1809
Country:	Austria
Refer to:	Chapter 7
Composition:	*Symphony No. 29* and *Symphony No. 104*
Genre:	symphony
Musical Era:	Classical
Did you know?	W.A. Mozart referred to him as "Papa" Haydn.

Holst, Gustav

Dates:	1874 - 1934
Country:	England
Refer to:	Chapter 14, 15
Composition:	*The Planets*
Genre:	program symphony
Musical Era:	20th century
Did you know?	This work does not contain a movement for "Pluto" because in 1914, when the piece was composed, this planet had not been discovered.

Ives, Charles

Dates:	1874 - 1954
Country:	United States
Refer to:	Chapter 16
Composition:	*A Symphony: New England Holidays*
Genre:	program symphony
Musical Era:	20th century
Did you know?	A graduate of Yale University, Ives was an insurance salesman. He created "Term Life" insurance.

Janácek, Leos

Dates:	1854 - 1928
Country:	Czech
Refer to:	Chapter 15
Composition:	*Sinfonietta*
Genre:	program symphony, but more like a suite
Musical Era:	20th century
Did you know?	His passion for a married woman 38 years younger than him was partly responsible for his inspiration and incredible musical output that began when he was already in his sixties.

Josquin des Prez

Dates:	c.1420 - 1521
Country:	A Burgundian town near France
Refer to:	Chapter 9
Composition:	"Tu pauperum refugium"
Genre:	motet
Musical Era:	Renaissance
Did you know?	He is considered the greatest early Renaissance composer of the Netherlands School (Northern France, Belgium, and Holland).

Léonin

Dates:	Late 12th century
Country:	France
Refer to:	Chapter 9
Composition:	"Gradual"
Genre:	chant, organum
Musical Era:	Middle Ages
Did you know?	He was a monk at Notre-Dame Cathedral in Paris.

Liszt, Franz

Dates:	1811 - 1886
Country:	Hungary
Refer to:	Chapter 15
Composition:	"La Leggierezza" and "Waldesrauschen"
Genre:	concert etudes
Musical Era:	Romantic
Did you know?	As a composer, pianist, conductor, he inaugurated the recital as a popular form of musical presentation.

Machaut, Guillaume de

Dates:	c.1300 - 1377
Country:	France
Refer to:	Chapter 9
Composition:	"Hoquetus David" and *Messe de Notre Dame*
Genre:	motet, mass
Musical Era:	Middle Ages
Did you know?	He was a French composer and poet from the late Middle Ages.

Mahler, Gustav

Dates:	1860 - 1911
Country:	Austria
Refer to:	Chapter 8
Composition:	*Symphony No. 5*
Genre:	symphony

Musical Era: Post-Romantic
Did you know?   He was more famous as a conductor than as a composer during his lifetime.

Mendelssohn, Felix
Dates: 1809-1847
Country: Germany
Refer to: Chapter 8
Composition: *Symphony No. 4*
Genre: symphony, overture
Musical Era: Romantic
Did you know?   Started during a trip to Rome, the "Italian" symphony was completed in London.

Morley, Thomas
Dates: 1557 - 1602
Country: England
Refer to: Chapter 9
Composition: "Now is the Month of Maying" and "Farewell, disdainful"
Genre: madrigal
Musical Era: Renaissance
Did you know?   He was the author of the first treatise (manual) on music printed in England.

Mozart, Wolfgang Amadeus
Dates: 1756 - 1791
Country: Austria
Refer to: Chapter 4, 5, 6, 7, 10, 11, 15
Composition: sonata, symphony, opera, requiem mass, serenade, concerto
Genre: He excelled in just about everything he wrote!
Musical Era: Classical
Did you know?   Although he is credited with composing 41 symphonies, there is no *Symphony No. 37.*

Mussorgsky, Modest
Dates: 1839 - 1881
Country: Russia
Refer to: Chapter 14
Composition: *Pictures at an Exhibition* and *Boris Godunov*
Genre: program music, opera
Musical Era: Romantic
Did you know?   Only three of the movements in *Pictures at an Exhibition* correspond to the pictures at the actual exhibition in 1874 staged by Vladimir Stassov. The rest are from drawings that he had seen in Victor Hartmann's home.

Palestrina, Giovanni Pierluigi da
Dates: 1525 - 1594
Country: Italy

Refer to:	Chapter 9
Composition:	"Exulate Deo"
Genre:	sacred choral piece
Musical Era:	Renaissance
Did you know?	He is named for the town in which he was born, Palestrina.

Pérotin

Dates:	c.1160 - c.1220
Country:	France
Refer to:	Chapter 9
Composition:	"Gradual"
Genre:	chant, polyphony
Musical Era:	Middle Ages
Did you know?	He was a monk at Notre-Dame Cathedral in Paris. He was also influential in the development of the motet.

Praetorius, Michael

Dates:	1571 - 1621
Country:	Germany
Refer to:	Chapter 4
Composition:	"Courante"
Genre:	dance (suite)
Musical Era:	Renaissance
Did you know?	A prolific composer and important music historian, his book *Syntagma Musicum* is an important source for information on the musical instruments of the Renaissance.

Prokofiev, Sergei

Dates:	1891 - 1953
Country:	Russia
Refer to:	Chapter 2, 8
Composition:	*Peter and the Wolf* and *Symphony No. 1*
Genre:	program work, symphony
Musical Era:	20th century
Did you know?	Having left Russia after the Revolution (1918), he divided his time between France and the United States. He died the same day as Stalin.

Puccini, Giacomo

Dates:	1858 - 1924
Country:	Italy
Refer to:	Chapter 11
Composition:	*La Bohème*
Genre:	opera
Musical Era:	Romantic
Did you know?	He had originally planned on being a church composer. But when he heard Verdi's opera *Aida* at age 17, he enrolled at the Milan Conservatory to study opera composition.

Ravel, Joseph Maurice

Dates:	1875 - 1937
Country:	France
Refer to:	Chapter 2, 15
Composition:	*Boléro* and *Alborada del gracioso*
Genre:	ballet music
Musical Era:	20th century, Impressionism
Did you know?	During W.W. I he drove an ambulance on the front lines. Later, when Gershwin wanted to study composition with him, Ravel advised him to continue his unique style of incorporating jazz into concert music.

Reich, Steve

Dates:	born in 1936
Country:	United States
Refer to:	Chapter 16
Composition:	*Eight Lines* and *Electric Counterpoint*
Genre:	instrumental
Musical Era:	20th century, Minimalism
Did you know?	Was a classmate of Philip Glass during the 1950's at the Julliard School of Music in New York.

Rodrigo, Joaquín

Dates:	born in 1901
Country:	Spain
Refer to:	Chapter 6
Composition:	*Concierto de Aranjuez*
Genre:	concerto (for guitar and orchestra)
Musical Era:	20th century
Did you know?	Rodrigo has been blind since the age of 3.

Saint-Saëns, Camille

Dates:	1835 - 1921
Country:	France
Refer to:	Chapter 2
Composition:	*Carnival of the Animals*
Genre:	program work
Musical Era:	Romantic
Did you know?	He practiced for two hours in the morning the day he died.

Schoenberg, Arnold

Dates:	1874 - 1951
Country:	Austria
Refer to:	Chapter 10, 16
Composition:	*Pierrot Lunaire* and *Suite for Piano*, Op. 25
Genre:	vocal/chamber and solo piano

Musical Era: 20th century, Expressionism and 12-tone
Did you know?   He is the creator of the 12-tone system and was also a painter in the Expressionistic style.

Schubert, Franz
Dates: 1797 - 1828
Country: Austria
Refer to: Chapter 10
Composition: *Der Atlas, Erlkönig*
Genre: art songs
Musical Era: Romantic
Did you know?   His nickname was "little mushroom" because he was not even five feet tall.

Shostakovich, Dimitri
Dates: 1906 - 1975
Country: Russia
Refer to: Chapter 6
Composition: *Piano Concerto No. 2*
Genre: concerto
Musical Era: 20th century
Did you know?   His *Symphony No. 10* is a grim portrait of Stalin.

Smetana, Bedrich
Dates: 1824 - 1884
Country: Czech
Refer to: Chapter 14
Composition: *Má Vlast*
Genre: tone poem
Musical Era: Romantic
Did you know?   Smetana, considered the first composer of nationalist Czech music, was the son of a brewmeister.

Strauss II, Johann
Dates: 1825 - 1899
Country: Austria
Refer to: Chapter 15
Composition: *The Blue Danube*
Genre: waltz
Musical Era: Romantic
Did you know?   Angry with his father, Johann II gathered together some musicians, hired a hall, and began his own successful concert series.

Strauss, Richard
Dates: 1864 - 1949
Country: Germany

Refer to:	Chapter 5, 12, 14
Composition:	*Sonata for Violin and Piano*, *Salome*, and *Don Juan*
Genre:	sonata, opera, tone poem
Musical Era:	Post-Romantic
Did you know?	He was the first millionaire in music. He was famous for his conducting and his tone poems.

Stravinsky, Igor

Dates:	1882 - 1971
Country:	Russia
Refer to:	Chapter 13
Composition:	*The Firebird Suite*, and his ballets
Genre:	orchestral suite from original ballet music
Musical Era:	20th century, Primitivism
Did you know?	He was supposed to become a law student, but switched to music and studied composition with Rimsky-Korsakov. He is the author's favorite composer.

Tchaikovsky, Piotr (Peter) Ilich

Dates:	1840 - 1893
Country:	Russia
Refer to:	Chapter 6, 13, 14
Composition:	*Piano Concerto No. 1*, *The Nutcracker*, and *Overture 1812*
Genre:	concerto, ballet, tone poem
Musical Era:	Romantic
Did you know?	Tchaikovsky's patron had only one requirement—that they must never meet face to face.

Vaughan Williams, Ralph

Dates:	1872 - 1958
Country:	England
Refer to:	Chapter 15
Composition:	*Fantasia on Greensleeves* and *English Folk Song Suite*
Genre:	fantasia, band music
Musical Era:	20th century
Did you know?	His music for British bands is widely played throughout Europe and the United States.

Verdi, Giuseppe

Dates:	1813 - 1901
Country:	Italy
Refer to:	Chapter 12
Composition:	*Aida*
Genre:	opera
Musical Era:	Romantic
Did you know?	He raised 19th century opera to new heights with such works as *La traviata*, *Il trovatore*, *Rigoletto*, *Otello*, and *Falstaff*.

Vivaldi, Antonio

Dates:	1678 - 1741
Country:	Italy (Venice)
Refer to:	Chapter 6
Composition:	*Concerto No. 1 in F major* and *La Primavera*
Genre:	concerto grosso, concerto
Musical Era:	Baroque
Did you know?	Vivaldi was a famous Italian violin virtuoso, priest, and teacher who taught at an all-girl orphanage in Venice near St. Mark's Square.

Wagner, Wilhelm Richard

Dates:	1813 - 1883
Country:	Germany
Refer to:	Chapter 12
Composition:	*Ring Cycle, Tristan and Isolde*
Genre:	opera
Musical Era:	Post-Romantic
Did you know?	Wagner was married to Franz Liszt's daughter, Cosima.

Walton, William

Dates:	1902 – 1983
Country:	England
Refer to:	Chapter 10
Composition:	*Façade*
Genre:	poetry with accompaniment
Musical Era:	20th century
Did you know?	He was at first regarded as an 'enfant terrible' because of *Façade* and the 'jazz-age' influence on his early works.

Webern, Anton

Dates:	1883 - 1945
Country:	Austria
Refer to:	Chapter 16
Composition:	*Five Pieces for Orchestra*
Genre:	Expressionism, 12-tone
Musical Era:	20th century
Did you know?	In September of 1945 he was mistakenly shot and killed by an American occupation soldier. Why? Because he lit a cigarette outdoors during the evening curfew hours.

Expressive Elements

Dynamics

ppp	—	extremely soft
pp	pianissimo	very soft
p	piano	soft
mp	mezzo piano	moderately soft
mf	mezzo forte	moderately loud
f	forte	loud (strong)
ff	fortissimo	very loud
fff	—	extremely loud

Dynamic Changes

Crescendo	To gradually get louder.
Decrescendo	To gradually get softer (also, diminuendo).
Terrace	Abrupt changes; alternating forte to piano.

Tempo Markings

Grave	extremely slow, solemn
Largo	very slow, broadly
Lento	slow
Adagio	slow, easily
Andante	moderately slow, walking
Moderato	moderate
Allegretto	moderately fast
Allegro	fast
Vivace	very fast and animated
Presto	very fast

Descriptors

Agitato	agitated
Assai	very
Cantabile	in a singing style (melodic)
Con brio	with spirit
Con fuoco	with fire
Con moto	with motion
Grazioso	gracefully
Ma non	but not

Maestoso	majestically
Meno	less
Molto	very
Non troppo	not too much
Piu	more
Poco	little

Tempo Changes

Accelerando	To speed up.
Ritardando	Slow down.
Rallentando	To gradually slow down.
Rubato	Borrowed time, a flexible tempo indication.

Vocal Characteristics

Soprano	Coloratura - virtuosic, extended high range.
	Lyric - lighter.
	Dramatic - lower range, more powerful.
Alto	Lower range than soprano.
Tenor	Heroic, lyric.
Baritone	In between tenor and bass.
Bass	Baritone, lyric, profondo.

Timbre Classifications

Chordophones	Any instrument that has a string that is plucked, bowed, or struck.
Aerophones	Woodwind and brass families (from the flutes to the tubas).
Membranophones	Percussion instruments with a "head" or membrane that is struck. Pitched and non-pitched:
	pitched - timpani
	non-pitched - snare, toms, bass, tambourine.
Idiophones	Percussion instruments without a membrane head.
	pitched - xylophone, marimba, celesta, chimes, bells, piano
	non-pitched - claves, triangle, temple block, cymbal, gong, castanets, etc.
Keyboard	Often considered a separate family; piano, organ, harpsichord, etc.
Electrophones	Synthesizers, MIDI controlled instruments, drum machines.

Musical Terminology

A-PHRASE. The first phrase of a theme.

A-SECTION. The first section of a musical form.

ABSOLUTE MUSIC. Music for the sake of music, abstract music, the opposite of music that tells a story.

A CAPPELLA. A choral performance without any instrumental accompaniment, for voices alone.

ACCELERANDO. To gradually speed up, to get faster (tempo)

ACCENT. An emphasis or stress on a note or chord (harmony) either by playing it louder or by holding it longer.

ACCIDENTALS. Sharps, flats, and natural signs used to indicate a raised or lowered note that is outside of the main key (tonal) area.

ACCOMPANIMENT. The subsidiary or secondary parts that accompany or support a theme.

ADAGIO. A tempo indication for a slow, easy pace (speed).

AEROPHONES. The woodwind and brass families, any instrument that has a sound created by air.

AIR. A tune or melody for a voice or instrument.

ALEATORIC. A twentieth century style of music whereby the control of the piece is given from the composer back to the performer. It usually features elements of chance, randomness, and improvisation.

ALLEGRETTO. A moderately fast tempo indication.

ALLEGRO. An indication for a fast tempo.

ALTO. The vocal classification for the lowest of the female voices. Also called contralto.

ANDANTE. A tempo indication for a leisurely, walking speed.

ANTIPHONAL. An imitative type of texture whereby a call and a response between choirs occurs.

APPOGGIATURA. Italian "to lean." A melodic device used by Mozart (and others) where a dissonant interval or chord that is played on a strong beat is resolved on a weak beat.

ARCO. A string instrument bowing indication. This tells the performer to use the bow as opposed to plucking (pizzicato) the string.

ARIA. One of the big moments in an opera, oratorio, or cantata - the big melodies. It is a song for a solo voice and usually emphasizes vocal virtuosity.

ARPEGGIO. Notes of a chord that are played in sequence rather than simultaneously.

ARTICULATION. How a note is to be played or sung - legato, staccato, marcato, and pizzicato are common articulations.

ART SONG. A Romantic work (lied, or lieder) for voice and piano. This genre utilizes a high quality text and has an equal treatment of voice and piano—they are equal partners.

ATONALITY. The avoidance and lack of tonality, home base, or the key center. Derived from the music of Schoenberg (12 tone system, tone row).

ATTACK. The act of beginning a note, phrase, or melody. It is the starting place.

AUGMENTATION. In development, the process of making the melody longer or stretching it out by increasing the rhythmic value (length) of the notes.

AVANT-GARDE. A French term used to describe the radical or advanced works of various artists and composers. One composer of this style is Pierre Boulez.

B-PHRASE. The second phrase of a theme.

B-SECTION. The second section of a musical form.

BALANCE. The fine-tuning of timbres, dynamic levels, etc. in an ensemble so that no one voice or instrument overshadows another.

BALLADE. A typical Romantic piece for solo piano (Chopin) that is lyric and somewhat narrative (tells a story). One of the many types of character pieces or piano miniatures (genre) of the Romantic piano composers, especially Chopin and Liszt.

BAR. See MEASURE.

BARITONE. The vocal classification for the high register of the bass voice.

BAROQUE. Style period of music from 1600-1750. It begins with opera in approximately 1600 and ends with the death of J.S. Bach in 1750. Word comes from the Portuguese word "barocco" and was used by the Classical composers to designate works that were crude, overly emotional, elaborate, flamboyant, and excessively decorative.

BASS. The classification for the lowest range of the male voice. This term is also used to refer to the lowest instrument(s) in the orchestra and for the lowest instrument in a particular family (i.e., the bass clarinet).

BASS LINE. The lowest part of a musical texture. It serves as the foundation for the harmony.

BASSO CONTINUO. Baroque era; the harpsichord and the cello (perhaps bassoon and/or bass) that combine to provide a continuous accompaniment pattern. They are also used to keep the beat (pulse) and to the keyboard, in particular, it is expected to fill-in where necessary. See CONTINUO.

BEAT. The musical pulse, see RHYTHM.

BEL CANTO. An Italian style of singing that stresses the beauty of the voice as opposed to the dramatic interpretation of the melody. This is the opposite of the "declamatory" style of singing (Wagner).

BINARY FORM. A common two part form; A - B, two contrasting sections of music.

BITONALITY. The use of two keys (tonal centers) simultaneously. Used commonly in the twentieth century.

BOLÉRO. A Spanish dance in a moderate tempo in a triple meter.

BLUES. A vocal and instrumental style of "jazz" music that originated in the early twentieth century in America.

BOURRÉE. A dance of French or Spanish origin, stately in style, in a duple meter with a quick tempo. Generally found in the Baroque suites.

BOW. A mildly curved piece of wood with horse hair stretched between the ends, use in string playing.

BRASS. Family of instruments that includes the trumpet, horn, trombone, tuba, and their related instruments (cornet, flugelhorn, etc.)

BRASS QUINTET. A chamber ensemble consisting of two trumpets, horn, trombone and tuba. Common from the Baroque era to the present.

BRIDGE. A transition between two sections, commonly found in sonata-allegro form.

B.W.V. Catalog listing for J.S. Bach's music.

CADENCE. The ending of a musical phrase, a resting point (point of repose), release.

CADENZA. A virtuosic passage for a soloist (unaccompanied) in the concerto, may be improvised.

CANON. An imitative form of music, the use of the same melody in different voices with each voice entering at a later (different) time - similar to a round. It is polyphonic in texture.

CANTABILE. In a "singing" style.

CANTATA. A composition (genre) for solo voice(s), orchestra and chorus. It is the Lutheran equivalent to the Catholic oratorio.

CASTRATO. A male singer who has been "neutered" in order to keep his voice in the high soprano register and pure in quality. In the Renaissance and Baroque, many of these castrati became famous opera singers.

CELL. The smallest unit or part of a musical theme. Another term is motive or motif.

CHACONNE. A musical form in which variations are built on a short bass theme which is continually repeated. The bass has an ostinato effect.

CHAMBER MUSIC. Music designed for an intimate performance venue (literally, in the King's chambers). There are many types of chamber music including string quartets, woodwind quintets, etc. All of them generally feature one player on a part.

CHANCE MUSIC. See ALEATORIC.

CHARACTER PIECE. A programmatic work for solo piano.

CHORALE. A hymn tune with a German (vernacular) text. Through the reforms of Martin Luther

(German, Protestant), this music was composed for the purpose of involving the congregation in the singing of these hymns.

CHORD. Simultaneous sounding of three or more notes (harmony). The triad, composed of three notes, is one of the most common chords.

CHORDOPHONES. The family of string instruments (including guitar, harp, etc.).

CHOREOGRAPHER. The person who plans the dancer's movements and gestures.

CHORUS. A large vocal ensemble (soprano, tenor, alto, bass - SATB). Also, the refrain part of music AABA; the A section is the verse, the B section is the chorus or refrain. Also, a section of an opera or oratorio sung by the chorus members.

CHROMATIC. A scale or melody that utilizes all twelve notes available in Western music. It is composed entirely of half-steps.

CHROMATIC SCALE. The pattern that results from the successive movement of half steps—there are twelve half-steps found in Western music.

CLASSICAL. Style period of music from 1750 - 1820. It refers to the "Age of Reason" where the music was based not on emotions (Baroque), but on style, elegance, symmetry, balance, and proportion.

CLAVIER (Klavier). Term used in the 18th century to refer to a keyboard instrument.

CLOSING SECTION. The portion of the exposition or recap (sonata-allegro form) where the music is wrapped up with a series of closing themes.

CODA. The concluding section (ending) of a piece of music. It is the part that let's you know that the movement or the piece is about to end. Usually characterized by changes from tension to release and dynamic contrasts.

CODETTA. A short concluding section found within the music and not at the end of the piece. It is shorter than a coda.

COLOR. The tone quality, or timbre, of a sound.

COLORATURA. A virtuoso singing style that features the soprano voice in its extreme upper register. It is often associated with a light, high, voice that is capable of singing fast scales, ornaments, and arpeggios.

CONCERTINO. The group of soloists in a concerto grosso. It is also the name for a short work in the concerto style.

CONCERT MASTER. The first chair player in the first violin section of an orchestra. The duties of this person include assisting the conductor, establish the bowings for the string section, and making orchestra decisions regarding personnel, touring, etc. The concert master also has the responsibility of tuning the orchestra and in playing the solo passages in the music.

CONCERTO. A composition (genre) that features the interplay of a soloist and an orchestra (accompaniment). Usually in three movements - Allegro, Andante, Allegro.

CONCERTO GROSSO. A Baroque genre in which several soloists interplay with an orchestra (accompaniment). The concertino (soloists) are contrasted with the ripieno (full ensemble). Usually in three movements - Allegro, Andante, Allegro.

CONDUCTOR. The director of an ensemble. This person is responsible for coordinating the ensemble's performance, interpreting the music of the composer and in leading the orchestra in that musical interpretation.

CONSONANCE. Musical sounds that combine a harmonious (pleasing) manner. This is the "release" in the music.

CONTINUO. A Baroque texture that features a dominant soprano melody paired with a bass voice (foundation). The soprano and bass were supported by an improvised keyboard (harpsichord) part that is also called the continuo. See BASSO CONTINUO.

CONTRAPUNTAL. Featuring counterpoint, the style of using counterpoint. See COUNTERPOINT.

CONTRAST. A basic principle of music whereby two melodies, for example, are written in such a way that the audience can distinguish one from the other. In sonata-allegro form, the first melody is rhythmic with a contrasting second melody that is melodic. The principle of contrast also applies to form, see BINARY.

COUNTERPOINT. A simultaneous setting of two or more melodies against each other.

COURANTE. French dance from the Renaissance and Baroque eras. Can also be found in the Baroque instrumental suite. It is a lively dance in a triple meter with a fast tempo.

CRESCENDO. A gradual increase in the volume level.

CYCLE. A group of related pieces, usually songs (i.e., Schubert, Schoenberg).

CYCLIC. A process utilized by Beethoven (and others) whereby the movements of a piece of music are all related to each other. This is often done, as Beethoven did in his *Symphony No. 5*, by using a melody from one movement in another movement as a way of unifying the movements.

D. Catalog marking for the music of Franz Schubert.

DA CAPO ARIA. A solo vocal form in ternary form (ABA) in which the return to the A section is ornamented. Da capo literally means "to the head."

DECLAMATORY. Vocal style where the clear and correct pronunciation of the words is of the highest importance.

DECRESCENDO. A gradual decrease in dynamics, to get softer gradually.

DEVELOPMENT. The middle section of sonata-allegro form in which the principal themes from the exposition are expanded as the composer explores the various melodic, rhythmic and harmonic possibilities of the themes. Techniques such as fragmentation, augmentation, and diminution are used. Often there is a conflict between themes and keys (major and minor).

DIATONIC. The notes of the major or minor scale (seven notes).

DIMINUENDO. Another term for decrescendo, to get softer gradually.

DIMINUTION. The playing of a musical theme twice as fast. This is the opposite of augmentation.

DISSONANCE. Musical sounds that combine in a tense or displeasing manner. The resulting sounds are restless, unstable, and in need of resolution.

DOCTRINE OF AFFECTIONS. A Baroque concept that brought more emotion to the music. The idea was to have the music make you feel something—usually what the text (or theme) says or suggests.

DOLCE. To play/sing something "sweetly."

DOMINANT. A chord built on the fifth step of the scale. It usually requires a resolution back to the tonic (home base).

DOUBLE STOP. The simultaneous sounding of two notes on a string instrument.

DOWNBEAT. The accented first beat of a measure.

DOYLE. The author of this textbook.

DRAMATIC FORM. Used in Romantic music, the music follows the story in an attempt to portray the dramatic action. Sometimes it is quite literal, other times the music simply suggests the story.

DRONE. A rudimentary type of harmony whereby a note (or two) is maintained below the melody. Bagpipes are one example.

DUET. A composition for two players.

DUPLE METER. A rhythmic pattern in which a strong beat (accented) is followed by a weak beat (unaccented).

DURATION. One of the aspects of rhythm, it refers to the length of the notes - either long or short. Duration can also be applied to the silence or "rests" in the music.

DYNAMICS. The relative loudness or softness of the musical sounds.

ELECTRONIC MUSIC. Music in which sounds are created with, or modified by, an electronic instrument (i.e., a synthesizer).

ELECTROPHONES. A family of instruments whose sound is created or altered through the use of electronics (i.e., a synthesizer).

EMBELLISH. The musical technique of varying a theme by adding more notes to it.

ENSEMBLE. A group of performing musicians—either vocal or instrumental, large or small (chamber).

EPISODE. The section of the fugue in which the fugue themes are combined polyphonically.

EQUAL TEMPERAMENT. A standardized way of tuning that allows performers to move freely from key to key. This became the standard of Western music from the time of J.S. Bach onwards.

ÉTUDE. Literally, a study. As a piano genre, it was designed to explore a specific technical problem or sonority.

EXPOSITION. The first part of sonata-allegro form. In this section, the principal themes (usually two) are introduced. Frequently, the entire exposition is played twice, making it a "double exposition."

EXPRESSIONISM. An early twentieth century German art form that had a parallel in music. In style, it is highly emotional, hyper-expressive, and often morbid. The sounds are usually dissonant with jagged and angular melodies.

EXTENDED CHORDS or HARMONIES. Chords that contain more than the usual three notes (triad).

EXTRAMUSICAL. This refers to something that is non-musical - perhaps an idea, a character, an emotion. Usually the extra-musical ideas came from literary sources.

FANTASIA. An improvisatory-sounding character piece that is free in form. Often, it is a medley.

FERMATA. An indication in the music that a particular note or chord is to be held for an indefinite amount of time.

FIGURE. A general term for a short melodic pattern.

FINALE. The last movement of a work.

FOLK LORE (TALES). The stories and tales from the people of a certain country, region, nationality, religion, etc.

FOLK SONG (MUSIC). A song from the people. Usually the speech characteristics of the people are present in the melodies.

FORM. The organization of a piece of music—the internal architecture of music.

FORTE (F). A dynamic marking that denotes "loud" or strong.

FORTISSIMO (FF). A dynamic marking that denotes very loud.

FLAT. An indication to lower a note a half-step (half-tone). It can also mean playing somewhat under the proper pitch (out-of-tune).

FRAGMENTATION. The process by which a theme is broken down into smaller units (cells) for development.

FUGATO. In a fugue style. A passage or section of a piece that is fugue-like, but is not a strict fugue.

FUGUE. A complex, polyphonic style of composition. Developed during the Baroque era, this imitative type of music generally begins with a theme alone. It is then imitated (four times) and contrasted with episodic material.

GAMELAN. The percussive orchestra and music from Indonesia (Java and Bali). The word "gamel" means "to make with the hand."

GAVOTTE. A French court dance found in the Baroque suite. It is in a moderate tempo and a duple meter.

GENRE. A type of work—vocal or instrumental. For example, a concerto is an instrumental genre for a soloist and accompaniment (orchestra). An art song is a vocal genre for a solo vocalist with piano accompaniment.

GIGUE. A brisk and lively dance form from the Baroque suite. Generally the final movement in the suite.

GLISSANDO. A continuous sliding from note to note.

GLORIA. The second movement in the ordinary of the mass.

GRAVE. A tempo indication for a slow tempo in a solemn manner.

GRAZIOSO. Gracefully. It indicates a style of playing/singing. Usually found in conjunction with a tempo indication.

GREGORIAN CHANT. The monophonic liturgical chant organized by Pope Gregory during the sixth century. It became the musical form of worship for the Holy Roman Catholic Church until the rise of the polyphonic forms in the Renaissance.

H. (HOB.). Catalog listing for Franz Joseph Haydn's music.

HABAÑERA. A slow Cuban dance form in duple meter. Used in Bizet's opera *Carmen*.

HALF CADENCE. A temporary cadence that ends on the dominant harmony.

HALF STEP. The smallest distance between two notes in Western music.

HARMONICS. Pitches that sound in sympathetic vibration to a fundamental pitch. They have a glassy, ghost-like quality. These tones are produced by lightly placing a finger on a string and then plucking that string. Used at the end of the second movement from Rodrigo's *Concierto de Aranjuez*.

HARMONY. The simultaneous sounding of notes. The systematic relationship of consonance and dissonance.

HARPSICHORD. A keyboard instrument popular during the Baroque era whose sound is produced by a mechanical action that plucks the strings.

HEAD. The first few notes of a theme.

HISTORICAL INSTRUMENT MOVEMENT. A contemporary view whose advocates believe that one should use instruments from the historical period of the music. Some believe that the recordings should be made in the same hall and with the same amount of musicians as the composer had at his disposal.

HOMOPHONIC (HOMOPHONY). A musical texture that is basically chordal. It is the combination of a melody with all the other parts being in the background.

IDÉE FIXE. A fixed idea in the music. This refers to Hector Berlioz, who used a clarinet and a particular melody (theme) to represent "his beloved" in his symphonic poem *Symphonie Fantastique*.

IDIOPHONES. A family of instruments whose sound is produced by striking a non-membrane head. For example; a xylophone, cymbal, castanets, and marimba.

IMITATION. A texture in which successive musical entries echo the original melody. This is often the basic "device" in polyphonic music.

IMPRESSIONISM. A French style of art that originated in Paris in the late 1800's. In art and music it was a deliberate break from Realism. It features a shimmering orchestral color, flexible rhythm, and extended harmonies. Many of the musical ideas (i.e., pentatonic scales, additive textures) came from music of Indonesia and the gamelan orchestras.

IMPROMPTU. A short piano work that sounds as if it had been improvised.

IMPROVISATION. Spontaneous composition while performing. Found in jazz and in aleatoric (chance) music.

INCIDENTAL MUSIC. Music composed for performance in connection with a drama.

INDETERMINACY. See ALEATORIC.

INNOVATIVE ROMANTIC. A style of music in the Romantic era in which programs and literary sources provided the basis for the musical composition. These composers tended to utilize the brass and percussion instruments for dramatic purposes.

INSTRUMENTATION. The parts assigned to particular instruments in an ensemble.

INSTRUMENTS. Usually broken down into families (brass, woodwind, string, percussion, voice, electronics). May also be classified by timbre.

INTERIOR MONOLOGUE. Found in an opera. This is a piece of music that, although it is being sung aloud, the persons singing it are only thinking to themselves.

INTERMEZZO. An interlude.

INTERPRETATION. To take a melody and add your own "feel" or personal expression to it. The interpreted melody is similar to the original melody. In jazz, interpretation is not as creative as improvisation.

INTERVAL. The musical distance between two notes. Depending on the distance, the intervals may be major, minor, augmented, or diminished. If the two notes are sounded simultaneously (harmony), the interval may either be consonant or dissonant depending on its quality of sound.

INTONATION. The ability of a performer to maintain accurate pitch. To play or sing "in tune."

INTRODUCTION. A short section of a composition that is used to prepare the listener for the music to follow. Often found at the beginning of a symphony, sonata, or concerto.

INVERSION. The process of turning a melody or chord upside down. Used in harmony and in 12-tone music.

JAZZ. An American musical style. It is a combination of African melody and rhythm with European harmony and, to an extent, form and instruments.

JUST INTONATION. A system of tuning instruments according to the "pure" intervals found in nature. The predecessor to Equal Temperament.

K. Catalog marking for the music of Wolfgang Amadeus Mozart.

KAPELLMEISTER. German word for choirmaster or director of an orchestra.

KEY. A series of tones (notes) forming a major or minor scale (7 notes). It is the home-base; a composer begins in a certain key and, up until the late 1800's, returns to the home-base after making excursions to other keys for interest and relief.

KEY SIGNATURE. Sharps and flats provided at the beginning of a piece to indicate the Key of the composition.

KYRIE. The first movement of the ordinary of the mass.

LARGHETTO. An indication for a very slow tempo.

LARGO. An indication for a very slow tempo that is rather broad in feel.

LEAP. A sudden move or jump from a high note to a low note, or vice versa.

LEGATO. Smooth, an articulation that indicates a smooth connection between notes.

LEITMOTIF. A musical theme or motive that is used to represent an extra-musical character or idea. Leitmotifs were the basis for Wagner's music dramas.

LENTO. An indication for a slow tempo, between largo and adagio.

LIBRETTO. The story of an opera or oratorio; the words or lyrics that are set to music.

LIED (LIEDER, PL.). A German art song. Associated with Schubert and others.

LICK. The slang term for a tough musical passage. Taken from the jazz world.

LUTE. The predecessor to the guitar. It was popular in the Renaissance and Baroque eras. Generally with seven to eleven strings and a pear-shaped body.

MADRIGAL. A secular choral work from the Renaissance with a text in the vernacular. These madrigals were usually sung by the aristocrats and nobility, a form of entertainment music. Thomas Morley is an excellent example of an English Renaissance madrigal composer.

MAJOR SCALE. A series of seven notes with an arrangement of Half- and Whole-steps in the following order; W-W-H-W-W-W-H.

MAJOR TRIAD. The three note chord formed by the first, third, and fifth notes of the major scale. In C major, the major triad is C-E-G.

MARCATO. An articulation style that denotes a marked emphasis and distinction to the performance of a note or chord.

MARCH TIME. Duple meter in an allegro tempo.

MASS. A celebration of the main ritual of the Holy Roman Catholic Church. It is the enactment of the Last Supper of Christ. During the Middle Ages and the Renaissance, the mass was also an important musical genre.

MAZURKA. A Polish dance in triple meter. In the hands of Chopin, it became one of his most important genres for the piano.

MEASURE. A metrical unit of strong and weak beats.

MELODY. The tune of a piece of music—what you can sing. It is a series of tones sounded one after another in a linear fashion. Melodies have a wide ranges of types; from simple to complex, from smooth to angular, from narrow to wide in width. In each era, certain types of melodies were in style.

MEMBRANOPHONES. The drum family of instruments. The musical sounds of these instruments are created by striking a membrane that is under tension (stretched).

METER. The arrangement of measures creates a meter. There are two types of meters; duple (strong-weak) and triple (strong-weak-weak).

METER SIGNATURE. An indication at the beginning of the piece as to whether the music is in duple or triple meter.

METRONOME. A mechanical device invented in 1812 that can sound the beats of various tempi.

MEZZO. An Italian descriptive word that means "medium" or moderately.

MEZZO-FORTE. A dynamic marking that means medium loud.

MEZZO-SOPRANO. A vocal characteristic for a medium soprano—in between a soprano and an alto.

MIDI. An abbreviation for Musical Instrument Digital Interface. This device allows musical sound to be stored and used as digital information. A MIDI device allows a synthesizer and computer to "talk" to each other.

MINIMALISM. A twentieth century style of musical composition that is based on the repetition of musical ideas over a slowly moving harmony. Adams, Glass, and Reich are three composers in this style.

MINOR SCALE. A series of seven notes with an arrangement of Half- and Whole-steps in the following order; W-H-W-W-H-W-W.

MINOR TRIAD. The three note chord formed by the first, third, and fifth notes of the major scale. In the key of C minor, the minor triad is C, E-flat, and G.

MINUET AND TRIO. A stately court dance in a triple meter. As a form, it is A-B-A. The A sections are the minuets with a contrasting B section being the trio. Originally for only three instruments, the trio is lighter and softer than the A sections.

MIXED METER. The combination of duple and triple meters; frequently changing meters.

MODERATO. An indication for a moderate tempo in between andante and allegretto.

MODE. A scale that is not major or minor. For example, dorian and phrygian.

MODULATION. To change key; to shift from one tonal area (home base) to another. This adds variety and relief to music.

MONOPHONIC (MONOPHONY). A musical texture that is easily identified since there is only one melody and no accompaniment. For example, Gregorian chant.

MOTET. A polyphony, sacred, choral composition from the Renaissance era.

MOTIVE. A short musical idea that can be developed into a longer theme. It can also be a part of a theme.

MOVEMENT. A complete and independent section of an extended work. Synonymous with a chapter in a book.

MUSIC DRAMA. The original term for opera, as it developed in 17th century Florence, was "dramma per musica" (drama by music). Wagner used this term in the late 1800's to emphasize the dramatic elements in his operas.

MUTE. A device attached to an instrument to decrease the volume and to alter the timbre. Most commonly found in the upper strings and upper brass.

NACHTMUSIK. Night music.

NATIONALISM. Pride or patriotism. An important historical movement in the mid- to late 1800's which had a tremendous impact on composers and their music.

NATURAL. A musical symbol which cancels a sharp or flat.

NEOCLASSICALISM. A twentieth century style whereby composers return to a music style that is dominated by form and structure. Stravinsky was a pioneer in this style.

NEOROMANTICISM. A twentieth century style whereby composers return to music that is dominated by passion (similar to Innovative Romanticism). Many composers became involved in this style.

NOCTURNE. A piece of night music. Demonstrates the Romantic artists fascination with the night. In the hands of Chopin, the nocturnes are often dreamy and sentimental in feeling and rather free in form.

NOTATE. The process of NOTATION.

NOTATION. The process of writing a piece of music by utilizing symbols to communicate music and musical expression. These symbols indicate the pitch (melody) and the time (rhythm).

NOTE. The symbol(s) used to represent a particular pitch and rhythm.

OCTAVE. The interval encompassing eight notes of either the major or minor scale.

OPERA. A fusion of the arts; a dramatic spectacle; a libretto (story) is set to music with singing, acting, scenery, props, costumes, etc.

OPERA BUFFA. Comic opera.

OPERA SERIA. Serious opera.

OPERA VERISSIMO. An opera from the Romantic era that has a realistic plot, is seamless in form, and has a unified musical organization.

OPUS. The Latin word for "work." It is a number that is assigned in a chronological system cataloguing a composer's works.

ORATORIO. An unstaged opera with a Biblical text. It developed during the Baroque era as a replacement for opera during the Lenten season. It is the Catholic counterpart to the cantata.

ORCHESTRA.   A group of musicians; strings, woodwinds, brass, and percussion. The orchestra developed during the Classical era. It is synonymous with the terms "symphony" and "philharmonic."

ORCHESTRAL.   Pertaining to the orchestra.

ORCHESTRATION.   The art of writing music for performance by an orchestra.

ORCHESTRAL SUITE.   A Baroque suite (collection of dances) written for the orchestra. In reference to Tchaikovsky and Stravinsky, adaptations of their ballet music now appear at concerts in a concert setting with out the dancers (extract suite). Often, it is simply abbreviated as "suite."

ORDINARY.   Sections of the mass whose text remains the same each week. These sections are the Kyrie, Gloria, Credo, Sanctus, and Agnus Dei.

ORGANUM.   The earliest example of polyphony and harmony. It began in the Late Middle Ages and blossomed into the polyphonic style of the Renaissance.

ORNAMENT.   A musical embellishment or decoration such as a trill.

OSTINATO.   A short, repetitive rhythmic or melodic pattern that is used to hold the piece together; it is an important part of the musical organization (form).

OVERTURE.   An orchestral introduction to a larger work, such as a ballet or opera.

P.   Catalog marking for the music of Antonio Vivaldi.

PART.   The music played in a piece of music by a particular instrument. For example, the first violin part.

PASSACAGLIA.   An old Italian dance form. It is a continuous variation form characterized by a repeated (ground) bass.

PASTORALE.   A composition that suggests various scenes in the country.

PATRONAGE.   System by which composers were paid to work. Usually, the composers worked for a wealthy court or for the church, and received their wages in return for composing music "on demand" for whatever occasion required music.

PEDAL POINT.   A note sustained, usually in the bass, during a phrase of music.

PENTATONIC SCALE.   A five note scale (i.e., the black keys on the piano).

PHRASE.   A single, complete musical thought. Similar to a sentence in literature.

PIANISSIMO.   A dynamic marking for "very soft."

PIANO.   A dynamic marking for "soft." Also, a large keyboard instrument. Originally called a pianoforte because it was the first keyboard instrument to offer the dynamic possibilities from soft (piano) to loud (forte).

PIANO MINIATURE.   See CHARACTER PIECE.

PIANO TRIO.   A chamber ensemble consisting of a piano, a violin, and a cello.

PICKUP.   One or more notes that occur just before the downbeat of a musical phrase. See UPBEAT.

PITCH.   How high or low a sound is perceived; a note or tone.

PIZZICATO.   To play a string instrument by plucking the strings with a finger.

PLAINCHANT.   Another name for Gregorian chant.

POLONAISE.   A stately Polish dance in triple meter. One of the Romantic piano genres of Chopin.

POLY-   Many; more than one.

POLYPHONIC (POLYPHONY).   A musical texture that consists of two or melodies that are sounded together. Typical of Renaissance and Baroque music.

POLYRHYTHM.   A twentieth century device that combines two (or more) different rhythms or meters.

POLYTONALITY.   A twentieth century device that combines two (or more) different keys or tonalities.

POP FORM - AABA.   Also known as song form. It consists of a first verse (A), a second verse (A) with the same music but different lyrics, then a chorus section (B) that has both different music and different lyrics.

POPULAR MUSIC. Music created for/by a specific culture with the intent of mass marketing and wide "commercial" appeal through the media.

PRIMA DONNA. Italian for "first lady" and is associated with the principal female singer in an opera.

PRELUDE. A short introductory piece of music. During the Romantic era, the prelude became a genre for composers. In the music dramas of Wagner, the prelude became the new name for the overtures to each act.

PRESTO. An indication for a very fast tempo.

PRIMITIVISM. The rhythmic, percussive musical style of early Stravinsky.

PROGRAM MUSIC. Music that is based on an extra-musical (non-musical) idea. Typically, during the Romantic era, composers of this musical style based their music on literary ideas.

PROPER. The sections of the mass whose texts change from day to day.

QUADRUPLE METER. The same as duple meter, but written to contain four beats in a measure or grouping (strong-weak-strong-weak).

QUARTAL HARMONY. A type of harmony that utilizes the intervals of a fourth and fifth instead of thirds as in major and minor harmony.

QUARTET. A composition for four performers with the most common being the string quartet—two violins, one viola, and one cello.

R. Catalog marking for the music of Antonio Vivaldi.

RAGTIME. An American popular style of piano playing from the 1890's. It is characterized by "ragged" or syncopated rhythms.

RANGE. The distance covered, from top to bottom, by an instrument, voice, or melody.

RECAPITULATION. The third section of sonata-allegro form in which the exposition material returns.

RECITAL. A concert in which all of the pieces are played by one performer, or in which the music of one composer is featured. Usually suggests a more intimate setting dating from the Romantic salon culture.

RECITATIVE. The bridges between the arias and the ensembles. This is a solo song with a light instrumental accompaniment. It is used to forward the action and advance the story line.

REFRAIN. Music and text repeated between stanzas of a song.

REGISTER. How high or low the sounds are.

RELEASE. The point where a cadence occurs. Usually set up by tension (dissonance).

REPRISE. A repetition of a part of the music that was previously played.

RESOLUTION. The process whereby dissonance is transformed into consonance; tension becomes release.

REST. An indication for a specific amount of silence; notated in rhythmic values.

RHAPSODY. Free in form, with many changes in mood and feeling.

RHYTHM. The beat or pulse of music. Attributes include tempo, meter, duration, and their notation.

RHYTHMIC. Adjective used to describe music that contains assertive rhythmic patterns.

RHYTHM SECTION. In a jazz ensemble, the piano, bass, and drums. Used to maintain the harmonic and rhythmic support for the ensemble. In many ways, the Baroque basso continuo (or, continuo) functioned in the same manner.

RIFF. A short melodic idea or fragment of a melody.

RIPIENO. The full ensemble in a concerto grosso composition.

RITARDANDO. A gradual slowing down of the tempo.

ROCOCO. A transitional period between the Baroque and Classical eras.

ROLL. Rapid, repeated strokes on a percussion instrument.

ROMANTIC. The Romantic era was from 1820 to 1900. Music, art, and literature from this era was concerned with the outward expression of emotions. It is often seen as the opposite of Classical (balance, symmetry, form).

RONDO. A musical form characterized by the return to the first melody (A). One of the most common is A B A C A. Frequently found in the final movement of a concerto or symphony.

ROW. See TONE ROW.

RUBATO. A flexible tempo. The tempo pushes forward (speeds up) as the music becomes more exciting/emotional, and pulls back (slows down) as it relaxes. An expressive element in music.

RUN. A rapid sequence of notes going up or down.

SALON. In the Romantic era many of the composers entertained in the salons (library, drawing room) of the wealthy aristocrats. It became known as the salon culture.

SANCTUS. The fourth movement of the ordinary of the mass.

SATB. In choral music, this is a designation for soprano, alto, tenor, and bass voices.

SCALE. An ordered series of notes that forms the basic materials of melody and harmony.

SCAT. A jazz singing style using syllables and non-sense words instead of words. Often times the intent is to imitate the sound of an instrument. Louis Armstrong was one of the earliest scat singers.

SCHERZO. Literally, "joke" in Italian. This became the replacement for the minuet and trio in the third movement of the symphony (Beethoven).

SCORE. The music manuscript that a conductor reads from. It contains all of the notes played by all of the instruments. During the process of orchestration you create a full musical score.

SECTION. A large division of music - somewhat like a paragraph in literature.

SECTIONAL FORM. A piece of music that consists of large sections or blocks. For example, rondo, theme and variations, sonata-allegro, binary, ternary, etc. This is the opposite of imitative form, and differs considerably from dramatic form.

SEQUENCE. The repetition of a melody either higher or lower. The same melody is just repeated in either a higher register or in a lower one.

SERIALISM. A twentieth century mathematical system of composition pioneered by Arnold Schoenberg and the Second Viennese School (with Webern and Berg). The tone row is arranged in a sequence that is maintained (and manipulated) throughout the work.

SFORZANDO. A strong accent on a note or chord.

SHARP. A notation symbol that indicates raising a note one half step.

SIGHT READING. The performing of a piece of music without rehearsal.

SINGSPIEL. An 18th century German opera with spoken dialogue (i.e., *The Magic Flute*).

SOLO. A work in which one player or singer performs alone or is featured.

SONATA. A multi-movement genre (piece) for a solo instrument.

SONATA-ALLEGRO FORM. A sectional repetition form that is composed of an exposition, development, and recapitulation. Usually found in the first movements of Classical sonatas, symphonies, and concerti.

SONG CYCLE. A number of art songs that are loosely bound together by a central idea or a single author.

SONG FORM. See POP FORM.

SOPRANO. The vocal classification for the highest range of the female voice. Also used to designate the highest instrument in a family (i.e., soprano saxophone).

SOUND. Vibrations transmitted through the air and "captured" by the human ear.

SPRECHGESANG. Literally, singing speech. A twentieth century vocal technique which creates an eerie, hyper-expressive vocal quality. See Arnold Schoenberg's composition *Pierrot Lunaire*.

SPRECHSTIMME. See SPRECHGESANG.

STACCATO. An articulation marking in which the notes are separated from one another by a brief silence.

STAFF. The five parallel, horizontal lines upon which symbols (notes) are placed to indicate pitch.

STEP. The interval between two adjacent notes. There are two types; half and whole steps. The half step is the smallest distance between two notes in Western music. A whole step is the distance of two half steps.

STRING QUARTET. A chamber ensemble that consists of two violins, a viola, and a cello. Developed during the time of Franz Joseph Haydn.

STROPHIC FORM. A sectional repetition form in which the words change from line to line, but the music remains the same (similar to verse and chorus, see POP FORM).

SUBITO. Italian for "suddenly." Subito forte means suddenly loud.

SUBJECT. The theme (main melody) of a fugue.

SUITE. A collection of dances from the Baroque era. It can also refer to a series of loosely related movements drawn from a larger composition—the extract suite (i.e., *The Firebird Suite* is an orchestral version of the original ballet by Igor Stravinsky).

SWELL. A rise and fall in the volume level over a short period of time.

SYMPHONIC POEM. A single movement orchestral work of the Innovative Romantic composers. The subject matter is drawn from extra-musical sources (literature). One exception is Hector Berlioz; his symphonic poem *Symphonie Fantastique* has five movements. All five movements, however, are parts of one story.

SYMPHONIC SUITE. See ORCHESTRAL SUITE and SUITE.

SYMPHONY. A four movement work that originated in the Classical era. The four movement plan is generally Allegro (sonata-allegro form), Andante (theme and variations), Dance (minuet and trio or scherzo), and Allegro (rondo or sonata-allegro). Also, it is what the symphony (as a genre) was written for—a symphony orchestra, which consists of strings, woodwinds, brass, and percussion.

SYNCOPATION. The rhythmic feel that results from placing accented notes on unaccented beats.

SYNTHESIZE. To bring together, to blend.

SYNTHESIZER. An electronic instrument capable of generating a wide variety of sounds, timbres, and instruments.

TAIL. The final notes of a melody or theme.

TEMPO. The rate of speed that the pulse is moving at.

TENOR. The vocal classification for the highest male voice. It is also used to designated a certain range of instruments (i.e., tenor saxophone).

TENSION. The musical quality that sets up an expectation of resolution. Tension leads to release, dissonance leads to consonance.

TERNARY FORM. A three part form (sectional repetition) of A B A.

TERRACE DYNAMICS. The alternation of loud and soft dynamics without any use of crescendo or decrescendo. Common in the Baroque era. Usually accomplished by the sudden addition or subtraction of instruments.

TESSITURA. The characteristic range of a singer's voice.

TEXTURE. How many melodies; melody and how it is used; the layers of sound in a piece. There are three basic textures; monophonic, polyphonic, and homophonic.

THEME. A melodic idea that is used as the basis for development.

THEME AND VARIATIONS FORM. A sectional repetition form wherein a theme is first stated, and then is followed by a series of variations on the theme. In these variations, the composer will alter the melody, harmony, rhythm, instruments, etc.

THROUGH-COMPOSED SONG. A vocal form in which the text is set to continuously changing music. Non-sectional.

TIMBRE. The tone color of a musical sound.

TIME SIGNATURE. See METER SIGNATURE.

TOCCATA. A flashy, show-off piece from the Baroque era. Usually found as a prelude to a fugue, often it has an improvisational quality to it.

TONALITY. The home base; key center; often referred to as major tonality or minor tonality.

TONE. A musical sound; one note or pitch.

TONE COLOR. See TIMBRE.

TONE PAINTING. See WORD PAINTING.

TONE POEM. A one movement orchestral work based on a program or literary source. Developed by the Innovative Romantic composers. The tone poems are especially associated with Franz Liszt and Richard Strauss.

TONE ROW. The basic "melodic" ideas in a 12 tone piece. All twelve tones (chromatic) and their repetition and manipulation are the basis for 12 tone (serial) music.

TONIC. The home base note. In the key of C major, it is the note C. The tonic triad is built on the tonic note. Sometimes it is referred to as the "root."

TRADITIONAL ROMANTIC. Composers who were interested in carrying on the Classical tradition established by Haydn, Mozart, and Beethoven. Most often, Johannes Brahms is referred to as the renovator of tradition and is seen as the composer who most closely follows in the footsteps of Beethoven.

TRANSCRIPTION. The arrangement or adaptation of a piece for some voice or instrument other than for which it was originally intended. For example, Liszt transcribed many of Beethoven's symphonies for performance on the piano.

TREMOLO. A string technique in which there is a rapid repeat of a note or chord. It is Italian for "trembling."

TRIAD. A chord consisting of three notes (see MAJOR and MINOR). This is the basis for Western harmony.

TRILL. A melodic ornament; a rapid alternation between two notes.

TRIO. A composition featuring three performers.

TRIO SONATA. In the Baroque era, a trio sonata consisted of a violin (or flute) with a keyboard (harpsichord) and a bass line continuo (cello).

TRIPLE METER. A rhythmic pattern of one accented beat followed by two unaccented ones (strong-weak-weak).

TRIPLET. A rhythmic grouping of three notes.

TROUBADOUR. A wandering, vagabond musician from southern France during the Middle Ages. Today, it is a common generic name for all European wandering musicians from the Middle Ages.

TROUVÈRE. Same as troubadour, except from northern France.

TUNE. An informal term for melody.

TUTTI. An Italian word meaning "all" or everyone. Used in a concerto grosso to designate the full ensemble.

TWELVE-TONE SYSTEM. See SERIALISM.

TWELVE-TONE ROW. See TONE ROW.

UNISON. The performance of the same melody by more than one performer.

UPBEAT. The rhythms that immediately follow the strong beats of a phrase.

VARIATIONS. Ornamented or otherwise altered repetitions of a theme. See THEME AND VARIATIONS FORM.

VERISMO. A 19th century style of Italian opera that deals with the real world in real settings, rather than with history, legend, or traditional heroes.

VERNACULAR. In the language of the people. It was reaction to the use of Latin in the church service by Martin Luther (German Protestant).

VIBRATO. A slight fluctuation in the pitch; used to create warmth and color in the sound (timbre).

VIENNESE SCHOOL. First and second schools. The First Viennese School is represented by the Classical masters Haydn, Mozart, and Beethoven. The Second Viennese School is represented by the Expressionist and 12-tone (Atonal or Serial) composers Schoenberg, Webern, and Berg.

VIOL. A family of string instruments that were the forerunners of the violin family. Their sound, however, is much more subdued than the sound of the present day violins.

VIOLA. The alto instrument of the string family. It has a darker and more coarse tone quality than the violin.

VIRTUOSO. A performer with a very high degree of technical skill and proficiency.

VIVACE. An indication for a quick tempo with a lively character (quality).

VOICE. Used as a generic term for a line of music that is designated to a single instrument. For example, in a string quartet the viola voice is the viola part—the soprano voice is the soprano part.

WALTZ. A dance in triple meter. Typical of Viennese music from the end of the 19th century (see Johann Strauss, Jr.).

WHOLE STEP. The interval (musical distance) of two half steps.

WHOLE-TONE SCALE. A scale comprised of whole steps, no half steps. Used by Claude Debussy in *Voiles* and *La Mer*.

WIND ENSEMBLE. A wind instrument band that is smaller than the traditional band. Usually there is only one player per part.

WOODWIND QUINTET. A chamber ensemble consisting of flute, oboe, clarinet, bassoon, and horn.

WOODWINDS. Members of the aerophone family. These instruments include the piccolo, flute, oboe, clarinet, bassoon, and saxophone.

WORD PAINTING. A deliberate attempt by composers to capture the literal meaning of the text (words, lyrics) in the music. Can be seen as part of the Doctrine of Affections.

Musical Forms

Song form	A A B A
Strophic form	A A A A
Through composed	A B C D E, etc.
Free sectional	A B A B C, and many other combinations
Two part	A B or A A B B
Three part	A B A or A A B A
Rondo	A B A C A D A
Theme and variations	A A1 A2 A3, etc.
Sonata-allegro	A B A (overall; Exposition, Development, Recap)
Minuet	A B A (overall; Minuet, Trio, Minuet)

In detail:

Minuet	A A B B A,
Trio	C C D C C D C,
Minuet	A A B B A.

Instrumental Genres

The Symphony

A piece for the symphony orchestra featuring instruments from the string, woodwind, brass, and percussion families.

First movement	Allegro	Sonata-allegro form.
Second movement	Andante	Theme and variations, later Sonata-allegro.
Third movement	Allegretto	Dance style - Minuet, later Scherzo.
Fourth movement	Allegro	Rondo or Sonata-allegro form.

The Concerto (Concerto Grosso)

A piece for a soloist(s) and accompaniment. The accompaniment is usually an orchestra of some type.

First movement	Allegro

Second movement	Andante
Third movement	Allegro

Opera Overture (Prelude)

There are many different forms for this. Some contain many themes with contrasting moods and styles.

Concert Overture

Free sectional form. Similar to the opera overture.

The Suite

Two types:

1. Baroque dance-style movements. Typically an Allemande, Courante, Sarabande and Gigue. You can also find other dances including a Bourrée and a Rigaudon.

2. Extract suite. Excerpts arranged for concert performance that are taken from the original ballet, film score, or stage music.

Program Music

Descriptive works that are inspired by literature. The music follows and develops along the lines of the story. These include tone poems, symphonic poems, and character pieces.

Ballet

A story and music for dance purposes. Use of dancers, staging, props, and an orchestra.

Descriptive Music

Music that is absolute, yet has a basic idea behind it. Vivaldi's *Four Seasons* and Beethoven's *Pastoral Symphony* are two examples of descriptive music.

The Sonata

Most often, this is a solo work for an instrument. Frequently associated with keyboard music.

First movement	Allegro
Second movement	Andante
Third movement	Allegro

Character Pieces (Piano Miniatures)

One movement works for solo piano (generally). Atmospheric and programmatic in nature. For example, the nocturnes, ballades, mazurkas, and impromptus of Chopin. There are many different pre-set forms for these works.

Vocal Genres

The Mass

The Holy Roman Catholic service to commemorate the Last Supper of Christ. The "Ordinary" of the Mass is most often set to music.

I.   Kyrie
II. Gloria
III. Credo
IV. Sanctus
V.   Agnus Dei

One special mass is the Requiem Mass - a mass for the dead. The Credo and Gloria sections are omitted from the Requiem mass and a Dies irae section is added.

Two notable uses in an exceptional manner are *A German Requiem* by Johannes Brahms and *The War Requiem* by Benjamin Britten.

The Oratorio

This is an unstaged opera with a libretto based on writings from the Bible. It features the use of a narrator, soloists, chorus, and an orchestra. An oratorio is performed in a concert setting.

The Cantata

This genre is similar to an Oratorio. It is Lutheran in origin and meant to be performed within the actual church service. It also uses a narrator, soloists, chorus, and an orchestra.

Opera

This is grand musical theater. Based on a libretto, an opera features soloists, a large chorus, an orchestra, and many "extras" that add to the grandeur of the work. As in a play, the operas are broken down into various acts and scenes within an act. An overture begins the opera and functions to set the mood of the piece.

Index of Composers' Works

These works are not discussed in detail.

PRESENTED BY
LA PHIL

Keali'i Reichel

World Music **Tuesday, March 11, 2014, 8:00**

Keali'i Reichel
Shawn Pimental, *lead guitar*
Dana Pi'ilani Arias, *rhythm guitar*
Moses Kane Jr., *bass guitar*
Naomi Stephens, *vocals*
Nalei Pokipala, *vocals*
Lance Winston, *vocals*

Halau Ke'alaokamaile dancers
Henohea Kane
Oralani Koa
Hulali Canha
Anuhea Ho'opai
Chanel Souza
Marie Elena Juario
Ha'alilio Solomon
Devin Kamealoha Forrest

MC: Alaka'i Paleka – KPOA Radio Maui

The LA Supernova Ensemble is under the direction of Dr. William Doyle.

Guided Listening - Worksheet A

Name: _____

Day and time: _____

1. Describe the melody:

   simple & singable

   or

   complex & ornamented

   or

   dramatic & powerful

   or

   rhythmic & jagged

2. Meter: duple · triple · mixed

3. Tempo: fast · moderate · slow

4. Pulse: steady · non-steady (rubato)

5. Type of harmony: mostly major · mostly minor

6. Overall sound: mostly consonant · mostly dissonant

7. Type of texture: monophonic · polyphonic · homophonic

8. Range of dynamics: pp · p · mp · mf · f · ff   (circle lowest and highest)

9. Type of dynamics: crescendo/decrescendo · terrace effects · both

10. Instruments: strings · woodwinds · brass · percussion

    piano · voice

11. Type of ensemble: vocal · instrumental · mixed

Guided Listening - Worksheet B

Name: _____

Day and time: _____

1. Describe the melody:

    simple & singable
    or
    complex & ornamented
    or
    dramatic & powerful
    or
    rhythmic & jagged

2. Meter:

    duple · triple · mixed

3. Tempo:

    fast · moderate · slow

4. Pulse:

    steady · non-steady (rubato)

5. Type of harmony:

    mostly major · mostly minor

6. Overall sound:

    mostly consonant · mostly dissonant

7. Type of texture:

    monophonic · polyphonic · homophonic

8. Range of dynamics:

    pp · p · mp · mf · f · ff   (circle lowest and highest)

9. Type of dynamics:

    crescendo/decrescendo · terrace effects · both

10. Instruments:

    strings · woodwinds · brass · percussion
    piano · voice

11. Type of ensemble:

    vocal · instrumental · mixed

12. Genre (circle only one):

    sonata · symphony · concerto
    opera · lied · madrigal · chant

13. Era (circle only one):

    Pre-Baroque · Baroque · Classical · Romantic · 20th c.

Guided Listening - Worksheet C

Name: _____

Day and time: _____

1. Describe the melody: simple & singable
   or
   complex & ornamented
   or
   dramatic & powerful
   or
   rhythmic & jagged

2. Meter: duple · triple · mixed

3. Tempo: fast · moderate · slow

4. Pulse: steady · non-steady (rubato)

5. Type of harmony: mostly major · mostly minor

6. Overall sound: mostly consonant · mostly dissonant

7. Type of texture: monophonic · polyphonic · homophonic

8. Range of dynamics: pp · p · mp · mf · f · ff (circle lowest and highest)

9. Type of dynamics: crescendo/decrescendo · terrace effects · both

10. Instruments: strings · woodwinds · brass · percussion
   piano · voice · electronics

11. Type of ensemble: vocal · instrumental · mixed

12. Genre (circle only one): sonata · symphony · concerto · jazz related · world
music

   opera · lied · madrigal · chant · musical theater/ballet

13. Era (circle only one): Pre-Baroque · Baroque · Classical · Romantic · 20th c.

Final Exam

The "Mystery" Piece

Name: _____   Day and Section time: _____

1. Describe the melody: _____

_____

2. Meter: _____

_____

3. Tempo: _____

_____

4. Type of Harmony: _____

_____

5. Type of Texture: _____

_____

6. Range of Dynamics:_____

_____

7. Instruments: _____

_____

8. Form: _____

_____

9. Type of piece (genre): _____

_____

10. Era/Style Period of this work: _____

Bonus - A Probable Composer: _____

Concert Review # 1

Name: _____ Day and Section time: _____

Name of Concert Attended: _____

Date: _____

Location: _____

Type of Concert or Ensemble: _____

1. What was the most interesting selection in the first half? Why?

_____

_____

_____

_____

_____

_____

_____

2. What was the most interesting selection in the second half? Why?

_____

_____

_____

_____

_____

_____

_____

3. General Commentary

Types of musical selections on the program:

_____

Era/styles represented:

_____

Featured instrument(s) or performers:

_____

Anything interesting happen?

_____

_____

4. Any questions?

_____

_____

5. What was your overall opinion of this concert?

_____

_____

6. Your Rating: from **1** (low) to **10** (high)   _____

* **Note:** Attach a ticket stub and/or program.. **No credit for late reports.**

Concert Review # 2

Name: _____ Day and Section time: _____

Name of Concert Attended: _____

Date: _____

Location: _____

Type of Concert or Ensemble: _____

1. What was the most interesting selection in the first half? Why?

_____

_____

_____

_____

_____

_____

_____

_____

2. What was the most interesting selection in the second half? Why?

_____

_____

_____

_____

_____

_____

_____

3. General Commentary

Types of musical selections on the program:

_____

Era/styles represented:

_____

Featured instrument(s) or performers:

_____

Anything interesting happen?

_____

_____

4. Any questions?

_____

_____

5. What was your overall opinion of this concert?

_____

_____

6. Your Rating: from **1** (low) to **10** (high)   _____

* Note: Attach a ticket stub and/or program. **No credit for late reports.**

Concert Review # 3

Name: _____ Day and Section time: _____

Name of Concert Attended: _____

Date: _____

Location: _____

Type of Concert or Ensemble: _____

1. What was the most interesting selection in the first half? Why?

_____

_____

_____

_____

_____

_____

_____

2. What was the most interesting selection in the second half? Why?

_____

_____

_____

_____

_____

_____

_____

3. General Commentary

Types of musical selections on the program:

_____

Era/styles represented:

_____

Featured instrument(s) or performers:

_____

Anything interesting happen?

_____

_____

4. Any questions?

_____

_____

5. What was your overall opinion of this concert?

_____

_____

6. Your Rating: from **1** (low) to **10** (high) _____

* Note: Attach a ticket stub and/or program.. **No credit for late reports.**

Extra Credit Concert Review

Name: _____   Day and Section time: _____

Name of Concert Attended: _____

Date: _____

Location: _____

Type of Concert or Ensemble: _____

1. What was the most interesting selection in the first half? Why?

_____

_____

_____

_____

_____

_____

_____

2. What was the most interesting selection in the second half? Why?

_____

_____

_____

_____

_____

_____

_____

3. General Commentary

Types of musical selections on the program:

_____

Era/styles represented:

_____

Featured instrument(s) or performers:

_____

Anything interesting happen?

_____

_____

4. Any questions?

_____

_____

5. What was your overall opinion of this concert?

_____

_____

6. Your Rating: from **1** (low) to **10** (high)   _____

* Note: Attach a ticket stub and/or program. **No credit for late reports.**

Extra Credit Concert Review

Name: _____ Day and Section time: _____

    Name of Concert Attended: _____

    Date: _____

    Location: _____

    Type of Concert or Ensemble: _____

1. What was the most interesting selection in the first half? Why?

_____

_____

_____

_____

_____

_____

_____

2. What was the most interesting selection in the second half? Why?

_____

_____

_____

_____

_____

_____

_____

3. General Commentary

Types of musical selections on the program:

_____

Era/styles represented:

_____

Featured instrument(s) or performers:

_____

Anything interesting happen?

_____

_____

4. Any questions?

_____

_____

5. What was your overall opinion of this concert?

_____

_____

6. Your Rating: from **1** (low) to **10** (high)   _____

* **Note:** Attach a ticket stub and/or program. **No credit for late reports.**